Questions and Answers

by Frances Clark

*Practical solutions and suggestions given to
questions commonly asked by piano teachers*

Special thanks to Ryan Greene, Kari Krafft, and Kristen Landrum in assisting with the 2015 republication. Cover photo by Christian Steiner.

ISBN: 978-0692495315

Preface

For nearly fifty years, Frances Clark has been talking to piano teachers about common interests and concerns. Since 1966, some of the questions teachers ask, along with Miss Clark's sage answers, have made the back page of *Clavier* magazine a source of immediate and enduring value.

What has made this particular page so attractive to *Clavier's* readers is not only Miss Clark's profound knowledge and penetrating insights into the teaching-learning process, but her ability to cut through to the heart of a problem and offer a quick and practical solution. Her advice is straight from the shoulder and she doesn't mince words. Yet her warmth and wit, care and compassion, her eternal optimism and buoyancy have served as a source of renewed energy and encouragement to generations of teachers.

It has been my privilege to sort through twenty-six years of accumulated columns with her - to read, select, organize, update, and edit a mass of invaluable material. Not all duplicate questions have been eliminated, for often different answers shed a different light on the subject. By leaving most of the answers intact, it is also possible and fascinating to follow the direction and development of her thinking over the years. The date of the original column appears at the end of each answer.

I believe this book deserves a place in the library of every serious piano teacher today, and that it will continue to enlighten and enliven our profession for years to come.

Louise Goss
Editor

Table of Contents

Chapter One
Thoughts and Attitudes About Teaching

The piano teacher's goal. *Is it possible to state in one sentence your idea of our main goal as piano teachers?*

My primary goal as a piano teacher is to create a climate in which my students can experience continual musical, intellectual, and emotional growth, and to become increasingly dispensable to them in the process. Everything I do as a teacher, and every other teaching goal I have, relates directly to this first, most basic objective — to help my students grow by and for themselves. *(February 1988)*

Test of a successful teacher. *I have an ego problem! I have always considered myself a rather successful piano teacher. I have taught for 25 years, and always have a waiting list. When my students graduate from high school and go away to college they still keep in touch with me. Two of them have majored in piano at college. I love to teach.*

Recently in our city the emphasis has been on presenting students in contests or having them play for out-of-town judges. I haven't cooperated with this 100 percent, feeling no great need for it, but when I have entered students they haven't won any contests or received superior ratings when judged. I am left with the question, "Have I been a successful teacher?" I would greatly appreciate knowing what criterion you would use to judge a teacher's success.

If we were closer together, and I could hear your students play, my ears would be the only criterion I would need to judge your success. But even long-distance there is one almost fool-proof measure of a teacher's effectiveness: what do your students do with their music after they graduate from high school or discontinue music lessons? If they continue not only to play music they studied with you but to explore other music; if they are part of the musical life of their communities; if they attend concerts; if, when they have children of their own, they encourage them to study piano, not because it's the thing to do, but because they want their children to have the same musical experience they remember with such pleasure — then I think we can assume, without any reasonable doubt, that you have been a successful teacher. *(March 1971)*

Complete musicianship. *I have just attended a lecture on your concept of developing piano students who are complete musicians at every stage in their development. Do you believe this is possible even with elementary students? If so, what do you include?*

I do believe such musicianship is possible with elementary students, and indeed that it starts with the first lesson. In their first lessons our beginners have these experiences:

- they learn to read by direction — the notation is in large notes, off the staff, moving up or down or both;
- they experience rhythm, learning to move to music freely, to keep a steady pulse at various tempos, to swing, to chant, and to sing and play notes that last for one swing or for two;
- they experience technique: how to sit at the piano, the components of a good hand position, feeling a firm tip in their middle fingers, playing legato between hands;
- they begin to understand form by recognizing patterns that are alike and different;
- they begin ear training through clap backs, sing backs, and play backs;
- they experience ensemble through playing duets with the teacher;
- they even begin to compose, making pieces of their own that move up, down, or both, using the groups of two black keys all over the piano.

Beginning students have their first experience in how to practice by learning to follow a set of practice steps that leads them quickly and easily to an accurate performance of a new piece on the first playing. Even at the very beginning we work on projecting musical ideas and the artistic and convincing performance of each piece they are studying. In a microcosmic sense this is complete musicianship from the start.

We build this foundation in every area during every lesson. Slowly and naturally each new discovery is incorporated into every aspect of a student's musical experiences, first through its sound, then through its feel (the technique it takes to produce that sound), and finally through its sign and name. *(May-June 1982)*

Complete musicianship illustrated. *Please explain what you mean by developing complete musicianship from the very beginning, illustrating with the student's very first piece.*

For students to become complete musicians, they need to begin as complete musicians. This means that from the first lesson they need to start developing in four areas:

1) listening
2) sense of rhythm
3) understanding every sign on the printed page
4) ability to project the musical idea of every piece played.

To illustrate, let's look at the first piece in our students' very first book, *Time To Begin*.

In "Take Off," students discover that:

— the music is about something they are interested in (airplanes) and that this piece really sounds like an airplane taking off (as the plane goes up, the music goes up);
— there is a sign for every sound, and the picture (four groups of notes, each group exactly alike except that each successive group is higher) is an accurate graphic representation of the sound;
— the steady motion is a pleasant physical experience that helps students begin to develop a feeling of steady pulse;
— the introduction to technique features use of middle fingers (for balance within the hand) and alternating hands (for balance within the body);
— because the piece uses only the groups of two black keys, they can move easily over the keyboard, producing music that uses a wide range of sound;
— when they play their part with the teacher's accompaniment, they experience music as more than melody; through the duet they enjoy a big sound, the security of rhythmic stability, and the togetherness that is the heart of ensemble playing.

Students who understand and project the musical meaning of this first simple piece have already taken a big step toward becoming complete musicians. *(December 1984)*

Progress of today's students. *For several years I have wondered why today's students fail to progress as rapidly as they did 30 or more years ago. Many people, including my mother (now in her 70s) and my sister, took a few lessons adding up to less than a couple of years and can still play hymns at a church music program or sightread songs for pleasure. Now, regardless of the method, a child doesn't have the ability to play the above, mentioned things when he is a high school or college age person, or even an adult. What is wrong in this day when there are more readily available and attractive materials? Is it due to students not putting in as much daily practice? I didn't like to practice either, so that attitude isn't different, but I had to. Maybe that is the difference. I am speaking now of the average child whose parents want him to study a little piano as a good foundation just as my parents did with their three children. (I was the only one who went on to major in music and teach public school music for eight years; I now teach piano privately in my home.)*

My first reaction to this question is one of shock. On the basis of my experience with students all over the country, I can state categorically that on the national scene, progress among piano students is far greater today than at any earlier time. This not only includes higher standards of musical performance, but also the ability to sightread and play for pleasure. In our own school the situation is the same. Every year our students accomplish more than their counterparts did in the preceding year, and every year parents express their amazement at what their children know about music, and can do with what they know, compared with their own experiences as piano students a generation earlier.

My second reaction was to further consider this teacher's question in the hope of narrowing the gap between her experience and my own. I have asked myself two questions: How large is the student sample from which she drew her conclusions? What areas (other than the ability to read hymns) did she consider in evaluating her students' ability to "play for pleasure"? In addition to the worthy but limited premise on which she seems to draw, don't we also need to consider:

- the significant upgrading in performance standards all across the country. A person needs only to have judged auditions 30 years ago and today to see that the national standards are infinitely higher now.
- the many times a student brings in a new book we have assigned, having already read it through from beginning to end.
- the groups of students who get together all through high school for the sheer joy of reading ensemble music, such as the four- or eight-hand arrangements of Mozart symphonies.
- the hours that students spend spontaneously improvising at the piano, and the fine finished compositions they often create.
- students who work endlessly at capturing on the piano a tune they have heard on radio or television.

- the jamming that goes on at every party where two or three piano students get together.

Viewed in this broader context, I don't see how we can share the concern expressed by this teacher. Piano study in America is alive and well. *(September 1984)*

Progress of today's students summarized. *In the September 1984 "Questions and Answers" column a reader asked Frances Clark, "... why today's students fail to progress as rapidly as they did 30 or more years ago." Frances Clark responded, "My first reaction to this question is one of shock ... on the national scene, progress among piano students is far greater than at any earlier time." The huge volume of mail she received in reaction to her answer was so overwhelming that we thought it appropriate to devote this month's entire "Questions and Answers" column to Frances Clark's heartfelt reply to this mail.*

My response to the teacher who asked why students are not making as much progress today as they were 30 years ago has generated more feedback from readers than any other answer in the history of this column — so much feedback that at times I felt I had opened Pandora's box. The reaction to my original answer appeared in the Sounding Board. Both the opinions expressed by that teacher and the subsequent reactions to her letter have been invigorating. It proves that teachers are reading this column and the Sounding Board, and that when the subject is our students and their success, our level of interest and concern is exceptionally high. The various letters, from all sorts of teachers in all parts of the country, have demonstrated that there are two diametrically opposed points of view, with a wide range of viewpoints in between. Because there is supporting evidence on both sides, we naturally lean toward one or the other depending on our own experiences as teachers. I selected the original letter for reply because it reflected an attitude that has been in evidence throughout my teaching career, one that has troubled me for more than 40 years: "Things are getting worse." I had hoped to point out that things are certainly *different*, but that different is not necessarily worse and may in fact be better. Many of our readers have supported that position.

On the other hand, some of our readers support the position that things are not what they were 30 years ago and write with longing of the good old days. Various letters agreed that lack of practice is the basic problem and pointed to extracurricular activities, television, lack of discipline, working mothers, and the disintegration of the nuclear family as the major culprits.

On both sides of the question, all of us agree that times have changed, that "future shock" is *now* and that life today is dramatically different from the lives we knew as children. None of this is really new. The worry about activities that compete for a student's time, about lack of practice and lower performance standards has been around as long as I've been teaching. I remember concern that band (with the allure of uniforms, marching, and togetherness) would cut into piano study; I remember the panic when parents first rushed out to buy television sets and teachers were sure no one would ever be able to practice at home again; I remember the pressure of the Sputnik days and the hours of homework young piano students had to face for the first time; I remember the advent of after-school sports programs that kept many youngsters on the playing fields until supper time and made it a headache even to schedule their lessons. Now our latchkey children come home to empty houses where computers and V.C.R.s compete with homework (and endless telephone calls!) for time that might otherwise be spent at the piano.

All that's new today is that change is occurring faster, the list of activities that compete for a student's time is longer and family life as we once knew it has changed. But music is tough stuff. Piano students have survived all these changes; piano study has survived all this competition. Piano teachers must be a tough breed, too, for they have survived as well.

The good news is that for every new problem we face today, there are new solutions. To balance the lack of time, discipline, motivation and parental support, we have all the new insights into the teaching, learning process; all the new materials that stem from those insights; all the new tools for making piano study efficient and effective; all the new modes and approaches to capture today's students where they are, and give them the quintessential experience of actively creating something instead of always being passively entertained. Today we have unparalleled opportunities for increasing our teaching abilities, attitudes and skills. Thanks to the nature of music itself, to the nature of children, and to our own adaptability as teachers, piano study *is* alive and well. And it will continue to flourish, if:

- we discipline ourselves to stop looking back with longing to the good old days;
- we accept and love today's children just as they are, without longing to change them into the children we were;
- we try to avoid blaming our problems on the times or on our students, and instead take advantage of the resources available to help us adapt to the realities of today. (*March 1985*)

Preventive teaching. *Some teachers have an attitude that I find discouraging and psychologically bad – an approach that is preventive rather than constructive. Their emphasis is always on how to keep a student from doing something wrong, as if everything a student naturally does is going to be wrong. I'd appreciate your ideas on this.*

I'm interested in your premise and your reaction, but my response is different from yours. I fail to see preventing a problem as negative; indeed, prevention seems to me to be one of the most positive forms of teaching. All of our past teaching experience should alert us to potential problems ahead. Creating situations that help students avoid such problems is the very pinnacle of good teaching. For example, take a piece that begins in quarter notes but soon includes passages of sixteenth notes. To avoid the problem of a change in tempo at the entrance of the sixteenth notes we ask the student to set the initial tempo by counting a pulse at which he can play those sixteenth notes with control. Or take a piece that begins forte and later contains a section marked fortissimo. If we ask the student, before he plays the piece, to play an example of forte and an example of fortissimo so that the contrast is in his hands and ears before he begins, we can prevent lack of contrast when the fortissimo section appears. These are just two examples of teaching devices that avoid potential problems before they occur. I call this kind of teaching preventive rather than curative, positive rather than negative. *(November 1984)*

Preventive teaching illustrated. *I recently heard a clinician compare the work of a piano teacher to that of a doctor – we spend time diagnosing problems, then we cure them. I benefited from this analogy and thought you might like to mention it in your column.*

The analogy is an excellent one, but needs to be carried a step further. Today physicians put increasing emphasis on preventive medicine and avoiding health problems. Through the media, health professionals are trying to educate us to the many health problems we ourselves cause. They alert us to the dangers of obesity, improper diet, lack of exercise, mental or emotional stress, etc. If the way we live causes these health problems, then it follows that changing our lifestyle could prevent them from arising. In similar spirit, I like to teach what I call "preventive music education." It's a fine thing to be so aware of potential problems that we catch them at their earliest signs, but teaching in such a way that these problems never arise is even better. Here are some simple examples:

Rhythmic health

Emphasize the kinds of motion that involve the whole body, such as singing, walking, and dancing. If we make sure that students never begin to work on a piece at the keyboard until the rhythm is literally flowing through their bloodstreams, we can say goodbye to rhythmic insecurity and stumbling.

Technical health

Make sure that students have mastered the technique required to perform a piece easily and comfortably *before* assigning the piece for home practice.

Memory health

Start your students memorizing at the very beginning, and make it a regular part of every assignment and every practice period. If students understand that playing from memory simply means recalling what they have already understood and mastered, they won't have to experience the fear of performing without music.

Anticipating problems and preventing them is one of the tests of great teaching. Prevention is a skill even greater than quick diagnosis and sure cure, important though these may be. *(March 1987)*

Students who cry at lessons. *Occasionally I have students who cry at their lessons. This makes me feel terrible. I don't know what I do to make them cry and when I ask them about it, they cry all the harder. Sometimes they recover and we can go on with the lesson, but sometimes the lesson is ruined. What can I do?*

Try making two lists. One should include all the things you can think of that might make students cry, quite apart from what happens at piano lessons; the other should list all the things you might have done to cause the tears.

The first list might include such things as

— the student didn't get enough sleep
— is coming down with an illness
— had something go wrong at school had a fight with a friend
— hasn't practiced enough and feels guilty about lack of preparation
— played the piece much better at home and is surprised it didn't go well at the lesson, etc.

The second list might include such things as:

— the teacher didn't get enough sleep
— is coming down with an illness
— had a hard day and is tired
— stayed on a musical or technical point too long
— spoke in a voice too loud, firm or emphatic, or in a manner the student interpreted as cross
— didn't give enough praise for progress and improvement
— asked for higher standards than the student could deliver at the moment, etc.

Such lists can help us understand why students might cry for reasons other than what happens at the lesson or what we might do to make them cry despite our best intentions.

Teachers can often avoid tears by paying closer attention to the student's reactions. Avoid using a voice or manner that seems cross. Try to anticipate the limits of a student's tolerance for firmness, precision, or high standards and back off before a crisis is precipitated. If tears occur unexpectedly try ignoring them, move to a place in the studio where students know you can't see they are crying, and continue to teach as calmly and supportively as possible. It is often possible to weather brief showers without interrupting the lesson. Sometimes, however, it is necessary to leave the studio for a short while to allow time for students to collect themselves. In cases of severe distress, I would call the mother the next morning while the student is at school to explain what happened and get her insights into why the student was upset. *(March 1984)*

Plateaus in Learning. *I know that students sometimes hit plateaus at which they don't seem to be making any progress, but when this happens students often become discouraged and want to drop. I have had this experience over and over, usually about the end of their first year. How can this be avoided?*

Plateaus are a natural part of the learning process — forward leaps are followed by periods of slower progress during which the student is absorbing the concepts and skills which have been learned most recently. The only danger in this natural learning phenomenon is that we tend to lean on it as the excuse for poor teaching. A *natural* plateau is usually short in duration and should be nearly imperceptible, except to the teacher. It has been my experience that a more prolonged or obvious plateau is *not* part of the natural growth process, but the result of hurried learning or casual teaching during the preceding phase of development. Often students are allowed to move too rapidly, especially in the first year. Suddenly the music seems too difficult. Then they have to back up or stand still while they absorb the concepts and skills that have been presented too rapidly. Such a plateau is indeed discouraging.

Some students need much more time and much more music on each concept than others do, and for a variety of reasons — age, physical development, maturity, natural ability, practice skills, parental cooperation, etc. The pacing of new skills and concepts in the beginning method you use and the amount of music provided through which to absorb them may be about right for most of your students. But occasionally you will find students who can move more rapidly than the average and do not need to study all of the music in order to absorb and assimilate the new material thoroughly. The more frequent exception is the student for whom the amount of music provided in the basic method book is not sufficient. For such students, still more pieces are required at every step of the way. With these students we use supplementary books providing a large number of solos, some with optional accompaniment for teacher or parent. This provides the additional time necessary for slower or younger students to absorb each new learning phase in depth before moving on to the next phase. Because they are having quantities of new music each week, there is no feeling of standing still.

No matter what books you are teaching, if you are choosing supplementary music to reinforce new learning and avoid plateaus it is crucial that it include only the concepts and skills already presented in the basic material. We have been discussing the first-year student, but as teachers we should ask ourselves the same sort of question for every student we teach: is it better to forge ahead rapidly, appearing to make dramatic progress, then have to tread water while that ever-important absorption process takes place? Or is it wiser to move ahead slowly and steadily, providing for the absorption within the forward progress itself? The question really boils down to this: is it better to make show hastily or to make haste slowly? I find that the latter pays bigger dividends in the long run. (*December 1976*)

Body language. *I recently heard a fascinating speaker on the subject of body language. How can I use body language to make my piano teaching more effective? Do you know of a good book on the subject?*

This is an interesting and important question, one that all of us can answer for ourselves. First, I suggest you become aware of the extent to which you already use body language in everyday interactions outside your studio. Experts tell us that at least 70 percent of our day-to-day communication is nonverbal; when we shake hands, wave goodbye, shrug our shoulders, shake our heads (up-and-down or side-to-side), snap our fingers, move closer, turn away, touch, or any of a hundred other gestures, we give signals that communicate vividly and directly. What about our faces? An infinite variety of expressions communicate joy, sorrow, anticipation, anger, understanding, uncertainty, scorn, praise, disbelief, and limitless other reactions. Think of how many different meanings a wink can have, coupled with varying facial expressions, or consider the ways in which a smile can communicate everything from welcome to contempt.

In short, each of us is a walking encyclopedia of effective body language, but how can we apply this in our piano teaching? First, for body language to speak, it must be seen by the student. My first suggestion is to make sure that you teach from a place where students can see your face and body, at least in their peripheral vision. Second, why not consider that body language might do 70 percent of the work in the piano lesson, as it does in life itself? Why not try communicating less in words and more with your face, hands, and body? The posture you assume while listening to your students play, the way you lean forward or sit back, the tilt of your head, the expression on your face can all coach the student while he is playing, without interrupting him with words.

During active teaching, much of what you want to accomplish can be done by gesture and touch. Your hand on the student's shoulder can say, "Relax," "Don't rush," or "That was beautiful," just as effectively as words. Conducting is one of the most natural and effective means of nonverbal teaching. All of us teach tempo, dynamics, articulation, nuance, and a hundred other musical details just by what we do naturally without hands, arms, and body — providing the student can see us! The most effective nonverbal coach of all is our own performance of our students' music. So often when we perform a phrase or line or entire piece, students watch the music. They should be watching us — not just our hands, but the entire body to see the body language through which we communicate our interpretive suggestions.

Public performance has its own body language. The way a student walks onto the stage, sits down at the piano and prepares to play shapes an audience's expectations of success or failure. At the performance's end, how a student gets up from the bench, smiles, and bows is so effective a communicator that I have seen it change the amount of applause or even reverse the audience's reaction itself. Piano teachers who learn to make maximum use of body language will find that their students learn and grow by leaps and bounds, and that the studio is no longer filled with the unnecessary and intrusive sounds of our own voices. A good book on this subject, although not actually on its application to piano teaching, is *Kinesics and Context* by R.L. Birdwhistell, University of Pennsylvania Press, 1970. *(October 1987)*

Self-confidence. *My students seem to lack confidence — confidence in general and especially the confidence necessary to look at a new piece of music and feel they can dig right in and work it out. What am I doing wrong?*

A feeling of confidence is gradually built up over a long period of time and in many subtle ways. Without knowing you or your students, it is impossible to answer this question specifically, but I can suggest two approaches. First, the matter of lack of confidence in general. Our students need to feel secure with us as people and as teachers. They feel most secure with us as people if we are always consistent in the way we treat them. Of course, being entirely consistent is difficult in any human relationship, but it is particularly important for parents and teachers. If we are consistent, our students learn to trust us. It is also very important in teaching to impress our students with an honest approach to evaluating them and their work. If we say, "Okay!", "good!", or "great!" indiscriminately, students never get a clear picture of where they stand. It is important to say clearly how they are improving and why, and what needs improving and how.

In approaching new music, we can help students develop confidence in specific ways. We should always provide them with a balance between a sense of confidence in what they are doing now and a desire to discover more that is new. A student's confidence is based on sameness, his sense of adventure on difference.

Let's begin with a simple example from the first year of study. When a student is secure with quarter notes, eighth notes, and ties, and has a secure rhythmic response to their symbols, even including such a complicated combination as this,

then when we introduce a dotted quarter and eighth, we can present it as a new look for an old, familiar feel.

Confidence comes from knowing the feel, from being secure with the rhythmic experience. Adventure comes in seeing it written in a new way. Consider the case of intermediate students who have studied the *Adagio* by Bartók:

Adagio

In studying this piece, students quickly discover that it contains a great deal of sameness — the entire melody is based on the figure in measures 1-2 plus the cadential figure in measures 5-9. The left hand, too, is repetitious: the opening slur (perfect 5th to major 3rd) is used exclusively except for measures 16-17. Hence, there is very little to learn, and once the basic gestures are learned a great sense of security is established. The difference then comes from Bartók's subtle variation in rhythm, dynamics, and articulation — plenty of variety for a sense of high adventure. If we approach the *Adagio* in this way, the next time our students encounter a piece by Bartók they already have the feeling that they know something about Bartók's music. They expect a simple, folk-like melody with a great deal of repetition, and an accompaniment made of subtle rhythmic and harmonic changes. If their next assignment is a piece like the *Round Dance*, their expectations are fulfilled.

Round Dance

Introducing new repertoire to students this way may bring a wonderful question to mind: I wonder if all Bartók's music is written in this way? Doubtless this will lead to exploring other Bartók pieces, and of course students will find many cases in which this is true and many in which it is not.

Finally, let's illustrate this learning process with advanced students who are studying Mozart sonatas. When the teacher assigns another Mozart sonata, they already have some expectations, some sense of familiarity, which create a feeling of confidence. Their expectations include such things as the number of movements, use of sonata allegro form, Alberti bass, and the importance of silence. All of these expectations should be in mind because of what they have discovered in the Mozart previously studied. If, for example, they have studied the G major Sonata (K. 283) and the F major Sonata (K. 332), they have the confidence born of experience to expect that the new sonata will have three movements (fast, slower, fast). If the new assignment should be the Eb major Sonata (K. 282), they will have the adventure of discovering that at least one Mozart sonata begins with a slow movement. This might trigger the desire to learn if there are other sonatas that begin with a slow movement (more adventure). Of course we could cite dozens of examples, but the important thing is the realization that all our teaching is based on this concept of sameness and difference, security and adventure. It is this concept that helps determine what we teach, when we teach it, and how we teach it. (December 1970)

Teacher Motivation. *Every fall I feel the need for a shot in the arm to get me motivated for the year's teaching. Do you have a list of incentives for better teaching that might help me?*

The final assignment in my graduate pedagogy class this spring was for them to prepare a list of things they would do differently in their teaching this fall as a result of what they learned last year as student teachers. Following are a few excerpts.

- I will begin the year expecting a lot more from each of my students. I have learned that my students' potential is far greater than I originally thought.
- I am determined to create a situation in which all my students can be successful from the start and know they are successful.
- I will talk far less during my lessons this year. Taping myself and listening to the lessons made me realize how much I talked. I sometimes said the same thing three or four times; if I had had the student's attention first, or if I had given the instruction more careful thought, once would have been enough. If only I'd stop talking, I'd have time to hear and work on the entire assignment.
- I know now that asking the student to count will not necessarily solve his rhythm problems. I will be more aware of whether the student himself is counting or I am doing it for him.
- I will not assume that a student has mastered a particular rhythm pattern just because he can play it correctly in the piece of music he is practicing. He may

only have memorized the rhythm in terms of the melody. When he can play that same rhythm in other settings, I will know he has it.

- I will try to listen to my students' playing with the same ears I use to listen to everyone else's students. There is such a difference between what I hear and want to hear in other students, and I should be detecting it in my own.
- I will not work on everything at once for any one piece or any one lesson. Instead I will determine what is most important, concentrate on that, and see it through.
- I will begin to judge my success as a teacher by what my students can do on their own without any help from me.
- I will keep in closer contact with my students' parents, informing them of their children's progress.
- I will make sure at the lesson that new concepts are secure, remembering that students have to be able to recreate them unaided at home.
- I will try to do a much better job of preparing my students technically for their repertoire.
- I will spend more time on tone production: on playing with full, rich tone and developing the ear to distinguish between harsh and rich tone. The student can't make a difference until he can hear the difference.
- I will be more careful in my choice of repertoire for every student, in terms of balance of periods, styles, and forms.
- I will discover more ways to arouse my students' curiosity and develop their awareness of what to listen for.
- I will have a more definite idea of the piece I am teaching. I will not only study and analyze it more carefully, but I will be willing to sing it, conduct it, and verbalize everything about it: rhythm, phrasing, dynamics, tempo, touch, and tone. I will let my imagination do more in the process.

I feel certain that these excerpts from some very insightful year-end reports will trigger even more incentives and resolves for your own teaching. *(September 1989)*

Music in the public schools. *As one of the long established piano teachers in our community, I have been asked to make a statement before our local Board of Education, urging them to keep required music courses in our public school curriculum. Would you be willing to make a statement I could quote?*

I'll do better than that. Here is the best recent statement I have read on the subject. It comes from the Foundation for the Advancement of Education in Music, and appears in the June-July issue of *American Music Teacher* as part of an article on Excellence:

"... To understand music is to know an entire range of human expression, and to be able to play it means participating in that communication. As much as writing or mathematics, music represents a special form of literacy with its own repertoire of emotional and intellectual content. Perhaps as in no other discipline, to study music is to study a truly universal language, one that illuminates our culture as it connects us with other people and other times. It's no wonder, then, that the understanding of music and the ability to play it have long been regarded as marks of a well-educated individual, as much as music itself is the mark of civilization. It's in this context — the pursuit of the best possible education — that a sequential, balanced, comprehensive program of music study belongs." *(September 1988)*

Chapter Two

Lesson Plans and Assignments

Planning the lesson assignment. *Despite my excellent college pedagogy course I am still unclear about what I should include in my student's assignments. Could you offer some pointers on this subject?*

Planning the student's lesson assignment is one of a piano teacher's most significant responsibilities. A carefully thought-out, well-balanced assignment takes much time and thought, and it includes continual restudy and replanning as the lessons proceed. Broadly speaking, everything we teach falls into one of three categories: musicianship, a growing awareness of how the music should sound; technique, a growing physical ability to bring the music into sound; and practice habits, a growing mastery of the skills that make it possible to work out and improve repertoire, efficiently and musically.

The first question we need to ask ourselves is whether every assignment includes all three areas. The second question is whether we keep all three areas in balance from week to week and month to month. If a student's musicianship exceeds his technique, he becomes frustrated by not being able to play the music the way he wants it to sound. If technique gets ahead of musicianship, the result is a pianistic typist, whose note playing lacks musical beauty and understanding. If practice skills lag behind the other two areas, the student grows discouraged because it takes him too long to learn new repertoire. Ideal progress, then, results from balanced assignments that develop musicianship, technique, and practice habits hand-in-hand. The only sure-fire way I know to keep assignments in good balance is to begin by making a long-range lesson plan, from September to June. I then break those long-range plans into shorter segments — September to January and January to June, then month by month, and finally week by week. The shorter-range planning is a matter of continually adjusting and refining the longer-range goals. Every assignment has two aspects: what's new and what's to be continued or reviewed. Keeping these two parts in balance requires careful thought. What shall we assign that's new, and how much practice time will this take? Which part of the present assignment should be continued, and how should the student's practice be outlined for the coming week? We need to consider the entire review assignment in terms of new ways to work on and improve the review repertoire and technical materials, as well as to follow through in the areas of reading, rhythm, theory, practice skills, and so on. In balancing new and review materials we need to remember that every assignment is in itself a new experience and therefore does not always need to include new music. The new for some lessons can be new ways to practice or new ways to improve the performance of music the student is already studying. Many teachers have a tendency to keep adding new repertoire to the students' assignments, without considering the time it takes to hear, improve, and reassign the review music. New pieces probably need to be added in some sensible ratio to pieces being discontinued.

We can also examine every assignment in terms of the three stages of the learning process: romance, precision, and generalization. As a simple example, when we present a new piece, or enhance the student's musical understanding of a former piece, the student experiences romance. When we work on technical details or musical refinement, the student experiences precision. When romance and precision reach mutual fulfillment and the piece becomes part of the student's known repertoire, he has reached the stage of generalization. These three stages exist for all students, but the amount of time and emphasis on each stage varies with the individual student. Here again, balance is the keystone to success.

When the three areas are kept in balance, the student is encouraged and motivated, while a lack of balance causes discouragement and frustration. For example, romance can be overdone. The student can be presented with too much new music, too many new composers, forms, or styles, too many new goals, or too many new ways to practice. Periods for absorption are as necessary to healthy learning as time for digestion is to good nutrition. Precision can also be overdone. At times, the drill so essential to mastering skills and achieving musical refinement can appear to students as nitpicking, which they resent. We also need to maintain balance in other areas. Students need balanced experiences in style periods (Baroque, Classical, Romantic, Impressionistic, Modern), in moods (dramatic, poetic, humorous, sophisticated, popular), and in solo and ensemble playing. We need to remind ourselves daily that these balances vary from student to student and from time to time.

Finally, at regular intervals we need to restudy our students' last few assignments, to see how well we are balancing all of these considerations. We may be amazed to discover the stages we have gone through as teachers — the one composer period, the term devoted to Spanish music, the emphasis on virtuosic pieces, the summer spent on small gems, and so forth. We can learn much about our teaching and about our students' progress (or lack of it) regularly reviewing our assignments. *(January 1988)*

Making lesson plans. *My question concerns lesson plans. Are the teachers in your school required to put aside one morning each week just for planning? I, for one, cannot afford this much time. Is the lesson plan also used as the student's assignment?*

Our teachers are not required to put aside any specific amount of time for lesson planning. However, we have all found that making the plan for the student's next week's lesson can be done best the morning following the lesson, when it is still fresh in our minds. We make both a written plan for the next lesson and an assignment for the student to take home in his notebook. We prepare the assignment with a carbon copy and leave the carbon in during the lesson, so that changes, additions, and notes written on the student's assignment are automatically recorded on our copy. Then when we plan the following lesson we work from the copy of the assignment and the previous week's plan. The most important aspect of lesson planning, both for classes and for our private students, is an overview of the year and a detailed ten-week plan, both of which are made out before the first lesson is given. As we near the end of the tenth week we review our plans and assignments for the preceding weeks and make a new ten-week plan.

The overview is a general statement of our goals for this class or student in repertoire, theory, technique and such skills as sight-reading, transposing, accompanying, and memorizing. The ten-week plan lists specific music, technical etudes and exercises, and theoretical concepts and materials, with books and page numbers for everything we expect to assign. Also included are notes to ourselves about when to order new music. The ten-week plan is detailed and time-consuming, but it saves hours of time in planning weekly lessons. It is treated as a flexible program, subject to change and modification as the lessons proceed.

In general, I believe that planning a lesson consumes about as much time as giving it, a fact that ought to be taken into consideration when teachers determine their fees! *(April 1981)*

Assigning a new piece. *What are your guidelines for assigning a new piece? By the time I hear the student's current pieces and make corrections, the lesson is gone and I can only mention the new assignment.*

Two opposite approaches to assigning new material are:

- Merely make the assignment, leaving the student to work it out entirely on his own.
- Work the piece out in such detail that the student leaves the studio playing accurately and securely any portion of a piece you have assigned. Such a detailed work-out should result in your having nothing (or very little) to correct at the next lesson. On the other hand, assigning a new piece with no help from you should mean that the student already understands and can do everything the score indicates, knows how to make and follow a practice plan, and can develop progressive goals for a week's work.

If you find you are having to spend a great deal of lesson time correcting mistakes, your main emphasis should be on teaching your students how to practice: make practice plans with them and actually follow the plan with them at the lesson. The more time you spend developing wise practice habits, the less time you will have to spend in subsequent lessons correcting mistakes. Your time with the student can be spent turning accurate pieces into musical ones and going over new music in a variety of ways. *(October 1987)*

More about assigning a new piece. In the last issue I answered a question about guidelines for assigning new pieces, responding to a teacher who expressed the concern that by the time she had heard music on the current assignment and corrected the mistakes, there was time only to mention the new assignment. I suggested that there are many approaches to assigning new music, some more time, consuming than others. At opposite poles are:

- Merely make the assignment, leaving students to work out the music entirely on their own.
- Work out the music in such detail with the students at the lesson that they leave the studio playing accurately and securely any portion of a new piece you have gone over with them.

Of course our ultimate goal is to develop students who can work out music entirely on their own and return for the next lesson with the assignments as accurate and secure as if you had worked it out in detail with them, but this does not happen overnight. Developing students with this ability means using part of every lesson on detailed workouts, and because the process is so time, consuming, we need to select carefully the piece or sections of a piece for this kind of supervision. The minimal requirement is to make sure every assignment contains some music that the students are aware they are playing accurately, at least in rhythm, notes, and fingering. Meanwhile, other new music can be assigned in a variety of less time consuming ways:

- Look through the piece with the student, discussing what you expect to hear on the basis of the title, composer, rhythm, keyboard range, dynamic markings, and phrasing.
- If you play the piece for the student, do one or more of the following additional steps: ask questions about period, style, form, key, and rhythm; ask the student to listen, following along in the score, pointing and counting the rhythm, or tapping and counting the rhythm, expressing as much of the tempo, mood, touch, phrasing, and dynamics as possible; ask the student to mark the form; and ask him to find and mark the parts of greatest difficulty for special practice.
- Play the piece with the student, teacher playing one hand, student the other, then exchange parts.

- Make the assignment with the practice steps already written out for the student, with or without discussion, or applying all the suggestions to one section of the piece as an example of how to work on all sections.
- Discuss how to work out the piece, but let the student suggest his own practice steps.

Saving time in one of the above ways should allow you to do a detailed workout of at least some portion of a new piece each week with the student. In this way he always has at least one reminder of how important the first week of practice is and how important it is to begin correctly. Gradually, secure and accurate practice becomes the norm rather than the exception. *(November 1987)*

Preparation. *I believe that my teaching has improved greatly since I've been including the step you call "preparation," but I honestly don 't feel the need to prepare for everything six weeks before I plan to assign it in a piece of music the student will practice at home. Do you really feel a six-week preparation period is essential?*

I can't imagine where you got the notion of an arbitrary period of preparation. Like everything else in teaching, the time needed for preparation depends entirely on the individual student with whom you are working and what it is you are preparing.

First, let's consider what we mean by the step you are calling "preparation." Because music exists in sound and is perceived through listening, we believe that each new musical element should be presented first in *sound*, not in *reading*. When the student has heard the new sound, we ask him to describe it in his own words. Then we show him how it feels to make that sound at the piano (the technique required to produce it). It's not until these first two steps are completed and the student has heard the sound and experienced how it feels to produce it that we show him the sign that stands for the sound. In other words, the first time he sees the sign, he already has the *sound in his ear* and the *feel in his hand*. Then, last of all, he discovers the *name* for the sign.

Preparation is anything we do at the lesson with a new musical element before it appears in music the student is to practice at home. The goal of all preparation activities is to prepare the student so securely that we know he will respond accurately and musically to the new element when he is practicing alone at home. Much harm can come from lack of adequate preparation. For example, last week I was observing a lesson in which a young student was working on a piece by Bartók. It was filled with a variety of those accentuation marks Bartók loved so well. The student knew the name of every kind of mark in the piece and could answer any question the teacher asked with a good definition, yet his playing of the piece demonstrated that he had no real understanding of those signs. He had not been prepared aurally for the effect of the different sounds, nor had he been prepared physically for the technical feel of the various accentuations. Needless to say, the result was an inadequate performance of the piece.

To return to your question about the length of time that should be devoted to preparation, may I say again that it all depends on the element being prepared and on the individual student. We often spend as much as three or four weeks preparing for a new rhythm, but with a simple sign one or two weeks might be more reasonable. *(February 1974)*

Preparation, presentation and follow-through. *I'd appreciate more discussion of preparation. I think I see its importance, but I have only a vague understanding of what you mean by it and how to use it.*

It is difficult to explain preparation adequately without also in, eluding a brief explanation of the other two phases in the learning sequence, presentation and follow through.

Preparation

The purpose of preparation is to make students feel secure when they encounter a new musical element in their practice at home, and to enable them to respond to it accurately and musically. Because music exists in sound and is perceived through listening, we believe that students should first discover each new musical element through sound, not through reading. When students have heard the new sound, we ask them to describe it in their own words. Then we show them how it feels to make that sound at the piano (the technique required to produce it). It's not until we complete these first two steps, and students have heard the sound and experienced how it feels to produce it, that we show them its appropriate sign. Last of all, we let them discover the name for the sign, because without a name we cannot talk about it.

This learning sequence — sound, feel, sign, name — is exactly the way music notation developed historically. The musical sounds came first; the notation developed because of composers' needs to find a way to write down the sound of their compositions. We have found that students who make their musical discoveries in the same order that music developed historically better understand that notation is a sign language representing sound. It is only when students understand this that they develop respect for every mark on the printed page.

Presentation

Presentation takes place when all the steps of preparation have made students ready to use a new discovery in the music they read and practice alone at home. Knowing this readiness, we present the new notation or skill in a piece of music and begin to assign, for home practice, music that includes the new notation or skill.

Follow through

Follow through is everything we do to review and reinforce the new element at every subsequent lesson. It takes the form of written work, keyboard activities, drills and extensive use of the new element in the student's music, week after week. Students learn a new element only by using it repeatedly. Not to use it is to unlearn it. An understanding of these three phases of learning — preparation, presentation and follow through — is fundamental to the successful teaching of any subject. *(November 1984)*

Presenting new elementary pieces. *My class is made up largely of first and second year students, mainly beginners. I think these students should have a new piece each week, but what do you do when you give the new piece? I don't like to play new pieces for the students for fear they will begin to play by ear rather than learning to read. What should I do?*

Most elementary students, and especially beginners, need several new pieces each week. I think it is quite impossible to sustain interest and insure progress without quantities of new music in the first year of study. The catch is to be sure that every new piece is really at the right level of difficulty for each student — is it something he can read all by himself, something in which he is rhythmically secure, something for which he has the necessary technical facility, something for which he is musically and interpretively ready? If the answer to all of the above is yes, then we have selected the right music for that student. This brings us to the next question. If the music is right for the student in every way, then how do we present it at the lesson? To answer this, let me mention briefly three of the many ways we present new music to first-year students. I select these particular methods simply because they have worked successfully for us at the New School over a period of many years with hundreds of beginners.

1. *Rote-Notation* is the process we usually use with a piece that in, eludes some new musical element, one the student is taking home in a piece of music for the first time. The process is just what its name implies — first the teacher plays the piece, while the student watches and listens carefully; they discuss the piece, how it sounded, where it was played on the keyboard, what position and fingers were used, etc. Then the teacher guides the student to play it, imitating the teacher's performance. When the student has played it successfully, they either make the notation for the piece on the board, or find it in the book. In summary, this process begins with rote teaching and ends with reading.

2. *Workout* is the process we use when we are emphasizing practice steps, because it is exactly what the student has to do with a new piece whenever he is working it out by himself at home. So in every lesson we work out at least one new piece with the student, guiding him through the practice steps he is learning to use. In workout the piece is not played for the student first. In summary, this process begins with reading and ends with playing from the score.

3. *Play-Discuss* is the process we use to develop independence. The teacher plays the piece for the student; together they look it through to decide what might be difficult and how to work on it. Working out the piece is left for the student to do on his own at home. My belief is that the most successful teaching combines these three processes in every lesson. Rote-notation is the most efficient and immediately satisfying way to get at something new; workout is the best way to emphasize at every lesson the importance of following a set of practice steps; play-discuss is the safest way to develop independent work habits. A combination of these three processes makes a lesson really hum along and makes it possible to cover the quantity of music the young beginner needs to feel rewarded and successful and to make the kind of progress we know he can make under optimal conditions. *(January 1974)*

Playing new pieces for beginners. *Is it wise to play new pieces for beginners? Isn't there a danger that they may pick them up by ear and not learn to read?*

The only type of student for whom it is harmful to hear the new assignment is the beginner with an especially good ear, who might rely on your playing as a crutch and sneak by without really learning to read. In the case of students with only normally adept ears, one playing will not be sufficient to fix the impression, so that the hearing will be a helpful learning tool without interrupting his learning to read. It is also very challenging and inspiring to hear the new piece beautifully and convincingly played by the teacher. It tends to give impetus and enthusiasm at the time it is most needed, when the slow workout stage might be hard sledding. *(December 1968)*

New assignments. *How can I give a new assignment every week to a high school student who already has more music to work on than I can possibly hear in one lesson?*

A new assignment doesn't necessarily mean new repertoire, especially with students at an advanced level. Each week's assignment can include another scale or arpeggio, or other ways to practice scales and arpeggios already assigned. The same principle can be applied to technical etudes, theory assignments, and sight reading. Consider all the new insights that can be gained in the repertoire the student is currently studying; the student gains the insights at the lesson and needs to practice them at home. Insights in interpretation and musicality should be the most significant new elements of any lesson. In addition, there should always be suggestions for new ways to practice the more difficult passages, technically as well as musically. Consider assigning fewer pieces and going into them in greater depth. The student who leaves your studio with a new vision of how a piece, section, or phrase should sound or a new way to achieve technical mastery of a difficult passage has received a valuable new assignment from you, even though it may have come through work on repertoire already assigned. *(March 1981)*

Covering the entire lesson. *I began piano teaching with real enthusiasm. After three years I am questioning if it's the career for me, because I can't seem to stand the frustration. There is too much to teach in the time I have with each student, even though I give lessons longer than 30 minutes. Before I throw in the towel, I thought I would ask you if there's some time-tested way to cope with covering reading, rhythm, technique, theory, practice skills, fingering, phrasing, interpretation, meaning of music symbols, Italian terms, and on and on. Help needed, please reply!*

Your question indicates you are a serious teacher, and that's fine. Your problem is not uncommon among serious teachers. Three years is not enough time to learn to separate the woods from the trees. You are hung up on branches, even twigs, and need to learn to see the whole forest. Here are some suggestions which may help.

As you plan your next few lessons, consider that:

1. No conscientious teacher can cover everything in any single lesson. I would worry more about your teaching if you thought you could cover everything. Remember that each accomplishment with a student gives birth to a new accomplishment. There's a pyramid effect which should be viewed as a time-saver.
2. Everything you list (and much, much more) can be catalogued under general headings: musicianship, technique, practice skills. Part of your lesson planning should be to decide which particular aspect of each general heading you will emphasize in a given piece.
3. Whenever you work seriously on one piece of music with a student, you are, in essence, covering everything in your list.
4. Take a good, appreciative look at the forest (the music itself), then concentrate on a single tree (the piece you are working on), isolate a particular branch (perhaps one phrase), and work at it for total musicianship. In this way you can teach your entire list within the context of a single phrase, and all of the student's study will be affected by what is accomplished with that one musical detail. *(January 1983)*

Completing new music. *I have resumed teaching after a fifteen-year interval during which I raised a family. In that time I have followed closely my own children's piano assignments and feel critical of one aspect of their study. There seems to be no specific goal setting or* *deadlines for the completion of a piece of music. The possible exception to this is the yearly recital piece, for which the recital itself was the dead line. More often than not the assignment would read "needs more practice," "needs more technical control," "work on memory this week." Often these instructions were given over and over again for the same pieces. Now that I'm going to teach again, my hope is not to fall into the same trap. Do you have any solutions to this problem?*

You have brought to light a very important issue for all piano teachers. In school students get very specific assignments from their teachers. They have a certain number of arithmetic problems to be done at home and handed in the next day, or a certain number of paragraphs of Latin to be translated for the next class, or an oral report due a week from Tuesday, or a term paper to be finished before the end of the term, etc.

In piano, we too have our short-term and long-term assignments, our short-range and long-range goals. But how successful are we in communicating these assignments and goals to the student? Here are some of the techniques that have proved successful in my own teaching.

First, the weekly assignment sheet always includes the goal for that week for every piece the student is studying. If it is a new piece, the goal may be to bring it to the next lesson carefully and accurately worked out at a slow, secure tempo. If the student is reviewing a piece, the goals might include specific practice steps for problem spots, plus bringing the piece up to a moderate tempo.

There is almost always a piece on the assignment with one or more of these goals:

- finished musical performance next week
- ready for Repertoire Class
- securely from memory (with specific memory checks for security from analytical, aural, visual, and tactile standpoints).

In our situation every intermediate and advanced student attends a Repertoire Class every two weeks to play for one another and for the faculty. The lower-level students are expected to have something ready to play at every class; the later intermediate and early advanced students, who are working on longer compositions, are not expected to have something ready every two weeks, but are encouraged to play once a month, or as often as possible. The music to be performed at these repertoire classes is assigned well in advance and worked on in detail at the private lesson. Interestingly enough, the performance goals for these pieces are met in nearly 100 percent of the cases, for the classes provide invaluable motivation and inspiration for the students. *(December 1975)*

Detailed teaching vs. general. *There is a matter that has stumped me for years, both in my own teaching of piano students and with my pedagogy students in their practice teaching: when to be detailed. I find I'm often critical of student teachers either because they don't make enough demands on their students or because they are too detailed and expect so much. When and how is it possible to arrive at the proper balance between detailed work and working on a piece as a whole?*

Every serious teacher has to come to grips with that question every day. As you infer, it makes heavy demands on judgment, perspective, balance, and common sense. The ratio between the specific and the general is a major problem in all teaching, especially when training teachers. New teachers want answers to their questions immediately, but in matters such as this only judgment born of study and experience can be a guide. We know that a student needs detailed work to arrive at a musical performance. We also know that too much emphasis on detail, or detailed work that is badly timed, can be counter- productive. And we know that no two students need the same amount of detailed practice, and that no student needs the same amount every day or every week.

Perhaps these general principles can guide us:

1. Plan a lesson that balances specifics with generalities. For example, begin by having the students play pieces that are well along in preparation so that the lesson gets off to a musically rewarding start in which you work on broad outlines, not details. Follow this with some detailed work on technique or perhaps on working out a new piece. Relieve this with another sweeping musical experience, then return to detail.
2. Spend part of each lesson listening to and encouraging work that students have done on their own, which you don't ever plan to work on in detail.
3. For part of each lesson, listen to detailed work on pieces (or sections of pieces) to prove to students the effort of detailed work is valuable.
4. Ask students to work out their own practice plan for a problem section. Let the suggestions for detailed practice steps come from them.
5. Finally, plan a balanced lesson, but don't set your plan in concrete. The amount you do in each area and where you put your emphasis should depend on the individual student's preparation and reaction. Study the student; it's the student you're teaching, not the plan. *(October 1984)*

On-your-own pieces. *What do you mean by an "on-your-own piece"? I have heard it recommended by several teachers, each of whom described it somewhat differently. What do you expect the student to do? And what exactly is the purpose? It seems a bit like a lazy teacher's cop-out to me!*

Far from being a copout, the on-own concept demands as much or more from the teacher as any other part of the student assignment. Let me explain exactly what it is, how the assignment is made, and its purpose. I begin with the assumption that as teachers we all assign music the first week, hear it the second week to check on accuracy (using accuracy in its most all bracing sense) and make suggestions for the second week of practice, etc. This might run the gamut from assigning another week of slow, secure practice (paying still more attention to details) all the way to making a purely interpretive study of the piece in preparation for performance.

With an on-own piece, there is no hearing of the piece or help from the teacher up to the moment of its performance. In other words, the student's goal is to bring this piece to performance standards on his own in a specified length of time. The question then is simply what can the student do with this piece entirely on his own? Of course, the more searching question being asked is how much have we accomplished as his teacher? How successful have we been in teaching this student to practice effectively? How far along are we in helping him toward independence from us? Remember, the ultimate success of the teaching-learning interchange is how dispensable we are able to make ourselves. We know that the student's progress depends in large measure on how successfully he can work on his own at home in his daily practice. The conscientious teacher always looks toward that future when the student will no longer be taking lessons but will be able to use his musicianship and skills for a life-time of continuing enjoyment at the piano.

As you can imagine, choosing the pieces to assign for this purpose takes most serious consideration on the part of the teacher. Generally speaking, the on-own piece is at a slightly easier level than the rest of the assignment, and includes nothing that the student has not already experienced successfully in reading, rhythm, technique, and interpretation. The number of weeks the student is given for bringing the piece to performance standards depends entirely on the individual and on the teacher's really knowing where this student is in his growth toward independence. *(March 1975)*

Areas of study for intermediate students. *I have taught piano for 12 years, and I'm still not sure what an intermediate student's assignment should include — what areas, and how much of each. Can you help?*

Although it is never possible to be specific without a certain student in mind, our intermediate students always have the following general areas in each assignment:

Music, both new and review.

Keyboard literature from at least two different periods in music history and ideally from several different periods, but at least two. We put considerable emphasis on the period and the composer being studied. It is also important to include lighter repertoire in one of many popular idioms.

Technique.

At least one technical etude, and exercises (scales, arpeggios, legato thirds, etc.) according to the individual student's particular technical needs.

Keyboard theory, including traditional harmony, accompanying, improvising, transposing, composing, and form and analysis.

Most assignments also include sightreading and memorizing. *(May-June 1976)*

Budgeting lesson time. *Our study group has been involved in a heavy discussion of how to divide lesson time into the following categories:*

Amount of time to spend on hearing last week's assignment.
Amount of time to spend on presenting new material.
Amount of time to spend drilling, especially with flash cards.

This disagreement among us is vehement, especially in the case of one teacher who seems to believe that practically an entire hour should be spent on flash-card drills. I have been appointed a committee of one to ask if you will please indicate in some general way the division of time we should be spending in each of the three areas, for first-year students, second-year students, and third-year students.

To make the answer to your question more representative, I have not only included my own recommendation but have asked seven teachers from around the country to reply to your request. Each of them is a superb teacher of young students, and the recommendation of any one of them could be taken as fine advice. The interesting thing to me was the general agreement among them.

The chart below indicates a composite of my answer and the replies received from the seven teachers to whom I sent a questionnaire. In studying the chart, please keep in mind that this division of time does not represent all lessons, or even one lesson. It represents an estimated average over a period of a year. (January 1971)

Average number of minutes per hour	1st-year students	2nd-year students	3rd-year students
Hearing assignment	33	38	40
Presenting next assignment	22	20	20
Flash cards	5	2	0

Choosing supplementary music. *I need reassurance on the way I choose supplementary music for my second-year students. I assign sheet music that uses only the notes they can read and the musical signs they already understand, and I insist that my assistant teachers do the same. But I encounter disagreement on the necessity for this. Can you back me up?*

I'm happy to back you up on the absolute necessity for not assigning music that contains anything the student does not already understand. However, I would add three more criteria (you mention only reading and musical signs). It is equally important that our students be wholly secure with the rhythmic experiences they will meet in the new music; that they be technically prepared to play the music with ease and enjoyment; and, above all, that the music lie within the range of their present musical maturity — is it music they can understand and project with full musical meaning? *(March 1976)*

First lessons in the Fall. *Up until three years ago I taught all summer as well as throughout the school year. Then, because I felt that I needed summers free for myself, I began teaching only from September through June. This gives my students two months without lessons. And that's my problem — when they return in September, they seem to have forgotten everything they had learned the previous year. As a result I have used the first four to six weeks each fall as a review period, working on music they had studied in the spring. At least in that way they had something they could play; other, wise they'd have nothing for weeks. The students don't like the review pieces, and I've received some flak from parents, too. What else can I do?*

The reaction of your students and their parents seems wholly normal and healthy. A return to music lessons, after two months of vacation, should be a big moment with much new music, new goal-setting, and lots of reason for excitement and motivation. Instead of considering your review as review of music your students studied the preceding spring, why not consider reviewing the concepts or skills learned, but in the context of new music. To accomplish this, you could choose music having the same reading range and rhythmic experiences and requiring no new technical skills. To make sure the student has pieces to play at once choose music not more than a page or two in length that includes no major problems. Then use the first few lessons as directed practice periods, working out with the student portions of his new music so that he leaves the studio feeling capable and therefore eager to practice. In my opinion, a new school year necessitates new music for *every* student. *(October 1974)*

What suggestions do you have to help teachers make a big event out of beginning lessons in the fall?

The resumption of lessons in the fall can't be a big event if it represents merely the next lesson. So the first step in making it an "occasion" is to precede it with a vacation, both for you and for the students. The last lesson before such a vacation should include an evaluation of what your students have learned throughout the year, emphasizing the ways in which they have improved musically, technically, and in practice habits. This can be demonstrated most dramatically by contrasting what they are doing now with what they were doing a year ago. This evaluation should be followed by your great expectations for the year ahead.

The beginning of a new school year should mean new music, new approaches to technique, more advanced theory, etc. So, except for the most advanced students, the first assignment of the new season should include no "hold-over" music, nothing they were studying before vacation. In the first fall assignment it is wise to include at least one piece that is short (just one or two pages in length) and that sounds impressive, so that students experience an immediate musical reward that satisfies both their ears and their egos.

We have been talking about how to make the first fall lesson a big occasion for the student. It is also important to make it a big occasion for ourselves. I have one suggestion that has worked well for our staff. We try to imagine that each of our students is moving out of town and about to transfer to another teacher. When each student is inter, viewed by that imaginary new teacher (who will see and hear them far more objectively than we can), how will the new teacher rate the student in musicianship, technique, and practice habits? Where will that teacher begin? What will be that teacher's goals for each of our students? A careful consideration of each student from this stand, point can add real zest to your plans for the coming year. (September 1979)

Record keeping. *I know several teachers who have assistant teachers and who share with me the following question. Please understand that we are not pedagogy teachers, but each of us has from two to five assistants. They vary from year to year, because many of the assistants go on to have studios of their own. The result is that our students who study with these assistant teachers have a change in teacher very often. Our problem is, how can we possibly keep track of what the assistant teachers have assigned their students so that the next teacher will have some idea where to begin?*

We have a somewhat similar problem here at The New School for Music Study because of our teacher-training program. The simplest solution we have found is to maintain a complete record on all our students. There is a folder for each student who enrolls in the school, and included in the folder is everything that pertains to his study here — his original application, the interview form filled out by the teacher who interviews him, a record of exactly what he studies each year, a copy of each recital program on which he plays, etc. One of the most important items in the folder is a chart that shows exactly what music the student has been assigned and which pages in each book have been completed. Our format lists all the books the student is using, and under the book titles we list the page numbers on which each piece, exercise, etc., begins. When a student completes a piece or study, the corresponding page number is crossed out. A study of this chart does not indicate to what standards of performance the student was held, but it does tell the complete story of what material he studied. Such a record is invaluable in any teaching situation, but absolutely indispensable where change of teacher frequently occurs. *(January 1969)*

Sample Assignment Chart

```
LEVEL II
    KBT II   -  pp.  1, 8, 6, 7, 8, 9, 10, 11, 12, 13, 14, 15,
                     21, 22, 23, 24, 25, 26, 27, 28, 29, 30, 31,
                     37, 38, 39, 40, 41, 42, 43, 44, 45, 46, 47,

    Tech. II -  #    1, 2, 3, 4, 8, 6, 7, 8, 9, 10, 11, 12a, 12b
                     17, 18, 19, 20, 21, 22, 23, 24, 25, 26, 27,
                     34a, 34b, 35, 36a, 36b, 37, 38, 39a, 39b,
                     42b, 43a, 43b.

    Lit. II  -  pp.  3, 4-5, 6-7, 8-9, 10-11, 13, 14-11, 14-15#2,
                     23, 24, 25, 26-27, 28-29, 31.

    Cont. II -  pp.  5, 6-7, 8, 9, 10, 11, 13, 14, 16, 17, 18-19
                     25-26, 26-27.
```

Assignment books. *Our music store carries many different kinds of assignment books for students. Do you have any particular one that you use or recommend?*

Our students don't buy assignment books as such. Instead, each student brings a looseleaf binder (8½ x 11). I prefer this method for three reasons:

> The amount of paper needed for an assignment depends on the detail of the practice outline and varies from lesson to lesson and student to student.
> We prepare as much of the assignment as possible before the lesson, to save lesson time.
> Carbon copies of all assignment sheets are kept as a reference for planning the next lesson.

If at all possible, the assignment for the next week is prepared the evening of the lesson or the following morning, while the lesson is still fresh in memory. If this is not possible, at least jot down notes on the carbon copy as reminders of what needs to be done at the next lesson. *(November 1977)*

New piece expectations. *In presenting new music to intermediate students, I have been experimenting with the concept of setting up an expectation of how the piece will sound before beginning to practice it. I find it such an excellent preparatory step that I'm wondering how I can apply the same principle to beginners' pieces.*

Perhaps the best way to answer your question is to suggest the steps that will help beginners develop an expectation of how a piece will sound. In presenting *Bear Dance*, I might ask beginners these questions:

"Would a piece about a dancing bear be loud or soft?"
"Would it be played high on the piano or low?"
"Would it be fast or slow?"

With only a few such questions, we can lead students to expect a piece that sounds loud and low on the piano and has a motion that is slow and somewhat clumsy — just the way a bear dances.

Next, help the student realize that the two lines are exactly alike except that line two is played an octave lower. This sets up two expectations: the second line sounds exactly like the first, but lower; and this piece will be a cinch to learn. Lead the student to notice that every measure begins on bass F and that the entire piece is "F, up a 5th, same," or "F, down a 2nd, same," (same is shorthand for repeated note). Finally, point out the time signature (3/4), noting that the whole feeling of the piece is in threes and that the rhythm pattern consists entirely of quarter notes except for the dotted half note that ends each line.

If students observe all these things before they play the piece for the first time, they not only will have an expectation of how it will sound, but will be able to play it accurately on the first reading.

Here is a more difficult elementary piece, "Tall Pines."

Tall Pines

Jon George

By now students will be making their own observations without as many questions from the teacher. They will notice the title, the instruction "With quiet dignity," and the consistent look of all four lines. They will see that each phrase begins low on the piano and sweeps upward in broken 5ths, two notes to the pulse, with a gradual crescendo from bottom to top. At the top the figure turns around and descends in 2nds, primarily one note to the pulse, with a gentle decrescendo. They will observe that lines one and two are exactly the same except for a rhythmic change in the last two measures. They will notice that line three is exactly like line one but on the dominant, and they will see that line four is exactly like line two except that the last three measures are repeated an octave higher, the final right-hand note lasts much longer, and there is a final note for the left hand, an octave lower than low G.

The last step in setting up an expectation of how the piece will sound might be to experience it on the keyboard cover, actually playing the fingers and making the moves, but silently. During this playing the student should count out loud, beginning softly in each line, counting with crescendos and decrescendos as indicated, and counting the ending as softly as possible.

The more we look at music in this way, the more we excite our students' interest in how a new piece will sound. The expectations, and a natural desire to fulfill them, provide strong motivation for practice. *(April 1985)*

Before practice begins. *Ever since attending your one-week summer study course in Chicago, a group of local piano teachers has been meeting to discuss music and teaching. Would you be willing to answer some of our questions in your column? The problem with which we need the most help is this: what should a student see in a piece before he begins to practice? We will appreciate illustrations from your* Contemporary Piano Literature *books.*

I have selected three different compositions as illustrations of what we want our students to see in a piece *before* they begin to practice. We take for granted that they are aware of composer, title, key signature, etc. But beyond that, we want them to learn to look at a piece to develop an expectation of its sound, and to make a sensible practice plan.

Let's look first at "March" by Alexander Tcherepnin.

March
ALEXANDER TCHEREPNIN

The title and the marking "In march time" indicate the spirit and tempo of the piece. There are 4 lines (or parts). Lines 1, 2 and 4 are very similar, so we have marked them A, A^1 and A^2. The third line is different, so it is marked B. Let's look at the three A parts. Notice that the highest note in each line is E, but the fact that it comes earlier in each line changes the melodic shape and brings the climax at a different point each time. The left hand marches along in a C major 5-finger position. But now take a close look at the third line, marked B. Here there is not only a different look but a very different and special sound — suddenly our march has gone modern. This third line provides a complete contrast to the rest of the piece. Its dynamic level is utterly different (pianissimo instead of forte), the intervals are blocked rather than melodic, and the rise to that same climactic E is heightened and suspended by the use of the altered tone (Bb changing to B♮) and the natural ritard of those half notes. What a wonderful unsettled feeling we have on that open fourth in the last measure, and how exciting is the return to A at the beginning of the fourth line.

Here is a slightly more difficult piece by Tcherepnin.

Chimes

ALEXANDER TCHEREPNIN

Here the title tells us what the piece is about, and the composer tells us he wants these bells to ring vigorously, the chiming well marked. Furthermore, the abundant use of accents and pedal make us realize that this sound will really imitate the clanging, overlapping chime of large bells. The piece is made up of five parts which we have marked with numbers. There is no point in using letters since the en, tire piece is made of one small motif, but there is a clear rhythmic plan, and a clear plan for the accents. Let's look first at the rhythmic scheme the composer has used to give his piece intensity and momentum. Part one, in which the chimes are divided between hands, uses just quarter notes and eighth notes. The rhythm of part two is exactly the same, but it looks somewhat different because it is written entirely in the right hand with a slower accompaniment rhythm for the left. In part three the entire motion slows down to quarters and halves. In parts four and five the basic rhythmic motion gains momentum again and moves into the climax in steady eighth-notes, ending with a grand clang at the end. And what about the plan of the accents? In the first part the accent falls on the first beat of each measure. The second part starts out the same way, but in the third measure the accents begin to come twice in each bar, on the first and third beats. In the third part there are accents on beats one, two, and three. The fourth part is like the second, while in the last part the accent falls on every beat. Because the piece gradually ascends in register from beginning to end, each new part requires a new hand position.

The student who becomes aware of the gradual increase in basic rhythmic motion, of the continuous increase in accents, of the gradual rise in register, of the crescendo, and of the added effect of the pedal can experience the increase in tension before he ever plays the piece. In this way he is aware of what to listen for when he begins to practice.

Here is a still more difficult piece by Tcherepnin.

Hide and Seek

Here again the title and the composer's indication, as well as the general look of the page, tell us to expect an animated musical game. The piece is made up of four parts. The first three are made of the same basic figure, and have much in common. The last part, marked B, is wholly different. In the first two parts each measure is made of just one note, played at four different octaves; each part is made of the same notes but in a different order (in the first line, D, A, Eb, Ab, while in the second, D, Ab, AZ, Eb). In the third part the right hand reiterates D, while the left hand darts from D to BZ to Bb to F#. In the fourth line, the rhythmic figure changes to quarter notes; the first two measures are legato; the last two measures become dramatic leaps of more than five octaves. The student needs to see, then, that the piece begins with the feeling of darting here and there (the octave leaps and staccato). The third part begins to settle (those constant D s in the right hand) as if the seeker were getting closer to his prey. In the fourth part, he creeps up on him (the legato quarter notes) and, after a terrific leap, catches him in the last measure! *(December 1967)*

Presenting a New Piece in a Limited Amount of Time. *Will you please give some suggestions for what you would do if you have only a few minutes in which to assign a new piece?*

If I have only a few minutes in which to assign a new piece (and how often this happens!) I concentrate on the following areas:

Draw the student's attention to the composer and help him recall something about the other pieces he has studied by that composer. This fixes an impression of general style and gives the student a degree of familiarity with and expectation for the new piece.

Draw his attention to the title and interpretive markings and the expectations of sound these imply.

Work on the one thing that will help him most with his workout of this specific piece at home.

Let me illustrate with Schumann's "Hunting Song."

Hunting Song

From the *Album for the Young*, Op. 68

Robert Schumann

The one thing I want to be sure the student experiences before he goes home with this piece is the physical feel of each of the two basic gestures out of which the entire piece is made: the horn motif in measures I and 2 and the galloping motif in measures 3 and 4. I also want to be sure he understands that, rhythmically speaking, the entire piece can be expressed as the interplay between the horn pattern:

and the galloping pattern:

I would draw his attention to the fact that these two basic patterns are repeated alternately over and over until the beginning of the fourth score. At this point Schumann has thickened the texture — suddenly we have a feeling of three voices rather than two in unison octaves as before. In addition, the student needs to be aware that at this point Schumann has worked out an ingenious combination of the two basic patterns – the galloping motif appears in the right hand as melody, while against it the horn pattern enters in the left hand as accompaniment. Finally, the horn motif appears, this time in four voices, to bring the hunt to a triumphant conclusion.

If the student experiences the feel of each basic gesture and understands the way in which the two motifs or patterns are used throughout the piece, he is really ready to work the piece out alone at home. So these are the two things on which I would spend a few minutes.

Now let's illustrate the same principles in C.P.E. Bach's *Solfeggietto* in C Minor.

How many times have we heard Bach's immortal *Solfeggietto*, all 514 sixteenth notes clearly and cleanly played, like so many rounds of machine gun fire, totally devoid of shape, sweep, phrasing, and climax? Too many! For this reason, the one thing I would want to be sure the student understood when he went home to work out this piece is its structure.

The form can be expressed in the letter picture:

$$A B A^1 C A^2 D A$$

He needs to understand, too, that each of the parts is four measures long, except for D, whose ten measures provide a real climax before the final return to A.

He also needs to see that B, C, and D will require more practice than the sections of A material, for two reasons: first, each A section is made of two measures, repeated identically an octave higher in the next two measures; and second, each A section requires the same technical practice, except for the few places marked with a bracket in the score — at these spots the keyboard geography is different, so the feel of the technical practice is different, too.

Armed with this information, the student can make the most profitable use of his practice time, so it is this approach that I would stress in my few minutes with him. (*March 1970*)

What suggestions do you have if there are only a few minutes to present a new piece? Some teacher friends and I have prepared a list of pieces, easy to advanced, hoping you will continue this in future issues.

The problem with your request is only one of space, because the suggestions are meaningless to other readers unless accompanied by the music we are discussing. In this issue I will make suggestions for the first two of the easy pieces on your list.

The Broad Jump

In "Broad Jump" I would want students to see that it is made entirely of three consecutive 6ths, except where it closes to a 5th in measures 4, 8 and 16. They need to see that in the first three scores the sixths are played in contrary motion, which puts the accent either on both thumbs or both fifth fingers. In the last score there is a complete technical change — the motion becomes parallel so that the accent falls on the RH fifth finger and the LH thumb.

Playing Tag

In presenting "Playing Tag," I would want to make sure that before the student left the studio he could play smoothly and evenly the D and A major five-finger patterns (which feel alike) and the F major pattern (which feels very different) and that he could move from one position to another with ease. *(May-June 1970)*

What are your suggestions for presenting these pieces by Ross Lee Finney in a limited amount of time?

Each of the Finney pieces is constructed on the principle of the tone row. The specific row selected and the way in which the composer uses it are the things I'd want my students to discover first about each piece.

Let's look at "There and Back."

There and Back
From *25 Inventions*

Lively

Ross Lee Finney

The row Finney has selected for this piece begins with Middle C, and uses each of the 12 tones of the chromatic scale from C to C in this order:

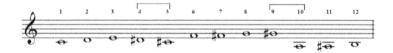

Tones 4 and 5 are played together, as are tones 9 and 10. The "game" of understanding this piece is to see how the row has been used. In line one, tones 1 through 5 appear in measure 1, are repeated in measure 2, and the row is completed in measure 3. Line two is the same except that the hands have exchanged parts. Line three begins with tone 12 and presents the row backwards, arriving at tone 1 at the end of the second measure. This is repeated an octave lower in the next two measures. Line four is a partial row. The student will enjoy figuring out which tones are omitted.

Berceuse
From *25 Inventions*

With gentle motion

Ross Lee Finney

In "Berceuse" the tone row consists of a right hand pedal point on D (tone 1) with the rest of the notes of the chromatic scale as a left hand melody, used in this order:

In measures 5-8, Finney transposes the row up a half-step, gives the pedal point to the left hand (D# now) and the transposed melody to the right hand. Also the row has undergone considerable rhythmic development. In the last five measures the left hand not only takes a sustained pedal point but also doubles the melody an octave below the right hand; again the melody is varied rhythmically from the two preceding statements.

"Skipping" presents a new treatment of the tone row.

Skipping
From *25 Inventions*

In strict tempo

Ross Lee Finney

If we consider the right hand, we see that the row is used in this order:

What about the left hand? It is playing the identical row a major third below the right hand.

All of the Finney pieces can be analyzed according to the same principle. Students love to play this musical detective game, discovering first the row itself and then how the row is used to construct the piece. Be sure to call the students' attention to the wide variety of styles and moods achieved by Mr. Finney. *(April 1970)*

In several issues last year you dealt with the one point you would make in presenting a new piece if you had only a short time in which to do it. Would you be willing to apply the same idea to the Chopin E minor Prelude – for example, what would you do with it if you had just a few minutes to present it at the end of the lesson?

PRELUDE

in E minor

I would hesitate to assign this Prelude if I had just a few minutes at the end of the lesson. It deserves more consideration whenever it is first presented, and I can't seem to reduce it to one thing I would do. The bare minimum for presenting this particular work seems to me to include the following:

Play the piece to make the student aware of its beauty and the mood it creates. I like to think of this Prelude as an exquisitely moving study of grief — the static, nagging quality of resigned despair from which fresh outbursts of grief occur three times, always returning to the sense of resignation.

Analyze the musical means Chopin employs to accomplish this — that is, what he has done to create a work that can be remarkably inactive melodically and rhythmically, yet so moving emotionally. We would note that except for the three places marked (1) (2) (3) the entire piece descends gradually by seconds. What's more, except for the same three places the rhythm remains very constant:

Even the dynamic level, except at the three points mentioned, remains the same.

To make sure the student is aware from the start of the gradual descent by seconds in the LH chords, ask him to circle the note or notes in each chord that descend (see measures 2 through 8). When he sees this he will have an insight into the musical means for the depression that overwhelms us — it is indeed a physical fact that the piece's foundation sinks ever lower. The three poignant moments of outburst can be understood only in contrast to this overall descent. In each successive outburst the dynamic range increases, the melodic sweep becomes wider, the rhythms freer and more intense. To emphasize the total contrast in the two moods, have the student compare the melody of measures 1 through 3 with that of measures 16 through 18. *(April 1971)*

Students come to lessons without all their music. What do you do when a student habitually comes to his lesson with only part of the music on his assignment?

Coming to a lesson without all the music indicates a disorganized and careless attitude, which all too often is reflected in disorganized and careless practice habits.

In fact, I strongly suspect that the student who comes without all his music also practices without completing his entire assignment. The sooner we can help the young person approach piano study in an organized and careful way, the sooner he will become a successful and happy student.

The well-organized teacher should have a copy of all the music he is teaching. He needs it both to prepare the lesson and to use during the lesson. So from a practical standpoint the lesson could be given from the teacher's copy of the missing music. But this makes it impossible to make notes in the copy from which the student will be practicing. When students come without all their music, I explain to both the student and parents the importance of having all the music at every lesson. If the problem persists, I help the student make a checklist to use before leaving home. In extreme cases I have resorted to sending the student home without giving the lesson. This means the inconvenience of a make-up lesson for me, but it certainly dramatizes the seriousness of the issue to both student and parents. I have never had a student forget music again after being sent home without a lesson! (*April 1979*)

Cancelling a lesson for lack of practice. *What do you do when students call to cancel a lesson because they haven't had time to practice all week?*

I tell them that if they haven't practiced they especially need the lesson, and that we will turn it into such a good practice session they'll be glad they came! Of course I'm disappointed when a student hasn't had time to practice, but it happens to almost everyone occasionally, and for good reasons — illness, being out of town, family company, a term paper due, rehearsals for the high school play, etc. Students who haven't practiced have two strikes against them — they are unprepared, and as a result they feel guilty. No wonder they want to get out of what they think will be an unpleasant experience. Our first job is to make them feel comfortable about corning for a lesson without preparation, and our second task is to make the lesson so productive they'll be glad they came. I usually devote such a lesson to detailed work on one or more of the pieces they are studying, focusing on what constitutes efficient and effective practice and on how much can be accomplished in a short period of time. My goal is not to get a week's work done in one lesson but to dig deeply into one or two compositions, enjoying the luxury of this lesson for which the only agenda is motivating the student to really constructive practice in the week to come. (*April 1979*)

Practices only part of the assignment. *What would you do if a student consistently practices only part of his assignment?*

First, we might consider whether or not the assignment is too long or too difficult for the amount of time this student has to practice. Then we might consider if the part of the assignment he fails to practice is always the same part — that is, does he always omit technique, theory, Bach, contemporary music, etc.? If so, this is probably an indication to us that he doesn't like that particular part of the assignment. Why not try to replace this part with something he does enjoy that still accomplishes the same goal?

If you have considered the above solutions and found them of no help, there is one further suggestion: spend the entire lesson on the unpracticed parts, until the student catches on that he is responsible for the whole assignment. (October 1966)

Students beg for new music. *What do you do with junior high students who beg for new music even though they can't really play the pieces on their last assignment? I have students who seem to be unwilling to finish music or to play it really well. They just want to read new pieces all the time.*

We all have students like that. Many young people, especially those of junior high age, are in a stage of adventure and romance, of wanting to explore the world, not only in music but in many areas of their lives. When students are in this developmental stage, I suggest reducing the amount of precision you require and increasing the amount of adventure you encourage. This can be accomplished by giving a double assignment: a few pieces they are to study carefully and bring up to high performance standards, and more pieces for browsing or sight-reading. Music in the browsing assignment is for them to read and enjoy without the necessity for meeting any demands from you as to accuracy or performance standards. We have found that there are students who blossom under this treatment, and that in a year or two they have grown out of the need for a browsing assignment and are again eager to meet high standards for most of the music on their assignment. (April 1980)

Big vs. small music. *After many years of teaching I still have the problem of the student who considers the music he is playing small and wants to play the big pieces that his friends are playing before he is able to play them well. I overcome the problem with one student and soon it pops up with another. Is this situation inevitable? What suggestions do you have for meeting and solving this problem?*

Yes, I do think there is a degree of inevitability about this problem. Young people (and often their parents) are not yet ready to understand that any good piece of music beautifully played is a "big" piece. That is the kind of wisdom we have to nurture, and we can expect it to develop faster in some students than in others. It appears to me from your question that you already have some very good answers to the problem yourself, for you apparently have solved it with many students. The best answers will be drawn from your own experiences, and of course all I can speak from are my experiences. But here are three suggestions that I hope may prove helpful to you.

1. Whenever possible, let the student hear what he calls "small" works played by a great artist, either in person or on recordings. An all-Bach recital by Rosalyn Tureck had a great effect on a group of our students recently, because her first group included several easy pieces they had studied. Their reaction was, "Why, even a great artist plays our pieces!" and the music obviously skyrocketed in their estimation.

   Last summer Sylvia Muehling opened her recital at The New School with a group of the "Little Preludes and Fugues" of Bach. Many of the students who heard her were working on those very pieces at that time. Suddenly these pieces seemed "bigger" to them. Just this summer, Elvina Truman Pearce gave the opening recital at one of our study courses. She included stunning performances of short Handel "lessons" and the Mozart Variations on "Ah, vous dirai-je, maman." When the students in the audience approach those same pieces next year or in the years to come, will it be hard to persuade them this is "big" music? I don't think so! When artist recitals such as these are not available, use recordings. The children's pieces of Bartok, Prokofiev, and Kabalevsky, for example, or at a more advanced level, Schumann's "Scenes from Childhood," take on added importance when recorded by an artist of stature.

2. During the year, have as many informal recitals as possible in which you arrange to have all of the students and their parents seated together in the same room. In this way each student hears all the other students play. Young people are very sensitive to the effect a particular performance has on an audience. When a student plays beautifully and artistically, whether it's a "little" Haydn Minuet or a "big" Beethoven Sonata, the effect on the audience is the same. When students hear that the "small" and the "big" produce the same effect, the separation into categories by size becomes less important in their minds.

3. Try to find out what "big" really means to these students. Often they mean a piece that is louder and more dramatic than the pieces they are currently studying, or one that covers the keyboard in a sweeping, splashy way. If so, there is much good music that when well played produces just that soul-satisfying effect for which they are longing. The trick is to find a piece that produces the desired effect without imposing unreasonable technical or musical demands. Such music exists, often not by the great composers but by those who have a knack for creating teaching pieces for these very needs. (*November 1979*)

Titles affect students. *I have had high school students look down their noses at two books I want them to study. Both are unfortunately titled "Scenes from Childhood," one by Schumann and the other by Pinto. I believe they would love the music if it weren't for the title of the collection and, in some cases, the titles of individual numbers. Do you recommend changing titles so that older students will be willing to study this music?*

In my opinion the collections you mentioned do not fall into the category of the many pieces that seem badly titled for high school students. Why not explain to your students that this is music written for adults who have lived long enough to remember scenes from their childhood? Children obviously can't look back on childhood; this is an experience only adults enjoy. The difficulty is that high school students may not be far enough removed from childhood to fully enjoy these reminiscences, either. But if you present the pieces and their titles as fully adult, I think you can interest them in these particular collections, especially if you let them hear some of the music as recorded by great artists. (July-August 1981)

The college student who won't practice. *I have been teaching a very gifted college student for six months and admit that I have gotten nowhere. He is pleasant and enthusiastic at the lesson, but practices only what and how he wants to practice, doing almost nothing between lessons with the suggestions I make. If I were to be firmer in my demands, I am sure he would quit. I can't run that risk, for he is far too gifted. At the moment all I seem to be doing is suggesting music for him to study, and study in this case means he merely plays as he wishes. What could I do differently?*

I wonder if your fear of his quitting isn't coloring your attitude toward him and, indeed, making it impossible for you to teach him? Wouldn't it be wise to ask him to come in for a conference, explain your view of a real teacher-student relationship, your feeling that you have failed him as a teacher, and your unwillingness to continue lessons on this basis? You could ask him to consider (between the time of the conference and his next lesson) whether he wishes to become your student, in the real sense, or whether he would prefer to have you recommend a teacher whom he could respect. Granted, this could be the end of your relationship, but more likely he will be shocked to discover your view of the situation and will decide to meet your demands once he understands them. Either way you are both better off. (March 1984)

When to drop a piece. How do you know when it's time to discontinue a piece and drop it from the student's assignment?

There aren't any rules, and I believe each decision is a judgment call. In general, though, there is a rhythm to the way pieces move through a student's assignment. This is true at all levels, but especially in the beginning and elementary years. At this level there are always new pieces to be worked out, last week's pieces to be worked up, and older review pieces that need further work to become more secure and musical.

Our beginning students usually have four to eight new pieces each week, some of which are short, one-line "discovery" pieces. These pieces make a specific pedagogical point and are usually not reviewed a second week, to make room for review of longer and more important repertoire pieces. The third week some of the repertoire pieces will move up to the category of special pieces for refined interpretive work, while others are dropped. The fourth week one of the special pieces may become a memory piece or a piece to be played for repertoire class. Others are dropped from the assignment. Of course, students continue to play their favorite pieces long after they have disappeared from the assignment.

One of the difficulties with this whole issue is that as teachers we are prone to say, "Well done! You've really got that piece now. Let's drop it." We drop it just at the moment when reviewing it would be most meaningful and most fun; yet, to make way for further learning, we must always drop pieces to add new ones. In carefully sequenced materials the same concepts and skills will be reinforced over and over, but always in new pieces.

For the more advanced student it's wise, before discontinuing a piece, to consider why you assigned it in the first place. For example, perhaps a student preparing to play the Mendelssohn Concerto in G minor is having difficulty with the octave passages. You might assign special octave studies. When the octave problems in the Concerto are cleared up, it would be appropriate to discontinue the special studies. Often when a student is seriously studying a Mozart Sonata (perhaps K. 283), we assign movements of other Mozart sonatas for browsing, to develop further acquaintance with Mozart's sonata form and style. These could be discontinued when their purpose is accomplished.

If a student comes to us for help on the Bartók Rondos, and we find that he has studied no easier Bartók pieces, we might loan him one of the Bartók collections to help him develop familiarity with Bartók's melodic repetition, harmonic dissonance, and accentuation. When this familiarity has been increased, the easier collection is dropped. A completely different issue is that of gracefully retreating from a piece that turns out to have been unwisely assigned. It may be too mature for the student musically, too difficult technically, or for one of many reasons is just not right for this student. In such a case it's usually easy to find a good reason for putting the piece aside for the time being and going to something more appropriate instead.

The world is filled with good music for teaching. If a certain piece doesn't work for a particular student, or even if the student simply doesn't respond well to it, there's no dishonor in dropping it in favor of something that works or that the student likes. (*March 1989*)

Chapter Three

Fundamental Subjects

Reading

Confusion about line-notes and space-notes. *I graduated from college last June and have been teaching piano for one year. I am having some real problems with beginners. Two of the students can't tell a note on a line from a note in a space, and all of them have trouble with up and down, and high and low. What am I doing wrong?*

The confusion about lines and spaces is very common. To most children, a note "on a line" means ——. They have experienced on-ness as a cup on a saucer, a hat on a head, sitting on a chair, lying on a bed. In other words, most of their previous experience with "on" has associated "on" with "above." So, from the beginning, when using the term "note on a line," make a new association —— and do it dramatically. Incidentally, it is far less confusing to use the expression "line-note." Watch out, too, for confusion over space-notes. If you present them as notes in space, a child may think ● . Space, especially in this day and age, is a kind of nothingness to float in. Its confines should be defined, and used as part of its description. For example, space-notes can be written three ways:

between 2 lines —— above a line —— below a line ——

I think the second problem you mention, confusion between up and down and high and low, is even more common. Again it is probably a matter of verbal confusion, because a child's previous experience with up and down has been purely spatial — up the steps, down the stairs, up the ladder, down the slide, and so on. The keyboard is horizontal and has no look of up or down. So, from the beginning, there must be emphasis on associating up the keyboard with moving to the right (——→) and down the keyboard with moving to the left (←——).

Above all, be aware of a built-in contradiction, and the problems that arise because of it. When a child plays an ascending passage (♪♪♪) he reads to the right and plays to the right on the keyboard. But when he plays a descending passage (♪♪♪) he reads to the right but plays to the left on the keyboard. This alone is the root of many reading problems.

A similar problem exists regarding pitch, and for the same reason. Pitch is not spatial. Again, only after associating the words high-low and higher-lower with their sounds for a long time can we expect a child to understand the words without the corresponding sound. Of course, if you find that your problem with a child is not one of verbal confusion, but a basic perceptual problem, I suggest you contact the school teacher to find out if he has related reading problems in the classroom. If a student confuses *b* and *p*, *n* and *u*, *v* and *w*, or rearranges the letters of a word (reading *spot* as *pots*, or *bird* as *brid*), the reading problem may be a basic one which should be referred to a reading specialist. Or it might be as simple as a need for glasses. (September 1966)

Ledger lines. *How do you explain ledger lines to young students? They occur in their music between the staffs long before they are ready to understand them above and below the grand staff. What do you tell them?*

Like many areas of learning, a student doesn't need an explanation if you adequately prepare and guide the experience. Rather than talk, do.

For example, students first experience ledger lines when they begin reading on a five-line staff. Whenever the right hand goes down to middle C, or the left hand goes up to it, an added line is needed. In preparing this ask the students to play and name notes up from bass F (or down from treble G) while you write them on the board, adding a ledger line for C as you come to it, without explanation. When you have done this several times, with students always playing and naming the notes as they are written, add the B below middle C for the right hand, and the D above middle C for the left hand in the same way. Later, add the A below middle C for the right hand and the E above middle C for the left hand. By this time he understands that whenever you need another line, you add it.

Once a student can read well on the grand staff, give him pieces in which he sees that middle C for the left hand is written closer to the bass staff, and middle C for the right hand is closer to the treble staff. Again, students accept this pragmatically, without any explanation. When a student has had a great deal of experience reading and playing music with ledger lines between staffs, assign written work such as the following examples to back up the understanding.

Here are three ways to write the notes from middle C up to E and from middle C down to A. Trace the notes in each measure, then play and name them

Before playing, you may want to have students add upstems for right-hand notes and downstems for left-hand notes, emphasizing the general rule that notes written on the treble staff are played with the right hand and notes on the bass staff with the left hand.

Later, give the same experience in ledger line notes across the staff and ask students not only to trace the notes but also to copy them on another staff:

There are four ways to write A-C-E across the staff.

Trace the notes in each measure.

On this staff, copy A-C-E each of the four ways across the staff.

Then play and name the notes in each measure.

Still later, they are asked to prove their understanding of ledger lines by transcribing notes from one staff to another like this:

Write these treble staff notes on the bass staff below them.

Write these bass staff notes on the treble staff above them.

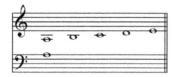

When the students' reading range expands, assign pieces that include ledger lines around high G and low F. They also have written drills in which ledger lines within the new reading range become a secure part of their reading experience. For example, mark the intervals (3,4,5). Then play and say the direction and interval ("G, down a 3rd, up a 5th," etc.).

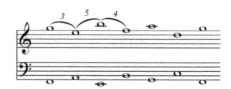

Ultimately, ask him to copy music from one staff to another, which requires him to read music with many ledger lines and to transcribe it to another register: on the upper staff, mark the intervals. Then play and count the melody, using the right hand.

On the lower staff trace the G clef and time signature. Copy the melody one octave lower. Then play and count what you wrote, using the left hand. Does it sound the same, except an octave lower? Now play it hands together. *(July-August 1988)*

Interval reading. *I am not sure I understand your approach to reading music by intervals. For example, in Music Tree A, when students have learned only 2nds on the grand staff, how are they able to read the interval of a 6th between hands?*

It is best to approach interval reading in two steps: find the first note in each hand by its interval relation to the nearest landmark (treble G, bass F or middle C); then, within each hand, read by intervals.

Let's look at a beginner's piece such as "Sailing."

We want students to see that the LH plays nothing but 2nds up from bass F and the RH plays only middle C. That's all they need to know to read the pitch notation accurately. To give students skill in interval reading, ask them to point and say the direction and intervals, like this:

"Bass F, up a 2nd, up a 2nd, middle C I bass F, up a 2nd, up a 2nd," etc.

Before playing the piece go through these additional steps:

> scan the score, seeing time signature (4/4), dynamic mark (p), and two identical phrases, except for the last note (which they circle as a reminder);
> practice the rhythm (point and count or tap and count);
> find the position for each hand: LH finger 4 on bass F (all other fingers lying on adjacent white keys); RH finger 2 on middle C (all other fingers lying on adjacent white keys).

Even though students need to know only landmarks and 2nds to read the notes, to play the piece *musically* they need to hear and feel not only the rising 2nds but also the lift (up a 3rd) between LH and RH, and the wider leap (down a 5th) between RH and LH.

In "Whippoorwill," too students need to know only landmarks and 2nds to read the notes.

Whippoorwill

Before playing, they go through the same preparatory steps: scan the score, practice the rhythm, and find the position for each hand: RH finger 3 on treble G-up a 2nd-A; LH finger 2 on middle C. Again, in both hands, all other fingers should lie on adjacent white keys.

Here it is important for a student to see that the entire piece is made of just 3 notes (A,G in RH, middle C in LH); but to play the piece musically, there is much to hear and feel:

> 5 phrases of varying lengths — 8 beats, 7, 4, 4, 9
> the first 2 phrases end with a 5th between hands (G-C)
> the last 3 phrases end with a 6th between hands (A-C)

Be sure not to overlook the pun.

In a piece such as "Walking Like Elephants," students should know landmarks, 2nds and 3rds.

Walking Like Elephants

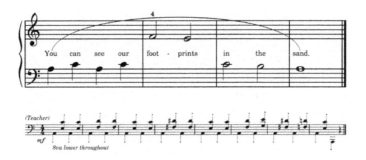

You can see our foot - prints in the sand.

(Teacher)

mf

8va lower throughout

Use the same preparatory steps to end in finding the position.

> LH: finger 3 on middle C-down a 3rd-A.
> RH: finger 2 on middle C-up a 2nd-D.

For a musical performance, students should hear and feel 3 phrases – 2 measures, 2 measures, 4 measures. Each phrase begins with LH 3rds and ends with RH 2nds and the third phrase is the longest and most active - the interval between hands stretches the ear to a fourth, followed by a calm descent in seconds and a natural ritard in half notes. *(October 1988)*

Careless readers. *I have problems with the majority of my students and it isn't the problem of getting them to read. They are good readers; in fact most of them read as well as I do. The problem is that they are careless and pay little or no attention to fingering, dynamics, slurs, staccato, etc., and lack a consistent sense of rhythm.*

If your students pay little attention to fingering, dynamics, slurs, staccato, etc., can we really agree that they are good readers? Your premise seems to be that playing the correct pitch is the beginning and end of good reading. In reality, it isn't even the beginning, is it? The beginning of good reading is developing students who listen, are aware of and understand everything they see in the score, and have the technique to bring what they see into sound at the piano.

This emphasis on reading music, not just notes, must begin at the first lesson. Only if we start by developing students who listen, who see and understand, and who have the technique to bring this understanding into sound, can we hope to develop students who are good readers in the complete sense.

If you start new beginners this fall, you have a built-in opportunity to try this approach. The problem with more advanced students, whom you describe as careless, is more difficult but it can be solved with time and patience. I suggest that using a portion of every lesson to work on a new piece, either a very short piece or a small portion of a longer work, setting the highest standards for listening, awareness, and accuracy. Pursue these goals with the utmost vigor and enthusiasm, supplying bravos for every success. When a student begins to see how this pays off, you are on your way.

During the year there should be at least one piece on each assignment to increase his capacity for listening, seeing, and understanding, and bringing his understanding into sound with more insight and beauty. *(November 1969)*

Rote teaching. *I have taught piano for twenty years and have yet to come to any conclusions about the value of rote teaching. I have taught some pieces by rote to some students, but still have doubts about its purpose and value. I have had students come to me from other teachers who, as a result of rote teaching, refuse to learn to read. The teachers with whom I have discussed this are either strongly for rote teaching or just as strongly opposed to it or, in some cases, share my confusion. We'd all appreciate your thinking on this matter.*

The word "rote" applied to music teaching is confusing in itself, and I suppose has nearly as many meanings as there are teachers. The literal meaning, found in any standard dictionary, includes such definitions as, "repetition of forms or phrases, often without attention to meaning"; "repetition in a mechanical, routine way"; "by memory without thought of the meaning." Any educator, considering one of these literal definitions, would naturally oppose rote teaching. However, in music teaching, a quite different meaning has come to be associated with the term "rote." When we teach pieces or parts of pieces by rote, we present them by sound and (at the keyboard) by feel, without first reading the notation which stands for those sounds and feels. I use and endorse rote teaching that includes such activities as these:

> Teaching songs by having the students hear them, then sing them by imitation without reading either the words themselves or the melodic notation.
> Playing a phrase and having the students sing or play it back by ear, imitating both sound and gesture, without reading.
> Tapping a rhythm pattern and having the students clap or tap it back.
> Playing a piece for beginning students, having them play the piece by imitating the sound, look, and feel before seeing the notation and relating it to what was just played.
> Teaching older beginners pieces that they can imitate without reading: pieces that provide the fun and satisfaction of a wider range of sounds than they can read at first, but sounds which they can nonetheless learn to play by imitating patterns and gestures.
> Presenting most discoveries (new signs and symbols) by rote — first the sound, then the feel (how it feels to produce that sound at the keyboard) and finally the sign that stands for that sound.

All of these activities, it seems to me, are valid uses of rote teaching at the piano. It should be added, however, that rote teaching is never an end in itself. In every example cited above, the teaching process moves from rote to note as quickly as possible. After experiencing the sound and feel, the student sees the signs that stand for that musical experience. I suppose the best possible label for this type of teaching is actually not just rote but, rather, rote-notation, because the significance is that the rote experience prepares for and leads to the essential reading skills that follow. Viewed in this light, I would say that rote teaching in music is both inevitable and invaluable. *(September 1976)*

The non-reader. *Recently a ten-year-old student came to me after three years of study elsewhere. At the interview he played musically all three movements of the Clementi Sonatina, Op. 36, No. 1. I was surprised to find, however, that he couldn't read music at all. His former teacher has students learn pieces by listening to records, and makes no attempt to teach reading. My plan for this student is to assign him* Music Tree A *and stay with* The Music Tree *series until his reading and other skills catch up to his playing ability. What will happen to his interest? He has been playing only big pieces. Please advise.*

The situation you describe is a growing national phenomenon, and a difficult one with which to cope. Here at The New School we, too, begin such students with *Music Tree* A, because there can be no long- term progress without learning the fundamentals of reading, rhythm, technique, and theory. Because aurally-trained students have such well-developed ears, however, they make fast progress if a teacher takes the following precautions. Seldom play a piece for the student. If he hears it, he won't need to read it; if he doesn't hear it, reading will be his only access. Use supplementary material of comparable simplicity to *The Music Tree* which he reads only at the lesson. For his home practice, assign a specific number of new pieces for each day's practice that he is not to repeat on subsequent days. Once he's heard them, his eyes might once again defer to his ears. In addition to all the rhythmic activities the *Music Tree* books provide, give weekly rhythmic dictation, in which you clap (or play) rhythmic patterns, asking the student to write the notation. Also, give melodic dictation beginning with exercises as simple as:

Then devise for each lesson a series of progressively more difficult dictation exercises.

In addition to all of the remedial activities outlined above, you will need to satisfy the student's need for bigger music. You may want to continue the former teacher's practice of teaching by rote (perhaps a single piece each week that will seem to the student like significant music). You may even want to have the student continue to learn from records until his reading skills begin to catch up to his level of technical proficiency. In your zeal to fill in missing basics, never forget the importance of his morale. *(November 1988)*

The student who plays everything from memory. *I have a very intelligent 11-year-old pupil who plays her lessons almost perfectly, but always entirely from memory. From the beginning she has played most of each lesson from memory despite the fact that no one plays her music for her at home. Because she is deficient in sight-reading, I wonder how she learns her music. I don't want her to grow up to be one of those pianists who can play well but cannot read well. Do you have any suggestions?*

Because your student comes to her lessons well prepared, despite the fact she is a poor reader, it's apparent that she has great powers of concentration as well as an excellent ear. Your challenge is to help her apply her strong concentration to her reading skills. Rather than beginning with a sight-reading program, I suggest you assign her six easier pieces each week, one to be worked out each day of the week. Because the six easier pieces are not assigned as sight-reading, she may work them out in any way she wishes: hands separately if necessary; divided into sections and learned section-by-section; or any other practice technique that makes it possible for her to play a new piece accurately after one day's practice. Make it clear to her that you will hear her regular assignment from memory (and to dramatize what you mean by memory, always close the music or remove it from the music stand) but that you will hear her read and play the six easier pieces. To demonstrate how differently you will treat this music, sometimes hear only the B section, or only the last phrase, or even the left hand alone. With so many new pieces and this emphasis on reading and playing at the lesson, you can gradually focus her concentration on reading. *(December 1982)*

Students who look back and forth from music to hands. *I am confident that students who continually look back and forth from the music to their hands will never become facile readers. Once the habit is started, though, how do you break it? Telling them to keep their eyes on the music doesn't work, nor does covering their hands.*

There is no immediate solution, but the problem can be corrected by spending two or three minutes at each lesson over a period of weeks or even months. Students first should learn to visualize the keyboard, to see it as clearly as they can see their bedroom in the dark. Second, they must be completely familiar with the topography of the keyboard, physically acquainted with how the mountains and valleys of the black and white keys feel under their hands and fingers. Then they should be able to find any specific key by feeling the groups of black keys, without looking at their hands. The result is they read without continually looking from the music to their hands because they have found they don't need to. The following are suggestions for developing this awareness.

To begin developing a mental picture of the keyboard, ask students to close their eyes (or look at the ceiling) and name specific keys; the key just below the two black keys; the key just above the three black keys; the two keys between the groups of two black and three black keys; the two keys between the groups of three black and two black keys, and so on.

To develop the ability to find a key by feeling the topography, ask students (again with eyes closed or looking at the ceiling) to find a group of three black keys and play B, up and down the keyboard; two black keys and play E, up and down the keyboard; three black keys and play F, up and down the keyboard; two black keys and play D, up and down the keyboard; two black keys and play C#, up and down the keyboard; three black keys and play Bb, up and down the keyboard, etc.

Drills and games of this kind can serve as correctives once the problem has occurred. How much better it is to use these drills and play these games from the beginning, and never have the problem develop. *(November 1987)*

High school students who are poor readers. *I recently inherited a group of high school students from a teacher who has moved to another city. These students have won many awards for their performances, but they are the poorest readers I have ever seen. It takes them weeks to work out a new piece. I have told them how poor their reading is, but they refuse to do any of the work on sight-reading I assign, indicating they feel superior to it. What can I do?*

In the first place, we should all campaign to have sight-reading included in the requirements for auditions and competitions. What a difference that might make in the winners. As to the problem of your students, I suppose they won't really know how poor their sight-reading is until they have an opportunity to compare their own reading with that of other students the same age. Why not have a repertoire class or special session at frequent intervals for all of your students of their age, and base the class on just reading four-hand or eight-hand music at sight. Teamed with other students, their own reading inadequacies will come into dramatic focus. Such an experience with their peers will do more than all the talking in the world from you. You might also assign the same new piece to all of the students in the class, asking all of them to be prepared to play it at the next session. Again, this will show them far more effectively than a lecture from you, how much the better readers can accomplish in a short time. As soon as your students become aware of what others can do, of their own shortcomings, and of the advantages of becoming good readers, you can begin a serious program of sight-reading for them.

To begin, find the level at which they can sight-read accurately and securely. Assign a book of pieces just a level higher for their sight-reading assignment at home and, if possible, assign one new piece to be read each day. At the next lesson, check on one or more of the pieces in the sight-reading assignment. As you hear the pieces, direct the student's eyes ahead by covering each measure as he plays the first note of the measure. So often the problem is not that he can't read, but that he has not been encouraged to look ahead or to read in groupings. Then set a still faster tempo, and ask him to play just the first beat of each measure or the first measure of each phrase — anything to keep his eyes moving ahead as rapidly as possible.

As he progresses, of course, he can tackle music at a more and more difficult level for his sight-reading assignments. Slow readers are often note readers, rather than music readers. If this proves to be the case with the students you mention, try drawing their attention to the groups of notes or musical units in the repertoire they are studying at their own performance level, as well as in their sight-reading assignments. *(February 1969)*

Advanced students who are slow readers. *What would you do with an advanced student who is a very slow reader?*

First, question his level. Can he really be advanced, and still be a very slow reader? More importantly, consider why this student reads so slowly.

> Is he alert to what's alike and what's different in the music he is playing? Does he readily see in what way the differences are different? Is he at home with the keyboard, so that looking at his hands is not the problem?
> Does he look far enough ahead to read by entire phrases or groupings, rather than in terms of single notes or chords?
> Is he technically ready for the music he is playing?
> Is it possible that he needs glasses?
> Is it simply that he needs a much longer assignment at a much easier level? *(October 1966)*

Real sight-reading means just one chance. *I agree with you that developing good sight-readers is important. However, if sight-reading means just one chance, as you suggest, how can any student afford to buy sufficient music for the necessary home assignments?*

Few can, but there is always a solution to a problem. From your own music, ask students to sight-play one piece at every lesson; a piece easy enough to play accurately, in tempo without missing a beat, with attention to phrasing and all musical signs. Doubtless this would be a piece at a much lower level than the difficulty of the student's present repertoire. Arrange your schedule so that two students at the same level come one after the other. Take five minutes from the end of the first lesson and five minutes from the beginning of the second lesson and spend the ten minutes sight-playing duets. Using selections from your library (or flash cards), do sight-playing at each class session from which an appropriate assignment might be sight- playing one piece every day or five or six pieces per day (play each piece once a day only, do not practice.) Even if the student repeats the same pieces each day, with that number to read it will be almost like sight-playing each time he comes to them. Start building a lending library for the purpose of sight-playing assignments.

Research done to date indicates that students who continue to play and enjoy the piano long after they have stopped taking lessons are the ones who learned to play at sight. *(May-June 1981)*

Sight-reading vs. reading assignments. *In sample assignments handed out at your summer study courses, I've noticed that you differentiate between sight-reading and reading assignments. Will you kindly explain the difference?*

There are two basic differences between the two kinds of assignments — the level of difficulty and the pedagogical goal. Music assigned for sight-reading is usually about two levels easier than the student's repertoire, and is assigned to give him experience and skill in reading that is done literally at-first-sight. When a student reads at sight he looks the piece over briefly, sets a pulse, and determines how the note values or rhythmic patterns of the piece will fit that pulse, then plays the piece from beginning to end without stopping and with no change in tempo.

Pure sight-reading is done only at the lesson, under the guidance of the teacher. In addition, send home music to help increase students' sight-reading skills. Such music is usually a collection of easier pieces, one piece assigned for each day's practice, to be read at sight, following the steps listed above.

Music assigned for reading, on the other hand, is usually only a level easier than a student's repertoire. There are two goals for these assignments. Some of the pieces are assigned to come up to performance standards in just one or two weeks. Because this music is easier than his repertoire level, he is able to accomplish such a goal, and feel the satisfaction of a major musical accomplishment in a short period of time. It is also an excellent way to reinforce and increase his understanding of performance standards.

Other pieces are assigned for quite a different purpose: to enrich a student's background in repertoire, or to increase his understanding of a period, style or composer, without putting him under the pressure of performance standards for every piece. This type of reading assignment might be a collection of pieces to read through from which he is asked to choose one piece to work on seriously, or it might be a collection of pieces in a style or by a composer in which a student is particularly interested — music loaned for browsing. The advantage of such reading experiences cannot be overemphasized as the basis for musical literacy and insight.

To summarize, a student is working at all times on music at three levels: the repertoire assignment, at his performance level; the reading assignment, easier music that he can master quickly or in which he can browse; and the sight-reading assignment, much easier music in which he increases his ability to play at sight. *(February 1969)*

Eyes on the music. *Is it correct for a piano student (say age 9) to drop his eyes from the music and play a number of measures looking at his fingers, and then resume reading the music at the next section where he may not be as familiar with the notes? I was taught that pupils should keep their eyes on the music, especially for sight-reading, but I am not talking about sight-reading. Is this a good or bad phenomenon?*

I don't believe you're describing a phenomenon at all. Most young students will make a habit of looking at their hands, whether or not they are secure with the music, unless you make a concerted effort to train them not to do so. I would make this effort in every phase of reading, not just sight-reading. Many bad reading habits develop from just the problem you describe. Even when a piece is memorized, it should sometimes be practiced with the music and it should be read.

The only time students should glance down at their hands while reading is when making a wide leap. When possible, smaller moves and changes to new positions should be done by feel, with the eyes glued to the music. Most of the stumbles and almost all of the careless errors that creep into a student's performance are due to not really looking at the music. Your efforts to encourage eyes on the music will result in better readers and more secure performers. *(December 1981)*

Reading a memorized piece. *I have students who, once they have memorized a piece, can no longer read it unless they begin at the beginning. They are at a complete loss if I ask them to begin at other spots in the music, either to check for accuracy or to make interpretive suggestions. Do you have any suggestions for overcoming this problem?*

Solving this problem will require remedial work. Perhaps we should consider how the problem might have been avoided in the first place, to prevent it from occurring with future students. The fact that your students can read a memorized piece if they begin at the beginning points up two steps that may have been missing in their early training. From their first lessons, they should have been developing the ability to begin at any phrase or section, and they should also have been learning not to go back to the beginning when a mistake is made.

At the lesson, if a problem spot occurs, take it out of the piece and work on it until it is accurate. Then put it back into the piece but begin with the phrase in which it occurs. Students like to go back to the beginning, of course, because it is more satisfying to play the part they can do than to work on the part they can't. But going back to the beginning is a sloppy and inefficient way to practice. To help them see how wasteful this habit is, compare it to the student who has ten math problems and makes a mistake on the seventh. Would it be more sensible to do the six correct problems over, or to begin by reworking the seventh?

When a piece is memorized, it should always be assigned for two kinds of practice: playing from memory and practicing with the score, paying special attention to accuracy and musical detail. Both types of practice should be done at half tempo as well as up to speed.

At his lesson, ask the student to begin at any section or phrase, hands together or hands separately, with or without the music. In other words, when a piece is memorized, reading it never stops, nor does section practice or hands separate practice. These techniques contribute to secure memory, and to security in the technical and interpretive aspects of performance. *(October 1980)*

Fingering

The student who has no sense of fingering. *I have a transfer student this year who has no sense of fingering — not even an awareness of how to finger a five-finger pattern. It' s the worst problem I've ever encountered. The only way I can get any degree of accuracy is to write in every finger number. What can I do?*

Because the fingering of a five-finger position is reasonable, this is a good place to begin. Ask students to put their hand in a five-finger pattern on C. Be sure that there is one finger on each key and that the hand is resting comfortably over the five keys. Then dictate which finger is to play: finger 3, finger 5, finger 2, etc. Have them check their hand after each note to be sure that no finger has moved out of position. Do this exercise with each hand.

Prepare short musical phrases in five-finger patterns, and ask students to write in the fingering at home.

At first ask them to write in every finger. As they become more accurate, ask them to write only the first finger for each pattern, playing the balance of the pattern with the finger that is resting on that key· Always have them check to make sure no finger moves out of position. *(March 1980)*

Respect for fingering. *Many of my students are careless with fingering; some of them pay absolutely no attention to it. I am determined to avoid this problem with my new beginners. Do you have any suggestions to help me?*

The way to develop respect for fingering in your students is to make the procedure reasonable and important from the start. Beginning with the first lesson, have your students routinely prepare for every piece with their hands in their laps. Ask them to think and say aloud each hand's beginning finger and note before they place their hands on the keys; for example, "right hand, finger 2, treble G; left hand, finger 3, middle C." This habit sets the stage for careful preparation, and saying the words aloud provides a consistent process for thinking through which hand, finger, and note begin the piece.

While students are still working on pieces limited to five-finger positions give them additional drills that guide them to careful consideration of fingering. For example, "Put your right-hand finger 3 on E. Where is finger 5 lying? Where is your thumb lying?" Or, "Put your left-hand finger 5 on bass F. Where is finger 2 lying? Where is finger 4 lying?" The use of the term "lying" develops the concept that all five fingers rest on five consecutive keys.

A later step is to show students short musical examples and ask them which finger should play the first key. For example, ask the student to study the music and then write the finger number above the first note.

Send home additional short examples that ask students to choose fingerings without your help. Include some passages that could begin on two different fingers and instruct them to "Mark two different fingers with which you could finger the first note."

Understanding the principles of good fingering makes all the difference between interest in fingering and indifference to it. I believe that if you emphasize this awareness from the beginning, your students will develop an appreciation and respect for fingering. *(September 1986)]*

Wise fingering. *I have been reasonably successful getting my students to decide on all fingerings before working out a new piece. I am delighted with their progress but disappointed that they do not always choose wise fingerings. Do you have any suggestions for helping this?*

Your students are already far ahead of many I have observed. Their awareness of the need to decide fingerings before working out a piece is the first step in intelligent practice, but of course the essential ingredient is that the fingerings chosen be wise ones.

I have some suggestions. With music that is already fingered, make it a habit to discuss with your students why the editor chose that particular fingering and whether or not it is a wise fingering for their individual hands. If you need to change fingering, discuss the reasons for the changes and be sure to have them mark the corrections in the score. It is very helpful to give students short phrases to finger, illustrating specific principles. Begin with something as simple as the following five-finger patterns; ask them to study each pattern, then finger the first note.

In making the point of scale fingering, give students two fingerings for a given passage; ask them to choose the wiser one and explain why. For example:

Wisdom in fingering doesn't come by pressing a button. It grows slowly and consistently with the help of a good teacher who puts it high on the list of teaching priorities. Fingering is not art, but it does make art possible. Learning how to finger wisely should become one of our students' most useful skills. *(November 1982)*

When music isn't fingered. *Do you ask your intermediate students to work out the fingering for all the music that isn't fingered?*

All music must have at least minimal fingering, but whether a student works it out by himself or with help from the teacher depends entirely on the individual student. It also depends, to a certain extent, on tempo. I am most apt to help a student with fingering if the piece will eventually be played at a fast tempo. Fingerings that often seem wise when worked out at a slow tempo are not the best ones for the faster speed. Realizing what the final tempo will be, I usually help him find the right fingering for the finished performance if there is reasonable question as to his finding it for himself in the slow work-out stage. Aside from this one consideration, it is true of fingering as of so many other things: the more a student can do on his own, the better. (*February 1977*)

Fingering changes. *I would like to understand your reasoning for the change in fingering in the little piece, "Butterfly," from* Playtime A.

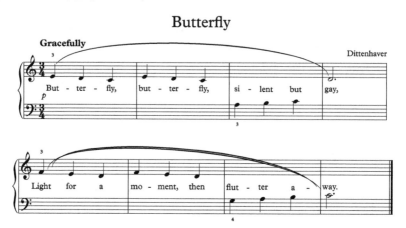

In the original edition, the second line began with finger 4 so the student did not have to move. In a more recent edition I notice that you have changed the fingering for that note to finger 3. It seems so simple to teach it without the move that I am wondering why you changed it. I've also heard that you recommend a finger change for the third Haydn German Dance in Piano Literature Book 2.

Both changes seem to make unnecessary moves for the student. May I ask you to explain your thinking?

Both changes are based on the premise that whenever possible it is wise to play parallel or similar gestures with the same fingers — to send in the same team for similar plays. In the two cases you mention, the same fingering is not only possible, but offers additional advantages.

In "Butterfly," fingering the second line like the first causes a move that encourages the correct phrasing.

In the Haydn German Dance in F major, the suggested change is really a necessity. The first phrase ends with the last beat of the fourth measure. The second phrase begins with measure five. The original fingering seems to imply that the quarter note at the end of measure four is an upbeat to measure five, and this is definitely not the case. The corrected fingering, written above the printed numbers, not only makes the two phrases parallel, but makes the correct phrasing absolutely clear. *(February 1975)*

Rhythm

Rhythmic preparation. *I'm beginning to see that with adequate preparation it is possible to develop students who have no rhythmic problems, or at least far fewer problems than in the past. However, I have two questions. How far ahead do you prepare a student for a new rhythmic notation, and what preparation steps do you use?*

There's no cut-and-dried answer to your question about how far ahead to prepare a student for a new rhythmic notation. The only sure answer is: far enough ahead to be certain he responds to the new rhythm securely before we assign it in a piece to be practiced alone at home. Just when this preparation should begin depends entirely on the age and ability of the student and, of course, on the teacher's standards for readiness.

In presenting any new rhythmic notation, some preparatory drills are necessary, but which specific drills, how many of them, and over how long a period depends entirely on the individual student. Let's use eighth notes as an example. Here are the preparatory steps used with 7 or 8-year olds. On paper they look cumbersome and time- consuming. In reality it takes only two or three minutes a lesson, if spread over a number of weeks. I much prefer to spend a very short time over a longer absorption period, than more lesson time crowded into a shorter time span.

- Hearing, and responding verbally.
  Nah-backs
  Teacher and student (or class) set a strong rhythmic pulse by swinging, using one full-arm swing (pendulum-style) to each pulse. Teacher chants brief rhythmic patterns on a neutral syllable such as "nah;" the student (or class) chants them back without a break in the pulse. The advantage of neutral syllables such as "nah" or "la" is that they provide a chance to sustain each note for its full value.

Count-backs

Same as above, but teacher counts brief rhythmic patterns, student counts them back without any break in the pulse.

- Hearing, and responding physically.

Clap-backs

Teacher and student set a strong rhythmic pulse by counting or "nah-ing." Teacher claps brief rhythmic patterns, student claps them back without a break in the pulse.

Tap-backs

Same as above, but teacher taps the patterns on the keyboard cover or a table top, student taps them back without a break in the pulse.

- Playing, without reading. Same as above, but teacher plays brief rhythmic patterns at the piano, student plays them back in a different octave (or at a second piano). The student is told on what key to begin and with which finger, then plays them back by ear. No reading is involved.

- Seeing and responding to the sign, without playing.

Teacher presents eighth notes using flash cards, and repeats any or all of the above steps (nah-ing, counting, clapping, tapping).

- Reading and playing simultaneously.

Teacher uses on-staff flash cards for the student to play. *(Feb. 1977)*

Swinging, clapping, tapping. *Please evaluate swinging, clapping, and tapping as aids to developing rhythm in young children.*

If evaluating means rating the aids, I'd give all three activities an A. If you mean to rank them, I'd say that all are equally important, but each has its own special purpose and value.

Swinging is a sure-fire way to develop a student's awareness of steady pulse. When a student allows his arm to become a pendulum, swinging with what we call a free-arm swing from as high as he can reach on the right side of his body to as high as he can reach on the left side, he is experiencing pulse with his entire body. As this arm-pendulum becomes free and steady, you will notice that he unconsciously begins to move with his whole body, to shift weight from foot to foot as he swings. This is an indication that the rhythm has become all-encompassing. With beginners we use "swing and say", swinging the pulse while chanting the words of their pieces. Later we change to "swing and count", swinging the pulse while counting the rhythm. Aside from dancing, walking, or running to rhythm, swinging is the largest physical activity students can have, and we always go back to it when a new note value or rhythmic pattern is introduced. In all swinging, the arm keeps track of the metric pulse, not of note values or rhythmic patterns.

In clapping, the pulse is felt while the note values or rhythmic patterns are clapped. Clapping, therefore, is the next step in rhythmic refinement; because a student feels the rhythmic patterns with his hands, it is muscularly one step closer to playing. Clapping is always done standing up, so the pulse can be felt in the whole body, arms hanging loosely, elbows free, motions large. When clapping a rest, students separate their hands with a rhythmic gesture of opening, and whisper the count.

Tapping is very much like clapping, but another step closer to playing the piano. Again, the pulse is felt, while the note values or rhythmic patterns are tapped. Tap on tables or on the keyboard cover. The hand and arm are free and the tapping is done with a light bounce of the finger tips. Right-hand notes are tapped with the right hand, left-hand notes with the left hand. Legato notes are tapped as smoothly as possible, staccato notes as short as possible; accents are tapped with extra stress; moves up or down are actually tapped higher or lower on the table or keyboard cover; and dynamic levels are expressed.

Whereas clapping is an important preparatory step in learning new rhythms, tapping is a basic practice tool in working out new pieces. Tapping is one of the best aids I know for developing coordination between the hands, and I consider it one of the most essential rhythmic practice steps. *(January 1982)*

Method of counting. *Do all your students use the same method of counting? When students come to you from teachers who have used a method different from yours, do you insist on the student's changing to your method?*

Yes, all students who start piano study with us count the same way. They count note values at the beginning and change to metrical counting later on. Once our students have developed a way to count, our concern is twofold: to make sure they do count (without relying on us to count for them); and to make sure that what they are counting is not notes but the pulses and divisions of pulses for which these notes stand.

With regard to transfer students, we change their way of counting only if their method does not result in a full, rhythmic response. *(December 1985)*

Counting 6/8 time. *How do you ask young students to count pieces in 6/8 time? I understand that your students count as if there were only two beats to a measure. How do you begin this and, if you start this way, how do you explain the time signature?*

The first and most natural preparation for compound meter comes when students experience playing pieces in 3/4 time at a rapid tempo, feeling one pulse to a measure rather than three. Later we present triplets, in which they experience that a pulse can be subdivided into three equal parts as well as into two equal parts:

$$\quad = \overset{3}{\boxed{}} \qquad \quad = \text{♫}$$

When the triple subdivision is easy for them in 2/4 time, we present compound meter as a familiar feeling with a new look:

(musical notation: 2/4 and 6/8 rhythm examples)

At first they count compound rhythms in two ways: counting in six, to make sure that each measure is really made of six eighth notes or their equivalent:

(musical notation: 6/8 rhythm example)

1 2 3 4 5 6   123 456   1 2 3 4 5 6   123456

and counting the natural rhythm, into, feeling the dotted quarter note as the pulse:

(musical notation: 6/8 rhythm example)

1 - a - la, 2 - a - la   1-a-la, 2-a-la   1 - a - la, 2 - a - la   1-a-la, 2-a-la

As soon as students are comfortable with step 2, we drop step 1. After the basic subdivisions of compound meter are secure, we introduce quarter notes with eighth notes, and also rests, counting them the same way:

(musical notation: 6/8 rhythm example)

1 - a - la, 2 - a - la   1-a-la, 2-a-la   1 - a la, 2 - a - la   1-a-la, 2-a-la

Syncopation. *How do you explain a syncopated pattern such as this to a young student:*

I would introduce syncopation in the same way I introduce any new rhythm: not by explaining it but by having the student experience it. Begin with clapping-back and then tapping-back rhythm patterns. You might start with quarter notes until you are sure the students are not just imitating you but actually feeling the pulse. When the pulse is secure, change to rhythm patterns that include eighth notes, for example:

Be sure students always count while clapping or tapping, that their arms and wrists are loose, with their elbows hanging freely from their shoulders. Then change to rhythm patterns that include the syncopation you illustrated above. When students are able to clap and tap the rhythm securely, have them play it by rote in simple diatonic patterns. After the rhythm is secure in your students' technique, show them the rhythmic notation, like this:

To make sure they have both the feel and the understanding, repeat the process with these rhythms: *(July-August 1982)*

Rhythmic Dictation. *Is there short-hand for rhythmic dictation that really works with young students? Most of the teachers I know agree with me that such dictation is impractical for young students because it takes them so long to draw the notes.*

I'm sure every teacher develops ways to accomplish more in less time, and rhythmic dictation is certainly worthy of our attention because it is so valuable yet so time consuming. We have devised a system we call "dash dictation." It involves these steps:

- Teacher taps and counts a short rhythm, for example:

- Students tap and count it back.
- Teacher taps and counts the rhythm again while students take it down in dashes, spacing the dashes to represent the rhythms they hear.

- Students add stems and change dashes into longer note values:

- Students add time signature and measure bars:

- Teacher taps and counts once more, as students point and count the rhythm they have written to check the accuracy of their notation.

I recommend staying with rhythms as simple as the example above until students can make the dashes while they hear the taps. Then increase the difficulty to a rhythm such as this:

Soon your students will be able to take four measures of dictation, including all the rhythmic patterns and symbols they have learned to date. As soon as rhythmic dictation is natural and easy, begin melodic dictation in an equally simple way. *(November 1982)*

Practice in various tempos. *Why do you ask your students to practice rhythmic activities in several tempos?*

In general, doing rhythmic activities in a variety of tempos is the best way to develop rhythmic flexibility and is the best test of rhythmic security. Specifically, there are three reasons:

Rhythmic symbols represent relative duration of sounds; the best understanding of these time relationships occurs when they are experienced at various tempos.

The music a student plays includes a wide variety of tempos. Experiencing rhythmic activities at a variety of tempos helps a student feel comfortable with slow, moderate and fast pieces.

When learning new music, a student necessarily goes through various tempos, from the slow pace of workout to the tempo of the finished performance. The ability to work out a new piece in a slow, secure rhythm, even on the first reading, is one of the key ingredients in successful practice. Later, when a piece is ready for public performance, one of the best tests of security is to play a fast piece at half tempo or a slow piece at double tempo.

Tempo variation in separate rhythmic activities helps a student learn to control the various tempos he will experience both in learning new music and in retaining security with music he has already mastered. *(May-June 1979)*

The student who understands notation, but can't play rhythmically. *I have a problem unique in my teaching experience. One of my students is an intelligent boy who understands rhythmic notation, yet seems unable to play his music with rhythmic security. I never assign a piece until he has proven that he can point and count the rhythm, both accurately and with a feeling of strong rhythmic pulse. I would appreciate help on this point.*

Without knowing your student, I can speak only in generalities, but here are some ideas that could relate to your question. The following four statements apply to any musical element you are teaching:

- understanding an element doesn't necessarily mean being able to perform it
- how a student plays a piece for the first time is more important than you may realize
- it is much easier to feel the rhythm of a piece at a moderately fast tempo than at the slow, secure tempo required for a first reading
- reading ability and technique are closely related to rhythmic control

To apply those four statements to your problem, I suggest that when you assign new music, you not only hear your student count the rhythm, but also ask him to play and count (at least part of the piece) at a tempo so slow that there are no errors. This can be done hands separately, if necessary.

In this first, very slow reading, you may make one or more important discoveries about your student: he is unable to feel rhythmic relationships at a slow tempo; the music you have assigned is too difficult for him to read with rhythmic security even at a slow tempo; or he can read the notes but lacks the necessary technique to play the piece — in other words, what seem to be rhythmic problems may actually be technical ones.

The only way to know which of these issues is the problem is to work out new pieces with him so that you can observe what goes wrong in the first reading. Perhaps the solution will lie in selecting easier music or in emphasizing some skill you may have been neglecting. *(April 1980)*

Presenting rests. *Why do you wait so long before presenting rests? I present quarter rests at the same time as quarter notes, half rests at the same time as half notes, whole rests at the same time as whole notes, etc. My students can name them at once and say how many beats each rest represents, so I see no reason to wait.*

There are two reasons for postponing rests. The first is the obvious one — a student should be wholly secure wit h a strong feeling of pulse in sound before he tries to maintain that same strong pulse through silence. The second reason is a little less obvious, but even more significant — the importance of phrasing.

One of the most important areas we teach (and we must teach it from the very first lesson) is the ability to carry a musical line from its inception to its end. This implies the experience of continuous movement and flow, and involves extended concentration. We believe this is developed more easily through continuous melody than through a melody interrupted by silence. Rests within a phrase must not be seen or felt as an interruption (a time not to play) but as moments of silence within the phrase that in no way stop the flow of the phrase from its beginning to its end. *(September 1974)*

Use of rests. *I have had it on my mind for some time to write to you concerning the use of rests in your beginning series. I should say the lack of rests. My question concerns not only your books but most of the first-year methods that have been published in recent years. I was taught that a rest was needed whenever one hand did not play. Please see the enclosed pieces, chosen from various courses, and note how I have added rests to conform to the rules as I understand them. I wouldn't be so concerned with music at the beginning, except that I believe students should begin correctly, so that they won't need to learn all over again when they advance to the classics. The rules you follow do not seem to apply to the classics.*

I can't agree with your basic premise that a rest is needed whenever one hand does not play. Musical notation falls into two general categories: signs that represent what the pianist is to listen for (pitch, rhythm, dynamics, etc.) and signs that give directions (RH, LH, finger numbers, etc.). Rests belong in the first category; they are signs for silence, something to be listened for — not signs for what a hand does or does not do. In the pieces you sent, rests are used for two purposes:

to represent silence in a melody that has already begun; and/or
to indicate the exact moment at which a second voice (or an accompaniment) enters.

As illustrations, I have chosen two of the eleven pieces you sent, with the rests you have added. Compare these two versions of "County Fair." The melody is a single line divided between hands. Since there is no accompaniment, rests are not needed except to show where there is silence in the melody. The rests you have added (version 2) only serve to confuse the notation and make the piece look harder than it is.

County Fair

Marion McArtor

With excitement

f Oh, this is the day of the fair, the fair! My

broth - er and I will be there, be there! We'll

try things, and buy things. What

fun we'll have at the fair, the fair!

Compare these two versions of "Paper Boy." Again, because the melody is a single line divided between hands, there is no need for rests. In the last measure there is a sudden entry of another voice, and the rest is required to show exactly where the second voice begins.

Paper Boy

Marion McArtor

Brightly

f Pa - per boy, pa - per boy, come this way! Tell me, what's the news to - day?

Here are three examples from the classic literature:

C.P.E. Bach's familiar *Solfeggietto* in C minor begins with a single melodic line, divided between hands (measures 1-12). No rests are used because there is no silence. But in measure 13, the texture suddenly changes to melody and accompaniment. The accompaniment occurs only on beats 1 and 3, so rests must be used to show silence on beats 2 and 4. In measures 13-16, a sixteenth rest is used in the melody to show the points at which the accompaniment enters.

In Scarlatti's Sonata, K. 29 (L. 461), the same situation occurs. During the passages of a single melodic line there is no silence, hence no need for rests. But in measure 4, the single line changes to two-voiced counterpoint. In measure 5, rests are used to show the point at which one of the voices drops out; in measure 6, they prepare for the entry of melody and accompaniment.

Sonata K. 29 (L. 461)

In this Bach Prelude, there is a clear example of music that changes rapidly from a single melodic line to a chordal texture. During the purely melodic passages, the melody passes from hand to hand but rests are not required because there is no silence. In contrast, in measures 2 and 4, rests are used as dramatic preparation for the chordal texture that follows. *(April 1973)*

Prelude No. 21 from WTC

Why wait to present eighth notes and 6/8. *I have just returned from workshops on both the Kodaly method and the Orff Schulwerk, and have found their teaching approaches very similar to yours, with one exception. They use rhythms including eighth notes and 6/8 time from the very beginning, instead of waiting until later as you do. Will you please explain this discrepancy of thought?*

I don't see any discrepancy here. In the Orff and Kodaly approaches the children are learning rhythms and performing them with their bodies and voices and on simple rhythm or melody instruments (drums, xylophones, etc.), not on the piano. I agree that in this context eighth-note rhythms are as simple to learn as any others. But as piano teachers, we are developing not just rhythmic understanding and response, but also hands and fingers that can play these rhythmic patterns with control. We wait to present eighth notes and 6/8 time not because they are difficult to understand or feel, but because a student's technical control may not have developed sufficiently to handle them easily. *(October 1971)*

Rhythmic notation illogical. *I spend too much time drilling rhythmic notation. Pitch notation makes sense to students because higher and lower are easy to see, and the lines and spaces simplify recognition of the distance between notes. In contrast, the symbols for rhythm are totally irrational. The basic problem is that notes are the same size no matter how long they last. How do you explain this?*

Granted, rhythmic notation is not as reasonable as pitch notation, but there is a system to it. We let our students discover that every time the value of a note is shortened, something is added to the notation. For example:

To cut the value of a whole note in two, add a stem.

To cut the value of a half note in two, fill in the notehead.

To cut the value of a quarter note in two, add a flag.

To cut the value of an eighth note in two, add another flag.

This approach, even though logically backward, is at least consistent. It always interests students, and makes rhythmic symbols more memorable to them, to realize that the system is the opposite of what they might expect. Where else in life do you get half as much by adding, or twice as much by subtracting? It's a fascinating paradox. *(March 1983)*

Use of the metronome. *At what age or level of study do you think it best for students to start work with the metronome?*

I never use a metronome with elementary students. When I use it with intermediate or advanced students it is usually in one of these ways:

- If the composer or editor has given a metronome mark, check the indicated tempo with the metronome. After establishing the tempo turn the metronome off and play at that tempo without mechanical assistance.
- Occasionally, we use the metronome to alert students to tempo changes they are making within a piece — changes they do not intend and of which they may not even be aware.

- Often, instead of assigning a piece to be practiced at "slow," "moderate" or "fast" tempos, we give recommended metronome settings for practice; but again, once the tempo is established, turn off the metronome before the practice begins.

A metronome is mechanical, rhythm is alive; a metronome cannot breathe, music must; a metronome has no inflection, rhythm is filled with it; a metronome doesn't allow for phrasing, music exists in its phrases; a metronome is outside the performer, rhythm is within. In short, consider the metronome a tool for checking tempo, not an aid to rhythmic control. *(April 1983)*

Walking rhythms. *When your students walk the rhythm of a piece, do they take a step for each pulse or a step for each note value?*

If your goal is a steady pulse, stepping the pulse is an excellent first experience. The ultimate goal, however, is to step the note values, because we are striving for physical expression of the piece's rhythm.

All too often, students feel the beginning of a longer note value but not its duration. They are more concerned with playing the next note on time than with holding the current note for its full value. Walking the note values helps correct this. At first, some children feel strange staying with a half note, dotted half note, or whole note. But once they have really experienced the full duration in their feet, their playing becomes truly rhythmical rather than merely expressing steady tempo. *(November 1983)*

Walking rhythms that include rests. *Having my students walk the rhythm of their pieces has been the best thing I've done this year, but what do you do about walking rhythms that include rests?*

We walk rhythms in two distinct stages: walk the rhythm as you say the rhyme, taking one step for each pulse; walk the rhythm as you say the rhyme again, taking one step for each note.

In the first stage students take a step on every pulse, regardless of whether the symbol for that pulse is a note or a rest. In the second stage they walk the rhythm taking one step for each note, or for each rest. In other words, rests represent duration just as notes do, so our students express the duration of the silence just as if it were sound. *(July-August 1988)*

From known to unknown in rhythm. *I have profited greatly from your emphasis on a student's making every new discovery on the basis of what is already known. I refer specifically to learning dotted quarter and eighth notes on the basis of knowing quarters, eighth, and ties:*

Could you give me an example of this principle at a more advanced level, especially in the area of rhythm?

The next logical example would be learning the various groupings of eighth and sixteenth notes as an outgrowth of understanding sixteenth notes and ties:

Another example would be learning to play two notes in one hand against three notes in the other. In the following technical etude, students experience the new rhythmic feel in a familiar notational setting, before repeating the same experience written in a new way. *(March 1975)*

Playing 3 against 4. *I have a student who has been studying this piece by Chopin for months and is still unable to play y the rhythm correctly. Playing four notes to a beat in the right hand, against three notes to a beat in the left hand, seems to be an impossibility for her. Where have I missed with her, and what can I do about it now?*

Fantaisie-Impromptu

Probably the mistake was in assigning this very difficult *Fantasie-Impromptu* in the first place. All too often we cause our own problems (and thereby our student's) by not making sure that he is thoroughly prepared in every way for the music we assign. In the case of this student, of course, the problem is control of the three-against-four rhythm.

Before even considering assigning this particular piece you should be sure the student has both the rhythmic understanding and the technical control for playing these passages, and at the necessary tempo — note that the meter is ¢ not c, so the student must feel eight notes to a pulse in the right hand against six notes to a pulse in the left. Since your student has been studying this piece unsuccessfully for months, my recommendation is to drop it as gracefully as possible, and go to a new piece for which she is really prepared.

The next time you present the *Fantasie-Impromptu*, these preparatory suggestions may prove helpful.

To play any cross rhythm, two preliminary skills are essential: students should be able to set and maintain an absolutely steady pulse and be able to alternate between various divisions of the pulse without losing the beat.

Let's assume that condition one is satisfied. Condition two may need some practice. Begin with an exercise like No. 1 below, and practice until a student can make the changes without any fluctuation in tempo.

This pattern should be transposed to provide practice in a variety of black-key and white-key patterns. When Exercise 1 can be played in many keys with no fluctuation in tempo, a student is ready for Exercise 2.

When Exercise 2 can be played in many keys with no fluctuation in tempo, a student is ready to tackle three-against-four rhythms such as those in the Chopin *Fantasie-Impromptu.*

Exercises 3 and 4 are excerpted from the *Fantasie-Impromptu* itself. Like Exercises 1 and 2, they provide practice of the difficult passages, first alternating hands, then hands together.

In later measures of the piece, each beat can be practiced like Exercise 4.

When each beat, or each half-measure, of the piece is secure, a student is ready to begin work on the piece as written, first measure by measure, then in formal groups of two or four measures, and finally as a whole. *(December 1974)*

Additional rhythmic material. *I have used every rhythm page in your* Music Workbooks *with all my students. I don't know how I could get along without them, but I also don't know where to go from there. Do you know of any similar rhythmic material at a more difficult level?*

May I suggest a recent book by Robert Starer (whose music you have undoubtedly taught), *Rhythmic Training*, published by MCA Music. The Preface states that in Mr. Starer's experience as composer, performer, and teacher he has come to the conclusion that inadequate grasp of rhythmic patterns is often the cause of poor sight- reading, and that insufficient familiarity with 5 and 7 time and changing meters has contributed to unjustified fears of performing 20th century music. This book was written in the hope of alleviating both these situations. *(September 1970)*

Theory

Memorizing major 5-finger patterns. *Many of my students pull away from memorizing the notes of all the major five-finger patterns. How long do you think it should take an eight, nine, or ten-year old to learn to do this? And then, when do you begin minor?*

I see no reason ever to ask anyone to memorize the patterns. As soon as a student knows half steps and whole steps, he should understand only that the major five-finger pattern is made entirely of whole steps except for one half step, and that this half step always comes between degrees three and four. That's all the information he needs to build a major five-finger pattern on any key: whole step, whole step, half step, whole step. The beauty of a pattern is that once you've learned it, you can move it anywhere on the keyboard and it works in exactly the same way. No memorizing is necessary. With young students you can begin minor five finger patterns as soon as the major patterns are secure. *(September 1975)*

Order of teaching major 5-finger patterns. *The lecturer at a recent piano teachers' clinic told us to teach the major five finger patterns in C, G, D, and A before teaching any flats. I have always taught them in the order of C, G, F, D, Bb, etc. How else would a student learn the circle of fifths? Isn't learning the circle of fifths important? Which order do you endorse?*

To answer your first question, yes, we want our students to under- stand the circle of fifths, but not necessarily at the elementary level. We consider that it is much more important for a student to be able to play major five-finger patterns with control of tempo, dynamics, and tone quality. To accomplish this, and to answer your second question, we would endorse the order your lecturer recommends. His order begins with the keys which best fit the young student's hand. C major and G major, where all keys are equi-distant from each other; then D major and A major, where the longest finger of each hand (the third finger) plays a black key. Playing the F major pattern in the right hand puts the wider distance between Bb and C in the weakest part of the hand (fingers 4 and 5); the Bb pattern presents the same problem for the left hand.

In summary, if your purpose is theoretical, continue with your way; if it is technical, I recommend you change to the lecturer's way. *(April 1969)*

Confusing the names for sharp and flat keys. *My students can build a major five-finger pattern beginning on any key by following the formula: whole-whole-half-whole. They love to do it, but when I ask them to name the notes they have played, they confuse sharps and flats. For example, if I ask them to play the E major pattern, they play it correctly, but when they name it they might say, "E, F#, Ab, A, B." What have I done wrong, and how can I correct it?*

Perhaps you have omitted sufficient writing of the patterns. To correct the problem, first make sure that your students understand that a major (or minor) five-finger pattern is built on five consecutive letter names. The best "proof of the pudding" is to have them write the patterns: since they are built on five consecutive keys, they should be written on five consecutive lines and spaces; no key is skipped, so no line or space is skipped. The lines and spaces help to clarify the consecutive letter names. A student who has played the E major five- finger pattern, and then has written it using five consecutive lines and spaces, sees instantly that the third note must be called G#, not Ab, because he wrote it on the G line. *(February 1975)*

Intervals: general and specific. *I follow your practice of first introducing intervals in a general way, and then going on to specifics (major, minor, Perfect, augmented or diminished)* *when a student can understand these details. Recently a colleague challenged me on this, insisting that introducing intervals only on white keys will prove confusing to a student later on. In my experience, this confusion has never occurred. Do you see any possible problem?*

None at all. I believe the confusion lies in the sophisticated and in, formed adult mind, not in the sponge-like receptivity of young children. Were we to introduce young children to specific intervals (not fifths as a general concept, but perfect, augmented and diminished fifths), we would have to postpone the whole concept of intervals for some time. There are rare exceptions to this rule, of course, but most children are not ready for the refinements as early as they are for the concept of intervals in general. Like you, I have never found any confusion later on, just increased interest when we draw the students' attention to the various kinds of seconds, thirds, a students' attention to the various kinds of seconds, thirds, fourths, fifths, etc. (*October 1972*)

Subdominant. *I was taught that the subdominant is the 4th degree of the scale and is called subdominant because it is under the fifth degree, the dominant. That's what I've been teaching for years. A speaker at our Music Teacher's organization recently gave a different explanation of sub, dominant, and I'm wondering if what I have been teaching is wrong.*

The only way in which you might be considered incorrect is your reason for the subdominant's name, a misunderstanding that occurs when we think in terms of scale instead of key. All notes of a key are determined by and named by their relationship to the keynote, or tonic. A key has two dominants – the 5th above tonic (called *dominant*) and the 5th below tonic (called *subdominant*, the dominant under the tonic):

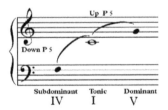

A key also has two mediants – the tone that's midway between tonic and dominant (called *mediant*) and the tone that's midway between tonic and subdominant (called *submediant*, the mediant under the tonic):

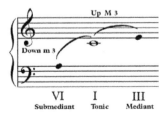

That leaves just two tones to be accounted for – the *supertonic* (the tone just above the tonic) and the *subtonic* (which we call *leading tone* because it leads so strongly to the tonic):

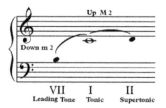

In this way, every note of the key is named by its relation to tonic. A scale results when you put the tones of a key in stepwise order from tonic to tonic. (*September 1969*)

Naming tonic in relative minor. *My young students don't understand why the first note of the relative minor scale of A major can't be called G♭ instead of F#. After all, G♭ is three half-steps down from A, too. They argue with me and I don't know how to explain it.*

I think the easiest solution is to make sure your students understand that a major key and its relative minor key are related in two ways; they have the same key signature and they use the same notes (but, of course, with a different tonic). Since there is no G♭ in the key signature or the scale of the major key, it cannot occur in the signature or scale of the minor.

A more dramatic proof is to ask them to build the relative minor, beginning on the sixth degree of the major scale, like this:

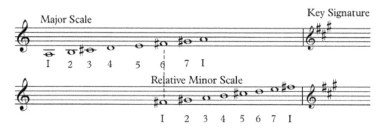

If you are teaching the harmonic form of the minor key, I would ask a student to build the scale in its natural form first, then to add the accidental to create the raised leading tone. (*March 1977*)

Transposing by finger numbers. *I have a student whose early training consisted of heavily-fingered music, all in major 5-finger patterns. She can transpose her pieces to many different keys, but I'm suspicious that she may simply be reading finger numbers in new positions. What should I do?*

Give her short phrases, such as the following, written without fingering, and ask her to transpose each phrase without having played it as written. In this way you'll be able to check that she is transposing, not by reading fingering or by ear, but only by reading intervals. *(February 1980)*

Studying form. *I notice that in your library a student begins to study form in the early books, and I think it's great; but you seem to drop it altogether later on. Doesn't a student need to know other forms, too, like sonata-allegro, rondo, minuet and trio, song forms, etc.?*

Yes, by all means. A student needs to continue the study of form as long as he studies piano. We take up the various forms you mention (and others) as they appear in the piano literature a student is learning. *(January 1969)*

Measure bar or barline? *I notice that in the* Music Tree, *you refer to measure bars whereas I have always used the term barlines. Which is correct or preferred?*

There is common agreement that a measure is a group of beats or a unit of musical time and that measures are marked off from one another by vertical lines, but there seems to be some confusion as to the proper term for those dividing lines.

Baker's *Dictionary of Musical Terms* defines a bar as "the vertical line dividing measures on the staff, and indicating that the strong beat falls on the note immediately following... hence, the popular name for 'measure.' Barline is a barbarism evoked by the familiar use of bar for measure."

However, the *Harvard Dictionary* claims that measures are marked off from one another by bar lines and defines a bar line as "a vertical line drawn through the staff to mark off measures."

In the *Music Tree* we attempt to define musical terms as simply and purely as possible. To avoid confusing a student with two different terms for measure or the apparent redundancy of bar line, we use measure bar to mean the vertical lines dividing music into measures and double bar for the ending bar. *(July-August 1986)*

The terms note, tone, and key. *I'm confused about the proper use of the terms note, tone, and key (when referring to one of the keys on the piano). How do you differentiate between them when talking to a student?*

A note is the written sign by which the composer ·indicates pitch and time duration. Tone refers to the sound produced when the key is played. Key refers to the key on the piano by means of which the tone is produced. Briefly stated, we see a note, hear a tone, and play a key. It's common to hear the word note used for tone or key as in put your 3rd finger on the black note. But in pure usage, we would say:

> What is the name of that note (pointing to the score)?
> Did you play the right key? (on the keyboard)
> Did all the tones in that passage sound even? *(February 1974)*

A sequence for teaching theory. *I'm confused as to the proper sequence for teaching various elements of theory in the first few years of study. I'm thinking of such things as triads and inversions, major and minor keys, and basic chord progressions.*

I'm sure there must be a variety of proper sequences, but I will be happy to give you the sequence we use as a general guideline.

Theory study should begin after a student has learned to read by intervals, using seconds, thirds, fourths, and fifths. Formal theory study begins with half steps and whole steps, using them as the building blocks for everything that follows. Once the steps are understood, use them to present major five-finger patterns. Students quickly learn to follow the pattern whole-whole-half-whole to build a major pattern on any keynote. When major patterns are secure, introduce minor patterns by lowering the third degree a half step. Use major and minor five-finger patterns to introduce transposing. Give students dozens of melodies in major and minor patterns to transpose to a variety of keys. Next they learn that degrees 1-3-5 of any pattern form a triad; that if the pattern is major they form a major triad, and if the pattern is minor they form a minor triad. As soon as this is secure, they learn to accompany five-finger melodies using degree I (the tonic) for measures composed mainly of triad tones (1-3-5), and degree V (the dominant) for those composed mainly of non-triad tones (degrees 2 and 4).

After extensive practice in accompanying and transposing melodies in major and minor five-finger patterns, present the major scale. Do this by adding three more tones to the five-finger pattern, using whole-whole-half. When major keys and key signatures are understood, present various forms of minor as altered patterns. Accompanying and transposition continue as new material is added. At this point a students' reading range expands through the introduction of sixths, sevenths, and octaves. They read and play these intervals within the key, without concern for whether the specific interval is major, minor, perfect, augmented, or diminished. This completes what we consider elementary theory.

In the intermediate years gradually introduce subdominant triad and accompanying with I, IV, and V, inversions of triads, basic chord progressions such as I-IV-I-V-I, dominant seventh chords, specific intervals (major, minor, perfect, augmented, diminished), modes, melodic development, and non-harmonic tones.

Students who master this body of theoretical knowledge by the time they graduate from high school are usually able to test out of freshman theory requirements in college, or simply to enjoy understanding the music they are playing for the rest of their lives. When we speak of mastering we mean, of course, both understanding the concepts and using them at the keyboard. *(February 1989)*

Composing

The difference between improvising and composing. *I know that you advocate creative work or composing for piano students, even in the beginning years. How do you distinguish between composing and improvising for elementary students?*

We don't use either word in the first year or two of study. Instead, we ask students to make some pieces of their own. When we hear these pieces at the lesson, they sometimes seem to have been carefully planned and practiced; other times they seem to be spontaneous developments of the materials or titles suggested in the assignment. If a piece has obviously been thought out, developed, practiced and memorized, we consider it a composed piece. If on the other hand, a student is still in the process of arranging musical elements spontaneously, we consider it improvised. A good test is to ask to hear the piece a second time. If a student can repeat it exactly, it is apt to be a finished composition, no matter how simple. These distinctions should remain in the mind of the teacher. We want to encourage real composing, but I don't think it is wise to make a distinction in a young student's mind between composition and improvisation. *(July-August 1981)*

Writing elementary compositions. *I have a six-year-old student who is extremely talented. Lately he has expressed the desire to compose, and his little pieces are really something! How can I teach him to write them down correctly? Is there a book which I can use to teach a small tot like this to write his melodies down with the correct rhythm, notes, etc.?*

I don't know of such a book, but even if I did, I would shun it like the plague. The fact that your student composes interesting little pieces at this age is wonderful, but the labor of trying to write them down would be vastly disproportionate to the rewards. Laboring to notate the pieces, especially if the rhythms are as complicated as those in most youngster's compositions, would only limit or perhaps kill the creative joy and spontaneity he now feels.

If a six-year-old had to write down the wonderfully imaginative stories he tells, he probably would stop telling stories rather than make the effort of recording them. Isn't the same thing true of music notation?

If you want a record of the pieces, why not jot them down for him, or tape record them? I wonder, however, if this doesn't spotlight his composing in a way that is unnatural and unwise. Why not just let him compose and compose — the more he creates, the more ideas he will have, and probably he'll be richer rather than poorer for not having a permanent record of his early achievements. Making a fuss about this entirely natural aspect of piano study may make it appear too important to the little boy and to his parents. *(April 1969)*

Why shouldn't students write the pieces they compose? *I have heard you say that you don't ask students to write out the pieces they compose. Would you explain this, please?*

It is only our elementary students who are not asked to write down their creative pieces, but they are encouraged to make their own pieces every week, using all of the new elements they are learning.

In addition, they are encouraged to use the entire keyboard (notation they haven't even begun to learn yet) and to work with complete rhythmic and stylistic freedom. They sometimes make pieces that sound just like the beginning pieces they are learning, but often their compositions are fresh and original, using intricate rhythms, irregular meters, crunched chords, and all sorts of exciting sounds which they wouldn't be able to notate for several years. To limit their composing to what they can write would be like asking a young child to tell stories using only words he can spell — a cramp to creativity and a damper to enthusiasm.

If a really first-class piece is created, it is easy to preserve on tape. Later, when notation is more advanced and secure, students are encouraged to write out their pieces. *(May-June 1970)*

Ear Training

Pitch awareness. *I have begun interviewing all new students, beginners as well as those who have studied previously, and it has been a big help in my teaching. However, I have not found a successful way to evaluate pitch awareness in very young students. I have interviewed students who aren't able to tell which of two notes is higher, for example, Middle C or the C an octave above. What can I do?*

Many young students are not able to distinguish pitch difference at the octave. Make the difference more dramatic: a 7th, 9th, or 11th. Your problem may be merely verbal. Young students have experienced high and higher, low and lower only in a spatial context (high on the hill, low on the ground) or as a degree of loudness (your voice is too high, please lower it). We should teach them what high and low mean in relation to musical pitch before we can test them on their ability to differentiate. Begin by making a visual association, raising and lowering one hand as you play tones that go higher and lower. Then have students copy your hand motions until they are comfortable with the terms high and low as they relate to the direction and sound of musical pitches. Be sure to play lower notes as loud as upper ones to avoid confusion between low and soft.

At the keyboard a student must also learn to associate going to the right with highness and going to the left with lowness. There are a lot of new concepts to consider before we can say with any certainty that a student can't tell differences in pitch. *(October 1981)*

How should ear training begin? *I have heard you say that training the ear is the most important single factor in developing complete musicianship. I agree, but do you mean that it should start with beginning students and, if so, how?*

Yes, ear training should start at the very beginning and should be part of every piano lesson. Following are some of the activities we use with both class and private students.

But before I list those activities, let me say that at its best ear training is not an isolated activity that occurs at a special time in the lesson. Ear training is the all-important component of everything we do in every lesson, and one of the primary aspects of all practice. All music teaching and all piano practice should be focused toward developing the ear. The following are a few of the specific ways to develop the ear:

Singing is probably the first ingredient of all good ear training. Students should sing at every lesson. They should sing all of the pieces that lie within their vocal range. They should hear you sing as you illustrate phrasing or dynamics. And they should come to use their singing voices as an indispensible tool in learning to play the piano. Students who are expected to sing from the first lesson on, are apt to be free of embarrassment or inhibition about singing later on.

Sing-Backs. The teacher sings a short musical idea and students sing it back (without any interruption in the rhythmic pulse). Sing on a neutral syllable, such as "la," and use hand motions to show direction, distance, and duration. Sing a series of 6-8 short phrases, varying tempo, dynamics and articulation. Following are a few samples:

Play-Backs. The teacher plays a short musical idea and students play it back (again, without any interruption in the pulse). At the very beginning, the play-backs can be done on black keys, using the middle finger and bounding along from key to key. Remember, this is ear-training, so we don't want any technical difficulty to interfere. As students progress, the musical phrases gradually increase in length and incorporate all the students' discoveries, including technical facility.

Question-Answer. The teacher plays a short musical question and students play an answer that complements or completes the phrase. When students are secure with playing answers, it is fun to reverse roles, letting them ask the musical question and the teacher answer it.

Sight Singing. The teacher puts short musical phrases on the board and plays or sings the starting pitch. Students sing the phrase at sight, using a neutral syllable such as "la."

Editing is our students' favorite ear-training activity· Put a short piece on the board (usually just 4 measures) and play it through while students watch and listen. After they have heard it once, play it again, making one or more changes. Students listen carefully through to the end, remembering the change and where it occurred. After the playing, a volunteer goes to the board and marks the change, editing the notation to conform to the change(s) heard. This process is repeated through several playings. Two examples of elementary editing drills follow.

Example 1

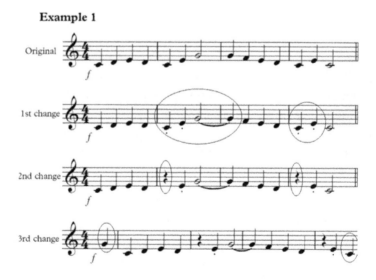

Example 2

Original

1st change

2nd change

As ear-training, editing has distinct advantages:

- it develops concentration and aural memory – no change is made on the board until the entire piece has been played.
- it focuses students' attention – they must not only hear the change, but remember exactly where it occurred.
- it combines rather than separates the various types of ear training – students must listen simultaneously for changes in pitch, rhythm, dynamics, etc.
- it skips the step of "naming" and connects the sign, pitch or rhythmic notation directly to the sound, without the step of naming in between.
- it culminates in writing the sign that stands for each sound.

No other type of ear-training includes all these features. Students view it as a game and, in group teaching, the challenge of being first with the correct written answer is keen and exciting. *(December 1973, November 1985)*

Chapter Four

Basic Skills

Position at the Piano

Moving freely at the piano. *In my class I have some students who are tense and awkward, unaccustomed to moving freely at the piano. Their upper arms, in particular, are stiff and seem glued to their bodies. How can I help them?*

A good playing position often solves other apparent technical or physical problems. Here are some suggestions to help achieve playing readiness:

- Adjust the bench to a proper height, keeping wrists and forearms parallel with the floor. (If students sit too high or too low, their forearms slant up or down and their sense of freedom and balance is lost.)
- Sit the proper distance from the keyboard, leaving upper arms hanging from the shoulders with forearms a comfortable distance from the body. (If students sit too far from the keyboard, they will have to reach for the keys; if they sit too close, they will feel crowded and cramped.)
- Maintain proper posture, sitting tall with shoulders dropped and relaxed, back straight (no slumping), leaning slightly into the keys.
- Balance weight, dividing it between the bench and the feet. (This division makes it possible to feel freedom in moving over the entire keyboard, without sliding on the bench or losing balance.)

These two simple exercises, done away from the keyboard will help students relax and loosen up:

Stand with feet slightly apart. Extend arms straight out from shoulders and enjoy awareness of the full length of each arm. Let hands hang freely from wrists. Drop arms suddenly with complete release; the hands will hit the sides of the thighs and rebound.

Still standing, swing arms from side to side, shifting weight from foot to foot as you swing. During the swing, continue to experience awareness of the full length of the arms. Swing to music or to a tempo set by the teacher.

To encourage students to develop flexibility in their playing, assign exercises and pieces that require moving over a wide range of the keyboard, from low positions to high and back — hands separately, alternating hands, and hands together. In all such music, the emphasis should be on moving to each new position directly, yet freely and gracefully; moving the hand and arm freely behind the finger that is playing; expressing the shape of each phrase with a loose wrist and elbow, supported by a good playing position. *(June 1984)*

Signs of tension. *When working with elementary students, where do you look to see if tension is developing, in addition to the playing mechanism itself?*

All too often we think of the playing mechanism as being the hands alone or the hands and arms. In reality, the entire body is our playing mechanism. Look for tension from the top of the head to the balls of the feet, because it is apt to show up in any part of the body. Watch especially for awkward and jerky motions of the head, facial contortions, pressed lips, drawn mouth, extended tongue, grimaces, raised shoulders, stiff upper arms, locked elbows, tense wrists or thumbs, and finally look closely at the feet (heels on the floor and toes in the air or vice versa.) All of these are among the most common symptoms of tension. *(May-June 1981)*

Benches. *I have a number of questions relating to piano benches: Where can I locate an adjustable piano chair or bench sturdy enough for day-to-day use? Is there some special way to check if the height of the piano bench is correct for each student? I use a great deal of ensemble music in my teaching, especially music for four hands at one piano and for this, of course, an adjustable chair or stool won't work. To date I have piled magazines on the bench for students who needed it higher. Do you have any other solution? How do you ask a young student to sit when he is too short for his feet to reach the floor?*

Illustration 1

Illustration 2

I'll answer your questions one by one:
The only really durable adjustable bench I have found is the artist bench, pictured in Illustration 1. It is available through piano dealers and, though expensive, will

last a lifetime. It is also possible to purchase an adjustable piano chair with a back, shown in Illustration 2. The bench is the correct height if the student's forearm is parallel to the floor. In Illustration 3, the bench is too low because the arm slants upward to reach the keys.

Illustration 3

Illustrations 4 and 5 show an inexpensive homemade solution to making full-size benches adjustable. In Illustration 4, using blocks of wood under the legs of the regular bench raises the bench nearly two inches. Even with the wooden risers, the bench is still a bit too low for this student — notice that his arm still does not form a parallel line with the floor. In Illustration 5, a bench pad has been added, and now his arm is horizontal with the floor.

Illustration 4   **Illustration 5**

The wood blocks can be made by any amateur carpenter. They arc standard 2x2s, cut to 16-inch lengths with little wells hollowed out to fit the bench feet. They must fit securely in order to hold as the bench is pushed in and out.

The bench pads arc made of styrofoam, cut to the proper length for your bench, and covered with contact paper. Each of our studios is equipped with a set of the risers and several bench pads of different heights. The easiest way to hold the pads in place is with hook straps, buckled to the underside of the bench lid.

Until a student is tall enough to sit on the bench with his feet firmly planted on the floor, ask him to cross his ankles, as shown in Illustrations 3-5. This does not accomplish the ideal division of weight between feet and seat, but it does provide a kind of anchor, and the feeling of balance so essential to good technique. *(February 1971)*

Position at the piano. *At what point or level do you stop discussing with students their position at the piano? Is it necessary to continue this at the intermediate level?*

I never stop emphasizing a good playing position no matter how advanced a student becomes, however, I don't usually try to accomplish the desired position by discussing it with him. Instead, my comments might run something like this: "Will you put your hands on the key, so we can check the height of the bench? Good! Your arm and wrist are exactly level and make a straight line with the floor." Or, "Look, your hand and arm are going uphill (or downhill) to reach the keyboard. Let's fix the bench." Then I would raise or lower an adjustable bench or add or subtract bench pads, as needed, to achieve the desired position. Or I might say, "You seem a little too close to the piano. Push the bench back a bit and see if it doesn't feel more comfortable. Now you look much more comfortable, and your elbow isn't pushing into your side. Does that feel better to you?" Or, "Are you sure you aren't sitting too far back on the bench? Try standing up. Can you get up comfortably? Sit back down. Now, does your weight feel evenly divided between the bench and the floor?"

If a student is playing a piece that covers a wide range of the keyboard, suggest that before he begins he try testing the highest and lowest positions of the piece to see if he can reach them with equal case. As he's testing the reach and adjusting his position to the exact middle of the piece, I might comment, "Be sure that your whole arm can support your fingers as you play the highest and lowest keys. Otherwise your tone will disappear as you get to the outermost reaches." Encourage our students from the beginning to lean to the right or left, behind the hand as it reaches up or down, never shifting position on the bench.

Often in the heat of performance, students' shoulders will rise as they come to a difficult or intense passage. Often just touching the shoulder is enough to remind the student to drop it. If not, I stop and ask the student to raise and drop his shoulders a few times, as a reminder of how comfortable dropped shoulders really are. The same goes for students who slump as they play. Often, just my hand in the middle of their back is sufficient reminder. If not, I may touch say, "Sit tall." If the wrist gets high or tense as a student plays, often just touching it (usually from underneath) is enough to insure relaxation, If not, stop and ask the student to put his elbow on the keys and dangle his wrist for a moment until he remembers the good feeling of complete release.

Position is equally important in more refined degrees. For example, a sudden bump in the melodic line is sure to result if a single finger has reached for a black key. Instead, the whole hand should prepare a position that accommodates that black key, long enough ahead of time so that the process is smooth and oiled.

Position is something I work on throughout every lesson with every student, usually not by discussing it so much as by making it a consistent point of reference, a kind of touchstone by which all performance is affected. *(September 1981)*

Playing technical patterns in 3 octaves. *What is your reason for ask students to play short technical patterns up and down the keyboard in octaves? Should they stop between octaves or play them non-stop?*

There are five reasons why students profit from playing technical exercises in several octaves:

- They become aware of the sound of the different registers on the 0, This is a good listening device in itself, and the change in helps to keep them alert and listening throughout several positions of the pattern.
- It multiplies the length of the pattern by the number of octaves assigned, so it helps to develop technical endurance.
- It is difficult to enter immediately into the rhythmic experience, short pattern. By multiplying the experience through repetitions of different octaves, momentum develops and the process becomes physically rewarding. This is also the answer to your second question: to develop rhythmic momentum, the patterns must be played non-stop.
- It provides much-needed movement over the keyboard, encouraging freedom of the upper arm, allowing the arm to carry the hand from high on the keyboard to low on the keyboard or vice versa.
- Then there is a practical psychological reason. Instead of asking students to play a specific phrase five or six times, ask them to play it once, in several octaves. *(May-June 1983)*

Playing on the keyboard cover. *What advantage is there to asking students to practice a piece on the keyboard cover? Could you give some examples of pieces in which you would use this technique?*

Playing on the keyboard cover frees students from the precision of playing exact keys, and allows them to give their full attention to the rhythm and motion of the phrase or piece. This is especially helpful if there is tension in the arms, awkwardness, or self-consciousness. When students discover the marvelous feeling of freedom that results from practicing on the keyboard cover, they are more likely to achieve the same feeling when they put the piece back on the keys. This technique is also useful for music that covers a wide range of the keyboard, especially if it requires crossing hands. Following are excerpts from two pieces in which we use this kind of practice. *(June 1984)*

Night Clouds

Knight's Tale

Scales

Why postpone scales? *I have always started my students on scales from very first lesson. I understand that you postpone scales for a long time. Please explain why.*

It's true that we don't start scales at the very first lesson, but I don't think we postpone them for a long time. Our aim is to start scales when the student is ready for them. Briefly, readiness for scales means that the student can play major 5-finger patterns with control of tone and tempo and that he has developed the ability to cross the third and fourth fingers over the thumb and to slide the thumb under the third and fourth fingers quickly and easily. These two aspects of technique take some doing. Generally our young students are ready for scales sometime in their second year of study. Of course with older students we assign scale practice much sooner. *(March 1967)*

Scale practice. *A paper on scale practice was read at our last piano teacher's association meeting, and it included the statement that scale practice should begin with the B major scale, not the C major scale. Most of us are up in arms over this recommendation, and would like to know what you think. How can an eight-year-old beginner play the B major scale when he hasn't read five sharps? How will he ever learn the circle of fifths if he begins this way?*

Before attempting to answer your question, I would like to clarify our position on scale practice, because it seems to differ from yours. Young beginners should not practice scales. When scales are introduced, students should not read them. Scale practice is technique, not theory. In teaching theory, begin with the key of C major and build the circle of fifths, going up from C in perfect fifths for sharp keys and down from C in perfect fifths for flat keys. The scale a student begins to practice as technique is a matter for each teacher to decide for himself, weighing the pros and cons of various approaches.

Now, to your specific question about the wisdom of beginning scale practice with the B major scale. There are two compelling reasons in favor of beginning with B major (or any scale that uses the five black keys).

The fingering is obvious. The thumb plays the two white keys; fingers 2 and 3 play the group of two black keys; fingers 2, 3 and 4 play the group of three black keys. I find B major preferable to F# or C# simply because it begins with the thumb.

Technically these three keys are far easier than those with fewer black keys since the longer fingers play on keys that are farther away. In proper position (the fingers curved and the fleshy pad on the edge of the black key) the student sees that he has a perfect bridge under which to slide his thumb, and, when he crosses the third or fourth finger over the thumb, he crosses to black keys.

To summarize, in scale practice, keyboard topography is of utmost importance when judging what is easy and what is difficult. *(April 1976)*

Beginning with black-key keys. *I cannot follow the logic of teachers recommend beginning scale practice with five, six, or seven sharps, so often students can't remember even two or three sharps. Does this make any sense to you?*

Scales that use all the black keys are the easiest to play for several reasons. Since all the black keys are used, there is nothing to remember. RH and LH use the same finger groups at the same time — fingers 2-3 always play the two blacks and 2-3-4 always play the three blacks. The keyboard topography fits a student's hands in a more natural and comfortable way — the longer fingers (2-3 and 2-3-4) play, black keys, and the short thumb plays the white keys. Because fingers 2,3,4 are always on the higher keys, they make a bridge under which the thumb can pass smoothly and easily. In the reverse direction 2,3,4 cross over the thumb (on the lower white key) to the higher black keys. *(January 1981)*

Scale practice for elementary students. *My problem with scales is getting the student to memorize all the fingerings, especially when they get to sharps and flats. I drill and drill but to no avail. In scales like Ab and Db and most of the students can't even remember what finger to begin on! What you do about this problem?*

Perhaps the clue to your problem lies in the word memorize. Why ask a student to memorize scale fingerings? All he should understand is the principle of scale fingering, a principle which will then apply to scales, major and every form of minor.

Briefly stated, here are the aspects of scale fingering he needs to understand.

Since there are 7 different keys involved in each scale, the group, of fingerings will always be: 1-2-3 and 1-2-3-4. The thumb never plays a black key. It is easier to pass the thumb under a finger that is a black key because the raised black key causes a higher arch in hand. Also, it is easier to cross fingers 3 and 4 over the thumb if they cross to a black key, again because the raised black key is easier reach.

From the moment a student has the D scale we ask him to diagram it according to its keyboard geography, the arrangement of black and white keys. He marks "B" for black and "W" for white, and the D scale diagram would look like this:

```
            B              B
     W  W       W  W  W
```

Then we ask him to mark the fingering groupings, like this:

```
            B          B        B
     W  W       W  W  W     W  W
     1  2  3   1  2  3  4   1  2  3  (etc)
      ‿‿‿       ‿‿‿‿‿        ‿‿‿
```

Next we ask him to block the groups of three's and four's, up and down the keyboard for four octaves, playing the 1 2 3 group as a unit, and the 1 2 3 4 group as a unit, all keys pressed down together. This helps him to see the arrangement in his eyes, even away from the keyboard. Not until this blocking is secure do we ask him to practice the scale as such.

One of the scales you mentioned, D♭, would be diagramed like this:

```
     B  B      B  B  B     B  B
           W            W           W
     2  3  1   2  3  4  1   2  3  1  (etc)
      ‿‿        ‿‿‿‿‿        ‿‿‿
```

Such a diagram makes it very clear to the student why the D♭ scale begins on finger 2.

I am afraid that in written form this all sounds wordy and looks complicated. At the keyboard it can be explained in just a few minutes. Once the principle is understood, the student will be able to figure out for himself any scale fingering and will be fascinated by the logic of the process. *(September 1974)*

Outline for scale practice. *When I visited the New School last year, I noticed that your students had outlines for practicing scales taped into the inside cover of their assignment notebooks. Would you be willing to reprint this outline in your column? Do you ask your students to do all the steps every day?*

There are different outlines for different levels of study, but as a middle ground, I'll reprint the outline we use for intermediate students.

Intermediate Scale Outline

1. Four octaves slowly (HS, HT)
2. One octave plus 1 note (HS, HT)

   Up
   Down
   Up and down
   Down and up
3. Two octaves plus 2 notes (HS, HT)

   Up
   Down
   Up and down
   Down and up
4. Beginning at the top of the keyboard. Same as Steps 2 and 3 (above) but beginning at the top.
5. Changing from quarter notes to sixteenth notes (HS, HT):

   One octave in ♩   Three octaves in ♪♪♩

   Two octaves in ♫   Four octaves in ♬
6. Playing quarter notes in left hand, while right hand changes from quarter notes to sixteenth notes.

   Left hand   **Right hand**
   One octave in ♩   One octave in ♩
   One octave in ♩   Two octaves in ♫

One octave in ♩   Three octaves in ♪♪♪ (triplet)

One octave in ♩   Four octaves in ♪♪♪♪

7. Same as No.6, but reverse hands and begin from the top of the keyboard:

Left hand	**Right hand**
One octave in ♩	One octave in ♩
Two octaves in ♩♪	One octave in ♩
Three octaves in ♪♪♪ (triplet)	One octave in ♩
Four octaves in ♪♪♪♪	One octave in ♩

8. Four octaves, HT — fastest possible tempo with complete control:

> Up
> Down
> Up and down — once
>   twice (non-stop)
>   three times (non-stop)

As you study the outline above, please keep the following considerations in mind:

- The outline is prepared only to save a teacher's time in writing out the student's assignment. By referring to the outline, a teacher need only list the key or keys, the dynamic level and the step or steps for that week's practice. For example, in the assignment, we might write:

  Keys: E Major, C# minor (harmonic form), *mf*
         Steps 1 and 5

- Step No. 1 is never omitted. It occurs in every assignment, no matter how well, how beautifully, how controlled or how fast a student can play a given scale. Step 1 is always the first step for all scale practice at this level.
- At the intermediate level we assume that there is no question whatsoever about scale fingering. Scale practice depends first of all on being wholly secure with fingering. This has been accomplished during the elementary years.
- No student is ever asked to do all of the steps in any given week of practice.
- There is little or no indication of tempo in the outline itself, although one of the goals is the control of scales at faster and faster tempos. Work for speed in two ways: from slow to gradually faster; and from slow to immediately fast, with the fast practice first done in short impulses, then in longer impulses.

The scope of the outline might seem to indicate that we spend a great deal of time on scales. In reality we don't. This is possible because, during the elementary years, a student develops real control of all the major and minor 5-finger patterns and, in addition, learns to make smooth crossings (3 and 4 over the thumb and passing the thumb under 3 and 4). This lays the groundwork for all future scale practice, and lessens the time and importance that must be placed on scale practice *per se* in the intermediate years. *(April 1974)*

Skeleton scales. *I have heard you discuss the use of skeleton scales in scale practice without ever fully understanding just what the skeleton of a scale is. Could you explain?*

I consider the skeleton of a scale to be those notes which outline top and bottom of each position and focus a student's attention to the pivotal notes involved in each crossing. In scale playing the thumb has a very special role, allowing fingers 2, 3, and 4 to roll into new positions. This is accomplished in one of two ways: either by using the thumb so that the other fingers pass over it, or by sliding the thumb under the other fingers, allowing them to pass over it. Because the thumb is crucial to playing scales smoothly, evenly, and cleanly, the points at which the thumb plays require the most refined practice. The thumb must be loose and curved, the knuckle bridge must provide an adequate arch, and the elbow should have no excessive motion.

The skeleton scale emphasizes practice of these pivotal points. For example, in Bb major, the skeleton scale for right hand looks like this:

Exercise 1 provides practice in crossing over the thumb.

Exercise 2 provides practice in sliding the thumb under:

Exercise 3 combines the over-and-under practice for finger 3:

Exercise 4 combines the over-and-under practice for finger 4:

The illustrations above include only two octaves. However, I strongly recommend that practice be done in four octaves and, of course, that it include similar practice for the left hand. *(September 1982)*

Scale skeleton. *When students practice what you call the skeleton of the scale, where they prepare fingers 4-3-2 and 3-2 as units, do they play these units silently or with sound? How long do your students practice the skeleton before playing the scale itself?*

When crossing over the thumb, our students practice the skeleton scale silently until they can cross 4-3-2 and 3-2 over the thumb easily and gracefully, preparing the next keys directly with no wandering or hesitation. When students can do this smoothly, they practice the skeleton with sound. Printed below is the skeleton of the Bb major scale for the right hand:

When sliding the thumb under fingers 2-3-4 and 2-3, the same emphasis on ease, grace, and direct preparation for the next keys applies. Again, when students can do this silently, with ease and comfort, they practice the skeleton with sound. The number of times students should practice the skeleton before playing the scale depends, of course, on the individual student. Assign continued practice of the skeleton even after a student is playing the entire scale. It's a wonderful warm-up before beginning the scale itself. *(February 1985)*

More about skeleton scales. *Please explain what you mean by the scale practice step you call the skeleton scale. Exactly which keys does a student play in this step?*

Skeleton scale practice is designed to put the emphasis on two aspects of scale playing: the crossings themselves, and preparing fingers 2-3 and 2-3-4 as a unit. In the C major scale, for example, the right hand would practice just the keys played by the circled fingers:

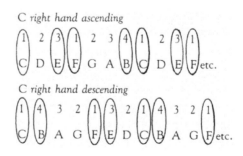

Students play only the fingers indicated, but are careful to prepare fingers 2-3 and 2-3-4 as a unit so that they lie on their keys immediately after the crossing. The order remains the same for all keys. In the sharp keys of G major through B major, the right-hand fingering is identical to that for C. In all other keys the order is the same, but the scale begins on different fingers.

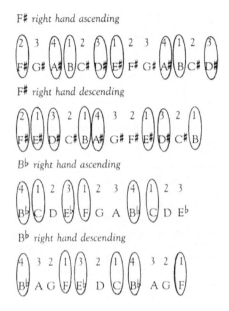

I believe that practice of the scale skeleton should precede all other scale practice steps. (February 1989)

Action of the thumb. *In scale crossings you put the emphasis on the action of the thumb rather than on the third or fourth fingers crossing over it. Please explain your view of the thumb's action and its importance.*

I view the thumb as the causal agent in a crossing. To illustrate —what I mean, let's consider a right-hand C major scale, descending. Put your right hand on five consecutive white keys, thumb on F. Now cross fingers 3-2 over your thumb to E-D. At the moment of the crossing, before bringing your thumb out to the new position, take a good look at your thumb. You'll see that it has collapsed, rolling over onto its nail. Now repeat the crossing, but this time concentrate on the action of the thumb as it rolls over — think the roll, feel it, watch it. Notice that the roll has caused fingers 3-2 to cross over the thumb. Now repeat the process with your fingers on five consecutive white keys, thumb on C. Roll your thumb with a bit more energy and stretch, so that fingers 4-3-2 cross over it to G-A-B. Again concentrate on the action of the thumb — think the roll, feel it, watch it. Notice that the roll has caused fingers 4-3-2 to cross over the thumb. Students soon

116

become sensitive to the degree the thumb must roll to cause a 4-3-2 crossing as opposed to a 3-2 crossing.

The action of the thumb is perhaps even more apparent in a right hand scale, ascending. Here there are two steps: first the thumb slides along the keys, ducking under the other fingers into its new position. Once on the new key, it rolls back into normal position, causing fingers 2-3 or 2-3-4 to cross over it. In short, in both ascending and descending scales, it is the rolling action of the thumb that causes the crossing, not vice versa. The difference is between putting fingers over the thumb, and a motion of the thumb which simply causes them to be there. *(July-August 1983)*

Why emphasize finger 2 in a crossing? *When a student is learning to cross the 3rd or 4th finger over the thumb, why do you also emphasize crossing finger 2?*

Since you can't cross fingers 3 or 4 over the thumb without also crossing finger 2, I assume your question relates to why we emphasize crossing fingers 3-2 or 4-3-2 as a unit. A common problem in crossing over the thumb occurs when the fingers do not prepare as a unit but pop up into the air. We've all seen crossings like that, and we know that the results are loss of rhythmic and tonal control, even inaccuracy of notes.

This picture illustrates the problem:

Compare it with this picture:

With a rolling motion of the thumb and a lateral motion of the wrist, fingers 4-3-2 cross over the thumb as a unit. This means that all three fingers are lying on their keys, prepared to play; excess motion is avoided and the whole hand is in a condition to support each finger as it plays. *(October 1985)*

Impulse practice. *I have had real success with teaching scales ever since I followed your suggestion for teaching impulses of one octave plus one note, but I do have some questions. Do you assign all steps hands together at once? What fingering do you use descending? What do you mean by practicing impulses non-stop? Do you also assign slow practice, or is this the only kind of scale practice you assign?*

When you speak of one octave plus one note, I assume you are referring to the rhythmic impulse:

A student must feel the impulse rhythmically — when he does, he plays one octave plus one note automatically. The note he ends on is a result of the rhythmic pattern.

All impulse practice is done right hand alone and left hand alone before hands together. Our illustrations are all for right hand. The same principles, however, can be applied to left hand and to hands together.

The following illustrations indicate fingering for impulse practice in the right hand ascending and descending:

Up and down once without stopping at the top:

Up and down twice or three times without stopping at the top or bottom:

To give a student experience in a different register, a different position of his body and a different grouping of notes, use the following impulse practice:

Playing four continuous octaves in this same rhythmic impulse is excellent practice.

It creates a situation in which there can be no doubt as to a student's security.

Non-stop practice consists of putting the ascending and descending impulses together, once, twice, and three times without stopping, as follows:

The final step is playing the scale four octaves in non-stop sixteenth notes.

This is by no means the only kind of scale practice we assign. Facility in scale playing can be developed in two ways: gradually increasing the tempo from very slow to moderate, to fast, to very fast; and an immediate change from very slow to very fast, but in short impulses as illustrated above. Slow practice is essential in either case.

We should add here that the rhythmic impulses illustrated above are only a few of many possible ones, and that the routine described here is only one of dozens of good ways to practice scales. No matter what practice routine is used for scales, always insist on practice that is strongly rhythmic, and on tempo, dynamic level and tone quality that are predetermined before the practice begins. *(September 1969)*

Outline for advanced scale practice. *I have successfully used the imaginative scale outlines for late intermediate students printed in your column. Will you please give some similar suggestions for advanced students?*

There are limitless ways to continue and vary scale practice with advanced students. Among the most important types of scale routines are playing all three forms of minor scales; playing all scales in thirds, sixths, and tenths; and playing all scales two-against-three (two notes in the left hand against three notes in the right hand and vice versa). When playing two notes in the right hand against three in the left, start the scale at the top of the keyboard descending, so that the hands can begin one octave apart. Then, play all major scales (and later all minor scales) in chromatic order, moving from one key to the next without stopping in between. Instead of returning the keynote of the scale you are playing, end each scale with the keynote of the one to follow. This kind of practice necessitates an adjustment of fingering in the last octave of the descending scale to accommodate the fingering of the next scale (see example).

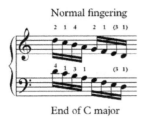

Normal fingering

End of C major

Adjusted fingering

Beginning of C♯ major

The student who can play scales non-stop, moving from C to C# to D to E♭, etc., is gaining valuable experience in changing leverage to accommodate black and white keys as well as in playing non-stop sixteenth notes.

Because of the numerous questions I receive on the subject, scales and scale practice have been discussed many times in this column; however, I do not put major emphasis on scales in my own teaching. Scales and arpeggios are only two ways of developing facility and control; equally important are practice of legato thirds and fourths; consecutive fifths, sixths, and octaves; fast repeated notes; voicing chords; playing full-octave chords (major, minor, dominant seventh, diminished seventh, etc.) with both hands up and down the keyboard; sustained and moving voices within the hand; and accompaniment figures. Scales are important, but we should be careful not to neglect other areas of our students' technical development. *(December 1978)*

Scales as trills. *I've heard that advanced students should practice scales as trills. What does this mean?*

To practice scales as trills, make a trill between each two tones of the scale as shown below:

Hands separately
Hands together (2 octaves apart)

When each exercise is secure as written, double the tempo by changing the sixteenth notes to thirty-second notes.

There are several advantages to this kind of scale practice: it helps produce scale playing in which there is tonal equality between all fingers; it allows extended practice on problem spots within a scale, such as the fingers involved at the crossings; it is excellent preparation for trills themselves; and it provides yet another way to practice scales, thus adding variety. *(April 1979)*

Chromatic scale fingering. *What is the correct fingering for the chromatic scale?*

There are three fingerings in common use:

The first example is good for developing each tone with equal richness. It's an easy fingering to remember because it uses only fingers 1 and 3 except between the two consecutive white keys E-F and B-C where fingers 1-2-3 are used.

The fingering in the second example, in which fingers 1-2-3-4 are used, is the best for developing tempo and facility. The thumb is used only on every other white key.

3.

I rarely use this example. (*March 1978*)

Additional questions on scales. *Your article in a recent issue of Clavier, on the subject of scale practice, was a great help to me. However, I have some additional questions about scale teaching. How fast should a student be able to play scales by the time he is in Level 6 of the Library? Do you ask your students to play all the scales in 3rds, 6ths, and 10ths as well as in octaves? Have you published a book on scales and chords? If you do not have your own book, is there one you could recommend?*

I am delighted that the article you mentioned was helpful to you, and will be happy to try to answer the additional questions about scale teaching that you have raised.

- Tempo

  I'm not as interested in how fast a student can play a scale as in how well he can control it. Scales are never assigned merely for facility. They are musical studies designed to increase finger independence and strength, control of passage work at various tempos, and every aspect of tonal control. Scale practice never has speed as its main objective and it is never divorced from intense and concentrated listening. For these reasons, I never impose absolute tempo requirements. On the average, however, Our Level 6 students are playing scales in sixteenth notes at a metronome mark ranging from M.M. ♩ = 80-120.

- Scales in 3rds, 6ths, and 10ths

  Playing scales in 3rds, 6ths, and 10ths is, in my view, a part of advanced technique that would be assigned only after a student has mastered thoroughly all major and minor scales in octaves. When you do teach scales in 6ths and 10ths, any or all of the same steps can be applied. I would leave practicing scales in 3rds till the very last, if I assigned it at all. It seems to me there are many more benefits to be derived from practice in 6ths or 10ths, where the hands are comfortably far apart. Also, passages in 6ths and 10ths are much more common in the music the early advanced student is likely to be studying.

- Scale Book

No, we have not published a book on scales and chords. I fail to see why scales or chord progressions need to be read. Of course they should be understood theoretically, but given minimum principles, any student readily learns to build all major and minor scales and to finger them wisely. The same is true of chords in root positions and inversions, and of simple chord progressions. It is my belief that if we spend the necessary time at the beginning to explain the underlying principles, we develop students who are free to work with scales and chords on the basis of understanding their structure. This seems infinitely preferable to depending on a reference book in which every scale and chord is fully written Out. *(January 1975)*

Variety in scale practice. *I have a problem in keeping my students interested in scale practice over a long period of time. By the time they have learned to play all of the major and harmonic minor scales, four octaves at a pretty good tempo, they are so tired of the sound and the repetition that they almost refuse to continue practicing scales. Do you have any ideas for other ways to assign scales that might hold their interest better?*

There are enough ways to practice scales to fill a book, certainly more than I can do justice to in the space of this column. But I will make a few suggestions here of ways to vary the practice of scales which should not only hold your students' interest, but also add greatly to the usefulness of their scale practice. Any or all of these suggestions can be incorporated as soon as a student is able to playa scale four octaves ascending and descending at a moderate tempo.

Dynamic Levels

Vary the dynamic level of the scale practice, from ***pp*** to ***ff***. Later, assign practice in which a student crescendos as the scale ascends and diminuendos as the scale descends and vice-versa. Still later, assign practice with a different dynamic level for each hand, right hand forte, left hand piano and vice-versa.

Direction

Scales should be practiced both in parallel motion and in contrary Then it is possible to make quite exciting scale routines by combining parallel and contrary motion — for example: ascend two in parallel motion; then play contrary motion for two octaves; ascend two more octaves in parallel motion and descend again, still in parallel motion; then change to contrary motion for two octaves; finally, complete the scale by descending the last two octaves in parallel motion.

This entire routine is done non-stop and students find it both stimulating and challenging.

Order

Students can be assigned in a number of different orders so that a student progresses from scale to scale by: circle of 5ths (C, G, D, A, etc.); chromatically (C, C, D#, E♭, etc.); major followed by parallel minor (C, c, D, d, E, e, etc.); and major followed by relative minor (C, a, D♭, b♭, etc.).

Rhythms

So often we assign scales to be played up and down 4 octaves in sixteenth notes, but how often does music run along in such simple rhythmic patterns? Isn't it better preparation for music, and more interesting, too, to use a variety of rhythmic combinations? There are, of course, dozens of possibilities, and again I will mention a few:

- up and down two octaves in eighth notes, changing non-stop to 3 octaves in triplets, changing non-stop to 4 octaves in sixteenth notes.
- four octaves up and down in a variety of changing patterns, inning with such simple ones as:

- playing the left hand one octave up and down in quarter notes, while the right hand plays two octaves up and down in eighth notes, then three octaves up and down in triplets and then four octaves up and down in sixteenth notes. Then reverse, so that the left hand gets the faster practice.
- use scales for trill practice hands together in sixteenths notes;

Later this same exercise can be practiced in thirty-second notes.

Impulse Practice

Impulse practice is one of the most productive types of scale practice. The impulses can be very short or very long, but the important aspect is to play the part of the scale being practiced on one impulse, to be sure that all of the notes come out of one gesture. Scales can be practiced in impulses as follows:

- to the crossing

- through the crossing

- one octave plus one note

- two octaves plus two notes

Every impulse should be practiced up, down, up and down, down and up. The practice can be first from the bottom of the keyboard, ascending; then from the top of the keyboard, descending.

All of the above suggestions can also be applied to a student's practice of scales in 3rds, 6ths, and 10ths as well as in octaves. I'm sure these suggestions will trigger your thinking, and that you will find dozens of other ways in which to vary a student's scale practice. *(March 1972)*

Traditional and non-traditional fingering. *I was taught the traditional fingerings for scales and have always taught them to my students. I'm hearing a lot of talk about scale fingerings that use the thumbs together, but I haven't been able to find any written material explaining just what these fingerings are. Can you help?*

The whole matter of traditional and non-traditional scale fingerings was presented in an article in *Clavier* by Mary Kathryn Cowles (March 1975, page 29). In it she discussed the relative merits of traditional scale fingering (five scales alike, the rest easily derived by a logical system, easy to memorize) versus the merits of two alternative fingering systems. The first alternative, developed originally by Tobias Matthay, provides the greatest possible ease in crossings. The second, advocated by Gallico, Mokrejs, and Randlett, is the one to which you refer. In it the thumbs are always played together, facilitating coordination between hands in playing parallel motion scales. In teaching the traditional fingerings you are already teaching this thumbs-together system for the major scales of B and Cb, F# and Gb, C# and Db and F (if you start the left hand of F major on 1 instead of 5). Here are the traditional fingerings, set up to demonstrate that they are already part of the thumbs-together system:

B   (Cb)   RH: 1 2 3 1 2 3 4 1
           LH: 1 3 2 1 4 3 2 1
F# (Gb)   RH: 2 3 4 1 2 3 1 2
           LH: 4 3 2 1 2 3 1 2
C# (Db)   RH: 2 3 1 2 3 4 1 2
           LH: 3 2 1 4 3 2 1 3
F   RH: 1 2 3 4 1 2 3 1
           LH: 1 4 3 2 1 3 2 1

If you translate this fingering principle to the key of C major, for example, you get a traditional RH fingering with an untraditional (but wholly workable) fingering for the LH:

RH: 1 2 3 1 2 3 4 1
LH: 1 3 2 1 4 3 2 1

The same principle can be applied to each of the remaining keys. The article includes a chart of the fingerings in all three systems. *(July-August 1980)*

Arpeggios. *When and how do you begin arpeggios? Your columns on scale practice have been of great help to me. When and how do you begin arpeggios?*

We begin arpeggios when a student has demonstrated his readiness through two preparatory steps: the ability to play, with control, broken chord passages that include the stretch of a 3rd between fingers 2-3, 3-4 and 4-5; and the ability to roll fingers 3 and 4 over the thumb into extended positions and to slide the thumb under fingers 3 and 4 in extended positions. See illustrations below.

1. For RH alone

2. For LH alone

When students have acquired both these techniques, they are ready for arpeggios. (*April 1975*)

When do you introduce major and minor arpeggios? *I am in doubt about when to introduce major and minor arpeggios as technical exercises. Is there an age or level at which a student should begin arpeggio practice?*

There are two basic considerations: first, are a student's hands physically ready for arpeggios?; and second, will his repertoire soon require the technique needed to play them? When the answer to both these questions is yes, then it's time to begin arpeggio practice.

Readiness for arpeggio practice includes two distinct skills:

- The ability to play legato with complete ease and a rich, full tone, and to play intervals of a 3rd and 4th between consecutive fingers.

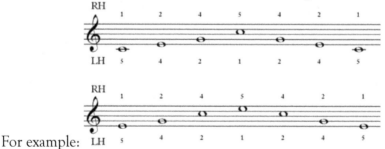

For example:

To play exercises such as these, the hand should not be stretched to an octave position, nor even slightly fixed or rigid. Instead, it should remain supple, preparing ahead for just one key at a time. To produce tones of equal quality and quantity, each finger needs the support of the whole hand (and arm).

- The ability to pass the 3rd and 4th fingers over the thumb, and to pass the thumb under the 3rd and 4th fingers, when the hand is in an extended position. This must be done legato (no thumb bumps), with ease and with no perceptible motion in the wrist or elbow. Above all, arpeggio practice demands that the thumb be loose.

The following preparatory exercises can be used before assigning an entire arpeggio. (*November 1977*)

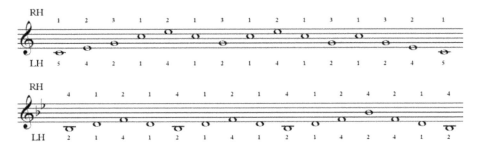

Teaching several arpeggios at the same time. *I have heard that you recommend teaching several arpeggios at the same time. Which arpeggios do you assign together and why? Which arpeggios do you consider the easiest?*

I don't necessarily recommend assigning more than one arpeggio at a time, however I always want students to understand that once they can play the C major arpeggio they can also play arpeggios in G major, F major, A minor, and D minor because they all have the same shape and feel in the hands. By the same token, I would want them to understand that D major, E major, and A major all have the same shape and feel in the hands, as do C, G, and F minor. Technically speaking, within each of the above groups, to be able to play one arpeggio is to be able to play them all.

The musical advantage in assigning two or three arpeggios to be played each day is the variety of sound. Despite the similarity of feel, the sounds of, for example, C major and D minor are completely different. This difference adds interest and variety to the technical practice and, of course, additional keys usually mean more practice.

As to which arpeggios are easiest, I consider those in which fingers 2 and 3 or 2 and 4 are on black keys to be easier than those in which all fingers play white keys. Fingers on black keys cause a higher arch allowing more room for the thumb to pass under. For this reason, the B major arpeggio is possibly the easiest of all. (*December 1981*)

Additional ways to practice arpeggios. *My intermediate students find practicing arpeggios a very dull experience. Can you suggest some ways to assign arpeggios in addition to playing them four octaves, hands separately and hands together?*

The reward from any technical practice comes when a student sees his own progress. The more variation we can introduce to technical practice, the faster students should progress. For starters, here are a few additional ways to practice arpeggios:

RH alone
LH alone (one octave lower)
HT (one octave apart)

Play four octaves in triplets (or in 6/8 time), beginning on each note of the arpeggio.

Play four octaves in sixteenth notes beginning on each note of the arpeggio. (*October 1980*)

Steps for arpeggio practice. *Could you outline the steps for arpeggio practice that were shown on video tape at the University of Houston last August?*

There are many possible procedures for introducing arpeggios and for practicing them; these steps represent just one way. The following examples are for left hand in the key of D major. The same steps would also apply to the right hand (with appropriate fingerings) and to any key.

Example 1. Depress the thumb silently and sustain it with minimal pressure. Play fingers 2 and 3 back and forth by rolling over the thumb. The exercise is written low enough on the piano so that a student sitting in the middle of the keyboard can see as well as feel the motion of the thumb that enables the hand to roll over it and reach from finger 2 to finger 3. Avoid putting the fingers over the thumb; instead the crossing should be caused by the thumb's rolling in the direction the hand is moving. The desired musical result is a melodic line that flows.

Example 2. Play each note very slowly and repeat the three-note figure: up, down, up and down, down and up. Listen for legato and avoid any accent with the thumb. Emphasize playing with a loose thumb and flexible wrist.

Example 3. This exercise adds an extra note at the start to give momentum. Practice up, down, up and down, down and up.

Example 4. One additional note has been added at the top to increase the sweep and provide follow-through.

Example 5. Now a student should be ready to play the arpeggio four octaves: up, down, up and down, down and up in running eighth notes. Our goal is to have a student feel, before playing the first note, that the hand is ready to play the entire four octaves as one phrase and on one impulse. Also play four octaves beginning on the second note of the arpeggio (5b – first inversion) and on the third note of the arpeggio (5c – second inversion).

Example 6. Play four octaves in sixteenth notes, four notes to a beat. *(February 1982)*

Chords

What chord practice should young students have? *I don't find any course of study that includes chord practice. Here and there I find a chord piece, but nothing consistent. What chordal experiences do you think young students should have?*

Our students' assignments include many pieces using chords. In addition, we use their theory assignment as an unending source of chord material. For example, when introducing triads, give them exercises such as this, to be played right hand alone and left hand alone (2 octaves lower).

A little later, assign an exercise to be played in three octaves, crossing hands, like this:

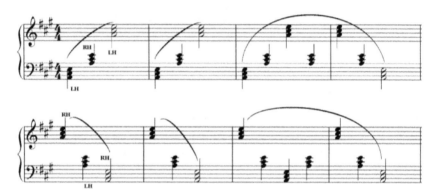

Exercises such as those above can be assigned in many keys, both major and minor, and the dynamic level can vary from week to week.

As soon as students are studying inversions, make up chordal exercises such as these, to be played right hand alone, left hand alone, and hands together:

Later, there are all the possibilities for playing chord progressions, such as these, in many keys:

As students progress, there is a wealth of material in diminished and dominant 7th chords. Diminished 7th chords are especially good, not only because they use all ten fingers, but because the notes are equidistant.

Transposed chromatically, diminished 7th chords provide a wealth experience in the many ways a supple hand can adjust to fit the black and white keys. *(November 1988)*

Learning diminished 7th chords. *I assign diminished 7th chords in various ways to give students handfuls of notes to play simultaneously. Some students learn these chords easily, but others fumble around and never seem to learn them. Do you have any suggestions?*

I assume from your question that you do not write out the chords for your students, and I agree that this should not be necessary; but for students who are fumbling, may I suggest two other approaches for your consideration.

Perhaps the easiest approach of all is to learn the diminished seventh chord on C, then transpose each successive chord by moving ach tone up a half-step.

Make sure the student understands that there are only three different chords to be learned:

but that each may be played in four different positions:

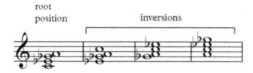

To learn all the diminished seventh chords, students should learn only the three different chords, and then learn to play each chord in its four positions. This approach is especially recommended for students who like to consider things theoretically.

A third approach is to present the chords in terms of their keyboard shapes. This topographical approach presents the chords as combinations of black and white keys:

(1) *Two white keys and two black keys:*
   C and G   – WBBW
   C# and F# – BWWB
   E and A   – WWBB
   Eb and Bb – BBWW

(2) *Three white keys and one black key:*
   D – WWBW
   F – WBWW
   Ab – BWWW
   B – WWWB

This approach is recommended for students who are architecturally inclined. *(March 1969)*

Reaching large chords. *I have an excellent student in level 5 to whom I want to assign "Intermezzo" (No. 21) in Piano Technic Book 5. She has small hands, can reach an octave, but cannot play a C major chord in an octave position. When I give students music that includes arpeggiated chords I usually ask them to play each arpeggio in blocked chordal style for the first week. The student whom I just mentioned is unable to do this because of the size of her hands. Is there a solution?*

I believe that any student who is able to play level 5 material will be able to play this etude, regardless of the size of her hand.

Blocking is often an excellent way to study chord shapes before playing them in arpeggiated form; but in this etude, where the emphasis is on legato shifts from one extension to another, I would not necessarily assign blocking the entire chord. The fingers need to know where they are going, but always in a fluid and flexible manner. Unless the hand is very large, extending over the entire chord before playing the first note is apt to produce a stingy tone and a tense wrist and arm. The kind of practice that insures even tone and flowing melodic line is to play the first note with the entire weight of the hand behind it; as the first note is played, rotate behind finger 4; as 4 is played, rotate behind finger 2; as 2 is played, rotate behind finger 1. Then, most important, as 1 is played, extend the hand again to are 5 on a new key, etc. As each new key is prepared, the fingers that have already played travel along with the finger that is to play. In other words, the hand doesn't need to reach for the top C until finger 2 plays G. This fluid, relaxed crawling over the keyboard allows the hand to support each finger equally and allows each finger to produce a rich and balanced tone.

For most students, the difficulty in this etude lies in passages like measure one where E-G-C are first played with fingers 4, 2, 1; then the hand has to reposition to play them with fingers 5, 4,2. If you still feel the need to block the positions, I suggest blocking parts of chords, emphasizing the points at which such a shift of position occurs. For example, in measure 1:

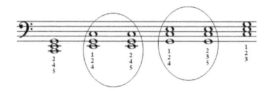

The kind of blocking outlined above points out and emphasizes the technical problem involved.

Another very helpful practice step is to highlight in motion the points at which this repositioning occurs:

The major practice should be done melodically with a relaxed wrist helping to support each finger as it plays.

Etudes like this are legion in the standard repertoire and these practice suggestions apply equally to hundreds of Czerny-type technical etudes and to much Romantic piano literature. *(December 1982)*

Other Technical Issues

Exercises for fingers 3-4-5. *What exercises do you give for fingers 3, 4, and 5? Do you give these exercises to all students, even those who can play scales and arpeggios four octaves at a fast tempo?*

I wouldn't give any technical exercise to any student unless I were convinced that he needed it. However, the ability to play scales and arpeggios at a fast tempo in no way tests a student's ability to control fingers 3, 4 and 5 (in any stepwise order) at a fast tempo. In fact, in many scales he never plays the combination 3-4-5; in others, these fingers are used only at the beginning in the left hand or at the end of the fourth octave in the right hand. In arpeggios, the stepwise pattern 3-4-5 never occurs.

One way to test whether or not a student needs the exercises for s 3-4-5 is to ask him to play fingers 1-2-3-2-1 in a rapid impulse once, then twice without stopping, then four times without stopping. Then ask him to repeat the impulses with fingers 2-3-4-3-2, and finally with fingers 3-4-5-4-3. This should tell both you and the student whether or not he needs special work on fingers 3-4-5 (most students do).

Following is an outline of the exercises we give our students, when and if they are needed. Keep in mind that the real issue here (as with all technical practice) is not whether the exercises are done, but how they are done.

Exercises for Fingers 3, 4, 5
    In all major and minor 5-finger patterns, play exercises for these finger combinations:
        3 4 5 4 3
        4 3 4 5 4
        4 5 4 3 4
        5 4 3 4 5
    Practice steps for each pattern:
        Play slowly and carefully, with attention on hand position, tension-release, and tonal control.
        Play at a fast tempo —
                once
                twice, non-stop
                4 times, non-stop
        HS
        HT in contrary motion
    Play each of these patterns at a fast tempo —
        HS
        HT in contrary motion
        5 4 3 4/5 4 3 4/5 4 3 4/5 4 3 2/1 2 3 4/5 4 3 4/5 4 3 2/1
        1 2 3 2/1 2 3 2/1 2 3 2/1 2 3 4/5 4 3 2/1 2 3 2/1 2 3 4/5
    Play each of these patterns HT at a fast tempo —
        RH: 5 4 3 2/1 2 3 4/5 4 3 2/1 2 3 4/5 4 3 2/1 2 3 4/5
        LH: 3 4 5 4/3 2 1 2/3 4 5 4/3 2 1 2/3 4 5 4/3 2 1 2/3
        RH: 3 4 5 4/3 2 1 2/3 4 5 4/3 2 1 2/3 4 5 4/3 2 1 2/3
        LH: 5 4 3 2/1 2 3 4/5 4 3 2/1 2 3 4/5 4 3 2/1 2 3 4/5

Incidentally, this last exercise prepares for the section of Czerny–Germer, Op. 740, No.1 (reprinted below) — a section which '"many students find impossible to play clearly at ♩ = M.M. 90. (September 1976)

136

Op. 740, No. 1

Czerny-Germer

Preparing for legato 3rds. *I have a problem developing students who can play legato 3rds well. What exercises might I use to prepare them for this specific technique?*

There are two basic techniques which a student must have mastered before beginning to play legato 3rds.

A student should be able to play a single legato line. It's amazing how many students who have trouble playing legato 3rds have never learned to listen to pure legato in a single line. Before ever approaching legato 3rds, establish the sound and feel of legato single notes in short diatonic passages. Secondly, a student should be able to play two keys exactly together — to depress two keys or release two keys at precisely the same time. The following preparatory exercises help a student develop awareness of balance within the hand and timing so that the two tones sound and release exactly together.

Begin with exercises that alternate 2nds with perfect 4ths in contrary motion:

For LH alone

Notice that these exercises are written so that the longer fingers black keys, to help with balance in the hand and to make playing legato easier.

The next step is exercises in which 3rds move to perfect 5ths in contrary motion:

Once this is easy, a student is ready for legato 3rds. Present them first in groups of 2, then in groups of 3. *(July-August 1983)*

Legato 3rds. *I feel that I have never taught the whole subject of legato successfully, especially between fingers 3-1 and 2-1. Do you have any suggestions?*

Most problems with legato 3rds have to do with balance. To play 3rds with fingers 2-4, for example, is fairly easy because the two fingers are approximately the same length and are balanced in the middle of the hand. Fingers 1-3 and 3-5 aren't the same length and deal with the outside of the hand, so they require much more care. With fingers 1-3, the hand must lean slightly toward the thumb and the thumb must curve slightly toward the 2nd finger. With fingers 3-5, the 5th finger should stand tall with its knuckle prominent, and the hand should lean slightly toward the thumb, thus lengthening the 5th finger. With fingers 1-2, the problems are still more exaggerated — the hand leans even more toward the thumb, and the thumb curves even more toward the 2nd finger in an attempt to balance two fingers of such different lengths.

To work on balance and precision, ask students to practice the C major scale in 3rds, using each set of 3rds throughout an entire octave.

This would be repeated with fingers 3-5, 3-1, and finally 2-1.

Before working on 3-1, 2-1, a student masters patterns in which every other combination of fingers is rehearsed:

When a student is ready for legato 3rds between fingers 3-1 and 2-1, the emphasis changes to listening for legato between fingers 3-2 and sliding the thumb from key to key as smoothly as possible to give the effect of legato. Exercises such as these help:

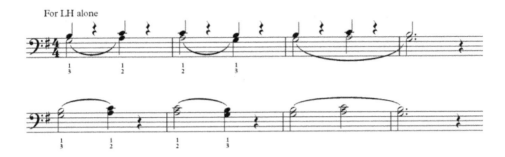

When such patterns are easy, a student is ready to tackle harder combinations:

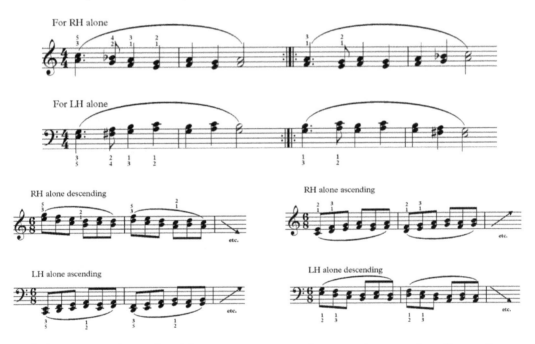

Still later, a student should master patterns that require crossing finger 3 over finger 5 and finger 3 over finger 4 in exercises such as these. Begin by playing each voice until it feels natural and comfortable, then play the two voices together as smoothly as possible. *(December 1986)*

Contrasting dynamic levels. *What do you do with a student who can't play loud in one hand and soft in the other at the same time?*

From the very beginning, students need to have in their ears a definite sound for *forte* and a definite sound for *piano* and, equally important, a definite sense in their hands of how *forte* and *piano* feel. Also needed is an awareness of the contrast between the sound and feel of *forte* and the sound and feel of *piano*. Simple exercises such as is can help develop awareness of dynamic contrasts.

Play on any key

In Example 1, the beat of silence in the first two measures can be used to prepare for the *piano* and then for the *forte* before a student goes immediately from *forte* to *piano* between measures three and four.

Assign easy pieces like Examples 2 and 3 in which there is dynamic contrast between melody and accompaniment.

Finally, assign music that requires continuous accompaniment at a different dynamic level from that of the melody, such as "A Little Song" by Alexandre Tansman. *(November 1979)*

A Little Song

ALEXANDRE TANSMAN

Voicing. *I would appreciate suggestions for helping develop the ability to play two voices in one hand, particularly in the early grades.*

As in all technical practice, the first emphasis should be on how the music sounds, then on what the hand must do to produce that sound.

To develop the skill of playing sustained and moving voices within one hand, assign exercises like these to students in the early grades: Play this pattern LH alone, then RH alone one octave higher.

Transpose to E major, F major, and A major.

Play the next example RH alone, then LH alone one octave lower.

Transpose to A minor and to C minor.

In *Piano Technic Book 2* of the *Frances Clark Library*, there are four etudes written expressly to develop the ability to play sustained and moving voices in one hand. In No. 27, the outside of the hand has the sustained voice while the inside fingers play the moving part: *(November 1979)*

Problems with octaves. *What shall I do with students who can play octaves only on the very edge of the white keys? They are likely to stumble when performing octaves in a piece.*

There is a vast difference between the ability to stretch to an octave and the ability to play octaves, especially octave passages. Playing octaves requires a span wide enough to allow both the thumb and the 5th finger to play on the flesh beside the nail with the first joint curved and firm. In other words, to play octaves necessitates the ability to reach a ninth. If students' hands can't span a ninth, they are not ready to play music with consecutive octaves, although they might be able to play broken octaves or an occasional octave in blocked position. In the meantime stretching exercises are in order, stretching between fingers 2 and 3, 3 and 4, 4 and 5. These should be done only under careful supervision by the teacher to avoid any possible strain from excessive stretching. *(February 1983)*

Playing octaves. *I have a high school student who plays very well and plans to make music her career. There is just one problem: she can't reach an octave comfortably enough to play consecutive octaves cleanly, and she also has trouble with chords that encompass an octave stretch. She has two more years in high school and I feel we must solve the problem soon or she will not be accepted in a music school. Is it possible she should change to another instrument?*

It may be wise to suggest she study a second instrument, while continuing to study piano. But before suggesting that she give up piano, I'd consider her growth pattern; her hands may still develop so that she will have less difficulty with octave stretches. Also, some carefully monitored stretching exercises might be helpful. I always hesitate to suggest stretching exercises for fear they will not be supervised carefully enough. They must be done for very brief periods of time, with constant checking for release. It is especially important to keep the wrist loose. Begin by asking her to play a third between fingers 2-3, 3-4, and 4-5. After that can be accomplished comfortably, with the wrist hanging loose, try stretching to a fourth. This should not be assigned for home practice until you are absolutely sure she knows how to do it without sustained tension.

Another type of exercise that you might find helpful is playing broken octaves as preparation for consecutive octaves. For example:

Play hands separately, then hands together beginning on every key in C scale (as shown) and then in every other key. *(January 1980)*

Where do etudes fit in? *I don't know what to include under the heading of technique in my teaching. I know Czerny and Hanon exercises are considered technique, as are warm-ups, scales, and arpeggios; where do the etudes or studies by Burgmüller and Heller belong?*

It seems to me that any music we teach, for any purpose, includes both technique and musicianship. They are flip sides of the same in. One side is how to bring the notation into sound (technique). The other side is how to bring the notation into sound with full musical meaning (musicianship). This is true whether we are teaching a Mozart sonata or a finger exercise. It's all a matter of emphasis.

As you suggest, the emphasis is technical in finger exercises, scales, arpeggios, and Czerny, but musicianship is not absent in the practice of any of these; the emphasis is more nearly equal in such materials as Burgmüller and Heller, or even in big etudes such as Moskowzski, Op. 72. The emphasis, however, is certainly on musicianship when we come to etudes such as those by Chopin, even though each etude is based predominantly on one technical problem. For example, in Op. 25, No. 5 is based on legato thirds, No. 8 on legato sixths, and No. 10 on octaves.

The real answer to your question lies in the reason for making any specific assignment. We practice finger exercises, scales, and arpeggios to be able to use those skills when they occur in the music we are studying. In the case of Chopin etudes, the main job is putting together musical and technical skills already acquired to realize the full musical content of each piece. *(December 1983)*

Moszkowski etudes. *I am looking for a collection of technical etudes for advanced students – not as difficult interpretively as the Chopin Etudes , and not as limited musically as Czerny's Op. 740. You once mentioned a group of Moszkowski Etudes. If you think these Etudes would be a possible answer to my need, please tell me the publisher and describe the collection.*

The complete title is *Fifteen Etudes de Virtuosité*, Op, 72. The collection is published by Enoch and Company (Paris) and is available in this country through Associated Music Publishers. An abundance of etudes devoted to less common technical subjects makes this collection unique and valuable. The collection is virtuosically demanding. All but two of the etudes consist of continuous sixteenth notes. Tempo and mood indications include allegro brillante, allegro energico, vivo con fuoco, and presto. Whole etudes devote attention to such Common technical hurdles as diatonic passages, arpeggiations, and consecutive repeated octaves.

The following examples show how the opening measures of each etude state the technical subject of the entire study. *(May-June 1986)*

145

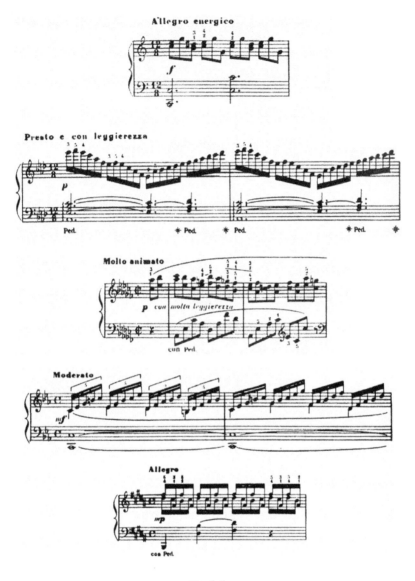

Pedal

Introducing pedal. *I do not consider myself successful in teaching pedaling to young students, and frankly don't know where or why I miss. Please some comments on introducing pedal in your column in* Clavier.

I am sure that every young student who has a piano in his home has experimented with the pedal. Our job, then, is to refine this experiment.

Pedaling, like anything else in music, begins with listening; we pedal by ear, just as we play by ear. The score is seen by the eye; which tells the ear what to listen for. This means that when we first introduce the pedal, we begin with listening. We might play a passage such as this without pedal, then with pedal, drawing a student's attention to the difference in sound.

When you are sure that a student is aware of the difference in sound, w him how to produce that sound, showing him what the dampers are and how the damper pedal affects the sound. Finally, show him the pedal sign.

In showing a student how to use the pedal, ask him to experiment with how far down he should push the pedal in order to collect the tones; also how far up he should release the pedal to lose the tones. This results in his learning to pedal with the ball of his foot riding up and down on the pedal (just as his feet remain on the floor as he rides and down on an elevator). This sensitizes both his ear and his foot, and eliminates that awful pedal hitting. I would not introduce the sign for syncopated pedal └──────∧──────┘ until this sensitivity is highly developed and until a student collects only the tones indicated by the composer, no more and no less. For instance, in a legato passage such as this:

A student is all too apt to pedal it like this:

Be sure that the effect of syncopated pedal is in his ear and the technique in his foot before assigning a piece that demands syncopated pedal. To aid in accomplishing this we often use little exercises such as these: *(May-June 1969)*

Students who pay no attention to pedal marks. *What do you do with students who pay no attention to pedal marks? I have some students who just put their foot on the pedal and leave it there. It drives me to distraction, yet nothing I say seems to have any effect. Just today I was teaching "First Love" from* Supplementary Solos 3-4. *As you know, syncopated pedal is crucial here, and again I was unsuccessful in making an impression on the student about the need for careful, consistent pedaling. Can you suggest any solution?*

The problem you mention is one of remedial teaching. All such problems can, I believe, be solved in just one way: take the student back to step one of whatever the problem is and, starting there, work your way forward until you reach the point in the original learning process at which things apparently broke down. Then, at this point, begin to rebuild.

From the moment a student begins to read music we are concerned with developing a direct connection between what his eyes see (all notation, signs, and symbols), what his hands do about what he sees, and above all what his ears hear. Eventually when a student looks at a score, he should have an expectation in his ear and a feeling in his before he plays the first note. Of course this does not happen overnight, but if it did not happen in connection with a certain concept or skill the first time around, there is no solution except to repeat al learning process again, beginning with the first step.

In the case of the damper pedal, we are adding to the other complexities of the score an additional sign; further, we have to add the technique of pressing the right foot down on the right-hand pedal at the right moment. But most important, we add one more element for the ear to hear and evaluate. We begin damper pedal with non-syncopated experiences. And we begin, as we begin all discoveries, with the ear. The teacher would play a simple example, like this one:

Play it first without pedal, then with pedal, and ask the student to describe in his own words the difference in sound. Then if you're at a grand piano, raise the lid and let him see what the dampers do in of the two situations. I've never met a student who didn't find this fascinating. Next, ask the student to play the same group of notes, first without pedal, then with pedal, listening to the difference in sound. It's at this point (when he first uses the pedal) that you make sure that the student feels his foot riding up and down smoothly, never banging down its inception or banging up its release. Eventually he finds that the pedal never really needs to go completely down or completely up. When he has acquired control of this operation, and the hand, foot and ear are working as one, show him the pedal sign, explaining that the sign shows exactly what his foot does when — down, hold, up. When this is secure, and he can react to the pedal sign with ease, assign pieces of music using it.

Not until non-syncopated pedal is really easy do we recommend teaching syncopated pedal. Here the same steps are recommended. Begin by playing an example such as this one:

Play it for the student two ways, first with non-syncopated pedal, then with syncopated pedal, and ask him to describe in his own words the difference in sound. Then have him play it, experiencing various stages: non-syncopated pedal (with a split-second break in tone between chords); exaggerated and slow syncopated pedal (with the first chord blurring into the second before the pedal is changed); and correctly-timed syncopated pedal (with the change occurring immediately after the second chord is played, producing neither a break nor a blur).

It is especially important to make a dramatic contrast between non-syncopated and syncopated pedal, both as to the technique required and the sound produced. We have found that the three stages above accomplish this most effectively.

Once the fingers, foot, and ear are working as one, introduce the sign for syncopated pedal:

Now, if these are the steps in the original learning process, it is easy to retrace them for the remedial student. For such a student, non-syncopated pedal will be easy, and you can probably move on quickly to the exercises in syncopated pedal. The important thing is not to skip any step in the process and not to move to the next step until the preceding one is really secure.

With the remedial student I would assign two specific practice steps for the piece you asked about, the first page of which is reprinted here.

Use no pedal until the performance of the piece is 100 percent secure without pedal. The danger with any pedal piece is that the pedal is often added before the performance is secure. This creates a false sense of security, and makes true security virtually impossible.

After the performance is secure without pedal, assign practice of the left hand alone with pedal until the hand, foot and eye are totally coordinated and you and the student are satisfied that each pedal change is exactly timed and perfectly smooth and clean. Then add the right hand part. Perhaps it's worth mentioning again here that the old adage "an ounce of prevention is worth a pound of cure" applies significantly and directly to the whole teaching-learning process at the piano. As piano teachers we must be constantly learning how to keep such problems from arising; that's a big part of the excitement of teaching. *(September 1973)*

First Love

Memorizing

Memory tests. *Do you ever ask a student to play from memory in public when he doesn't want to or sys he doesn't feel confident? How can I help such a student gain confidence?*

I wish I could answer your question with a simple "no," but the problem is a little more complicated. Whenever a student says he lacks confidence, we have to ask ourselves, "Is he saying this because it's the popular thing to say?" "Is he saying it because he has caught his parents' anxiety over the occasion?" or "Is his memory really as insecure as he says it is?"

Our job is to make sure he really knows the music and, if he is to play it from memory, that he really knows it from memory. If he has proven to our satisfaction that he really does know both, I recommend asking him to perform the music from memory to call his bluff (in the first case) or to prove to his parents that their anxiety was unfounded (in the second).

In answer to your second question, how to build his own confidence in his memory, I submit the following five memory tests.

Can he tell you in words, and demonstrate at the piano, what the piece is made of and how it is made? As an example, let's look at "March of the Trolls."

March of the Trolls
DAVID KRAEHENBUEHL

The principle rhythmic figure is: ♩ ♫ | ♩ 𝄽 |

The first part is made entirely of a major 3rd (C-E) and a perfect 5th (G-D), played in three different octaves. In the second part, the right hand plays four notes ascending (G,A,A#,B) and three notes descending (B,A#,G). The left hand plays two perfect 5ths: G-D and G#-D#. The third part is made of just two notes: F# and E#, played in three different octaves. The last part is exactly like the first part except for the last two measures.

Can he begin with confidence at any part? For example, in this piece, the form is designated with the letters, A,B,B,C,A^1 . Can he begin at part C, part A^1, part B^2, etc.?

Can he play the piece with confidence at half tempo, thus testing whether or not the piece is in his mind as well as in his ears and his fingers?

Can he play any part hands separately?

Has he played the music from memory with confidence for an audience you have created — a group of students in a repertoire class, for students who have their lessons just before or just after his, for parents or friends invited to the lesson just for that purpose, etc?

If he can pass these five memory tests, I am confident that he can feel confident, playing from memory in public. *(September 1967)*

When do memory problems begin? *My question has to do with memorizing. All of my young students memorize easily and play their pieces in recital with confidence, but by the time they are 12 or 13 years old, they develop a memory problem and beg not to have to play by memory. In my last recital several junior high students forgot and had to go back to the beginning of their pieces several times. Some teachers have told me that this is caused by age — as soon as students reach the self-conscious age they find it more difficult to play from memory. I'm sure there is some truth in this, but there must also be a solution to the problem. I'm hoping you can help me.*

Memorizing a piece of music means remembering it in four different ways: aurally (how it sounds), analytically (how it's made), visually (how it looks on the page), and kinesthetically (how it feels on the hand). When each of these processes is given sufficient emphasis, a student feels secure. This training is a continuous process that should begin early in the first year of study.

To experience real memory, a student should memorize a piece analytically and visually before playing it the first time. Of course this process needs to begin with a piece as simple as this:

Fish Market

In this piece, a student looks at the title, the time signature, and the dynamic marking. He then notices that there are no phrase markings; however, the words are a clue to the phrasing, with two short phrases followed by one long one. He sees that the piece is made entirely of fourths, so is played entirely with fingers 1 and 4. He experiences the rhythm (apart from playing) by whatever process this particular student needs (pointing and counting, tapping and counting, swinging and counting, or all three). He sees that measures 1, 2, and 4 are exactly alike except that the left hand plays an octave lower, and that the third measure is made of the same right-hand fourths, but upside down and all in quarter notes.

Now he is ready to play the piece. He prepares the right-hand and left-hand positions, and then we close the book. He counts two measures of 4/4 meter out loud, very slowly, then begins to play and count the piece from memory. Since he should think what he has seen and analyzed as he plays, he plays very slowly. With proper preparation of the visual and analytical steps, his first performance can be accurate at a slow tempo. This first performance, without looking at the score, lays the groundwork for the aural and kinesthetic aspects of memorizing. Notice that the process outlined here puts kinesthetic memory last on the agenda, rather than first. The piece is still not completely memorized until a student has played it enough to have memorized how it feels in his hands, but repetitions will secure the kinesthetic experience.

The entire process should be learned starting with short pieces at lesson after lesson until a student experiences how easy it is to memorize. Begun early, with simple music, the process of memorizing becomes easy and natural for a student. Soon he will be able to memorize a 16-measure piece like "Swinging" in just a few minutes.

Swinging

Sarah Louise Dittenhaver

Looking through such a piece he might see, for example, that lines 1 and 3 are exactly alike, lines 2 and 4 almost alike; so he should learn only line 1, line 2 and the part of line 4 that is different. When lines 1, 2, and 4 can be played securely without music, he plays the entire piece at a very slow tempo without looking at the score. Again, if the visual and analytical steps have been properly prepared, he will be able to play the piece accurately without music the first time through.

When memorizing is begun this way at an early age, and continued, a student not only learns how to memorize easily, but how to analyze any piece before he plays it. This is one of the most important, practice steps he will ever learn.

For students who were not taught this way, I suggest that they begin by memorizing pieces much easier than the ones they are currently studying. You can help a student quickly analyze the overall structure of the piece, noting any repeated lines, phrases, or rhythmic figures. With pieces that are easy to analyze, an intermediate student can be successful immediately with the sequence of experiences described above. Be alert to the fact that this process will not necessarily keep the piece in a

154

completely memorized condition. As a student plays the piece again and again, the kinesthetic process may take over unless the other types of memorizing are periodically reviewed. It is also important to play a memorized piece occasionally from the score as an aid to keeping the visual and analytical steps in mind.

Another good way to check on the condition of a memorized piece is to ask a student to practice beginning at specific places in the score. For example, ask him to begin at the fifth phrase, then to begin at the fourth phrase, then at the third phrase, etc. Or ask him to begin where the pedal changes on each beat, or where the pedal changes on the first beat of each measure, etc. For a more advanced student who did not begin memorizing this way, much the same process can be helpful. Teach the four steps of memorizing and then put a check at various spots in his music where you will ask him to begin, such as at the beginning of long phrases or formal sections, or at spots where he habitually forgets. At the lesson be sure to check on his ability to begin at these spots. This technique will not give him complete security, but at least he will have some places in the music that he remembers analytically, visually, and aurally, as well as kinesthetically. This will give him a feeling of security which may help the kinesthetic to carry him through; if problems do occur, he has starring points at which to recoup.

Mental practice. *Does mental practice away from the keyboard help a student achieve confidence in playing from memory for an audience?*

This is one of the very best ways to practice any piece, especially one we are preparing to play in public. Too much memory work is based on tactile memory only. Visual, analytical, and even aural memory can be reinforced away from the keyboard where tactile memory has no chance of operating at the level of habit, and the mind and ear are forced to recall structure, tonality, patterns, and shapes.

Your question reminded me of a delightful experience I had with a 13-year old student who took my suggestions about mental practice very seriously. I had occasion to call the student by long distance. Her mother answered the phone and explained that her daughter couldn't come to the phone just then; she was upstairs in her bedroom memorizing and had asked not to be disturbed. My first reaction was one of faint annoyance, but on further thought I decided my minor inconvenience was a small price to pay for an important lesson so thoroughly learned. *(April 1971)*

Memorizing versus reading. *After four years of teaching, I have come to the conclusion that most poor readers are good at memorizing. I believe the reason may be that, because it takes them so long to learn a piece, by the time they can play it, they have memorized it. Could this be true?*

No, I don't think so. In the first instance, instead of assuming that slow readers are

155

good at memorizing, I'd take a completely different approach: I would assign them easier or shorter music, putting the emphasis on developing reading skills. Nothing in an assignment should take so long to learn that by the time they can play it, they have memorized it. In the second instance the very qualities that make a good reader also make for good memorizing. Let's illustrate with a few musical examples. Look first at "Bear Dance."

Bear Dance

Jon George

From the very beginning, students learn to look at the whole piece for what is alike and what is different. They see that line 2 is exactly like line 1, except an octave lower — so there's just one line to learn. Looking at the rhythm, they see a 3/4 time signature and a pattern that consists of three measures in quarter notes followed by a dotted half note. They practice the rhythm until it is secure — swinging and saying the words, pointing and counting, tapping and counting, and so on. Then they see that every measure begins with bass F in the left hand, that the right hand plays only repeated notes on middle C, and that there are only two basic gestures: in measure 1, left hand bass F up to repeated middle Cs, and in measure 2, left hand bass F down a 2nd to repeated Es. Students who read new music in this way probably have a piece memorized before playing it the first time.

The next step would be to play and count, getting the sound in the ears and the feel in the hands. Students who grow up doing this kind of silent reading before beginning their practice not only become fine readers, but also find it easy to memorize.

How can these same techniques apply to music at a slightly more advanced level? Look at "Playing Soldiers" by Rebikov.

Playing Soldiers

Here we see that the right hand has only four measures to learn.

When the right hand rhythm is completely secure, students notice that the theme is based on two notes (C and G), extending to D in measure 2 and to high G in measure 3. In seeing this, students understand how the right hand of the entire piece is made. In the left hand, students see that they can master line 2 at a glance — a two-note slur, E to B♭. In line 3 the left hand descends from that B♭, down to A, to A♭, and then to every white key down to the next B♭. In line 4 a similar pattern in the top voice changes to half notes, beginning on B♭ and descending stepwise to bass C. The exceptions are tricky: the intermittent pedal point on bass C coming in on the second beat of each measure, and the surprise introduction of F#.

I have sometimes used "Playing Soldiers" to demonstrate that, even at this level, it is possible to memorize a piece before the first playing. Students are amazed to find that when rhythm practice and silent study have led to security, they can practice the piece from memory the first time they play it. *(April 1988)*

Practicing

Does practice make perfect? *If practice doesn't make perfect, what does?*

Whether practice makes perfect or not depends on the quality of the practice; and the quality of the practice depends largely on the practice habits a student has formed and is forming.

There are many mistaken notions about what constitutes practice. For example, students often think they are practicing when they play a passage, stopping to correct mistakes four or five times; then, on the next day's practice, stop to correct mistakes three or four times; the next day, two or three times, and so on, until they finally play the passage without a mistake. A student who practices this way has not formed the habit of playing the passage correctly but only the habit of making fewer mistakes each day. The playing has improved, of course, but the practice habit is to make mistakes (and correct them). This is a natural process into which human beings slip in all sorts of endeavors. Of course less wrong is a step forward; but the force of habit is worthy of our utmost respect. The time to build the habit of playing a passage accurately is when a problem has been solved and a passage has been played correctly. One definition of good practice is "the purposeful repetition of accuracy." In the purposeful repetition of accuracy, the habit of playing the passage correctly overcomes the habit of making fewer mistakes each day. All too often, when a student finally plays a passage accurately, we say, "Fine, you've got it!" as if the necessary practice had been completed. Sometimes we are guilty of dropping a piece, a study, or a finger exercise just when practice to make perfect could begin.

To help us and our students overcome this poor practice habit, I suggest one specific practice technique for problem spots or insecure ages. It is called "Oscar," a name selected half a lifetime ago by one of my young students who was tickled by the assignment and felt it needed a whimsical name. "Oscar" means to play a passage three times perfectly in succession. With young students, we often use three checkers or pennies. Place them at the left side of the keyboard, and each successive perfect performance, move one checker to the right side of the keyboard. If a mistake occurs on the second or third playing, all checkers return to the left side, and the practice begins in. Once "Oscar" has been completed (the purposeful repetition of accuracy), the passage may be put back into a larger context — mastering transitions into and out of the problem spot.

Like many good techniques, "Oscar" can be misused or overused. With elementary and intermediate students, I recommend limiting its use to short passages or problem spots that are no more than two to four measures in length; and assigning it for home practice only after it has been experienced successfully at the lesson.

"Oscar" is just one of many techniques that can help form good habits and insure that practice does make perfect. The very best practice is that in which the first reading of a new piece or passage is both accurate and musical. This sounds like an impossible ideal, but students can accomplish it if they carefully follow these three steps:

Plan. Instead of jumping right into a stumbling, trial-and-error reading, plan what and how to practice. Analyze the piece for parts that are alike and different; mark the form; circle similar parts where slight differences occur, noting what those differences are. Practice the rhythm (point and count or tap and count), until the rhythm is completely secure. Practice the technique silently (block chord changes or trace the melodic route) until the topography of the piece is completely secure.

Play and count out loud at a tempo so slow that there is no possibility of a wrong note or even a hesitation. Despite the slow tempo, this reading must have musical meaning as well as accuracy.

Repeat the slow, secure reading until it feels completely natural and comfortable, then gradually increase the tempo.

If students would follow these three steps faithfully in their approach to every new piece, remedial practice would become largely a thing of the past. (*October 1983*)

Students don't practice enough. *When you suggested giving students an outline of how to practice, it seemed like an answer to my prayer. Now that I have tried it for over a year, I am disappointed to discover that it has worked with only a few of my students. The majority still don't practice sufficiently or intelligently. I have the feeling that they get to the piano regularly, but for playing, not practicing. Any further suggestions?*

Motivating students to practice and developing students who know how to use their practice time wisely is our biggest single challenge as teachers. I say "our" challenge advisedly, because I believe that what all teachers desire most is students who make daily progress because they want to practice, and because they know how to practice intelligently. This is one of the hardest skills to teach.

Our widespread need for help in this area came home to me in a lecture I heard by Professor Edward Hugdahl of the University of Wisconsin at the National Conference on Piano Pedagogy in Madison last October. He reported on a survey of area piano teachers, conducted by the University, in which teachers were given a long list of topics and were asked to rank them in order of their importance to teaching. The topics ranged from group teaching to the interpretation of Bach, from developing good sight-reading to methods for teaching improvisation. The topic listed first by most teachers, as an area in which they needed help, was how to motivate students to practice and how to teach them intelligent practice habits. Among dozens of subjects, this one was given top priority.

There are many reasons why students don't do sufficient or intelligent practice. Some of them are reasons for which we, as teachers, are not responsible. Among these are too much homework, too many extracurricular activities, insufficient encouragement at home, a home environment that does not lend itself to regular practice, lack of privacy during the practice period, etc. However, there are also reasons our students don't practice for which we may be responsible. Among these are assignments that are too short to be challenging or too long to be accomplished, music that is too hard to read or too difficult technically, music that is too childish or too mature, music that is all of one type without contrast and variety, or music that a student simply does not like enough to bother to practice. I think we need to consider all areas for which we are responsible before being critical of a student.

Now let's assume that none of the above issues is the problem and that giving a student a practice outline is going to be the solution. How can this seemingly good idea go wrong? There are several possibilities.

- Is the practice outline for the week's assignment written in the student's notebook? If it is anywhere else, students are apt to ignore it.
- Is the practice outline too detailed for this particular student? If so, he won't use it.
- On the other hand, is it detailed enough? If it is too general, can it be of real help with a particular piece?
- Are you asking your students to follow a single outline with everything they are studying? Is it possible to make an outline that fits every piece? Of course not. Have you shown your students how to select the steps from the outline that they need for each of the types of music on the assignment, and how to adjust the practice plan as the week progresses? One of the biggest problems with practice outlines is that they need to be of two types: one for working out new music, the other for practicing music that has already been worked out. Wisdom in knowing when to shift from one of these practice modes to another is one of the most important things we have to teach our students about practice.

I believe the crux of the problem lies in whether we give our students a practice outline for use at home, and whether we do the steps with them at the lesson. If, by going through the practice steps at the lesson, students accomplish more in 20 minutes than they did at home in the entire week, you have made your point.

Certainly, making this point is worth a major part of the lesson for several weeks, and will pay enormous dividends in more successful home practice in the weeks and months to come. *(March 1983)*

"Tracing the route." *At your study course this past summer I heard you discuss "tracing the route," but I'm not sure I understand how to apply it to music.*

In addition to rhythm preparation, perhaps the most important practice step is one that is done silently, tracing the route the hands and fingers need to take as they play a piece. This first step helps avoid wrong notes in a first reading and contributes to physical security and control.

This silent practice is often referred to as blocking the positions. For example, look at the development section of this Haydn *Divertimento*.

A student would block the left hand by playing each new position as a chord, as shown in Example 1.

Example 1

Equally important, however, is an awareness of the route the hand and fingers must travel in moving from one position to another in continuous passages like this section from C.P.E. Bach's familiar *Solfeggietto* (Example 2).

In the bracketed section of measure 2, where continuous sixteenth notes are played by the right hand, students should see and be physically aware of the route. As the thumb plays the second treble C in beat 2, fingers 5-4-3-2 toll instantly to the keys to be played on the third beat. As finger 5 plays D on the third beat, the thumb slides rapidly and loosely to G, ready for the first note of beat 4, etc.

These three pictures of the right hand as it prepares to play a descending C major scale demonstrate how to trace the route,

In picture 1 the 5th finger is on C:

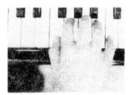

In picture 2 the thumb has rolled so that fingers 3-2 are on the notes E-D:

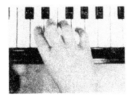

The instant this happens, the thumb slides out to C, as in picture 3:

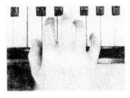

Let's consider tracing the route of this Haydn *Minuet* (Example 3).

Example 3

In the right hand a student prepares for the first two notes (G and C). As the 2nd finger plays C, the hand contracts to prepare for the C major triad that starts on beat 3. Once the thumb is on C, the hand is ready for the next 6 beats, then on the third beat of measure 3 the hand moves up to a D minor triad. As the thumb plays D at the end of the triplet, fingers 3-2 roll over the thumb as a unit, preparing the C and B in the next measure. As soon as the thumb slides out to G, the next triad is prepared. In the first four measures of the piece, then, the hand is in constant motion from triad to triad.

In the left hand positioning the 2nd finger on C, the thumb on E, and the 5th on G prepares for the first eight notes. As the thumb plays E in the third measure, finger 2 rolls over the thumb to play F. As F is played, the thumb slides out to play the upper G. As that G is played, the hand extends to the octave. During the rest, the hand moves so that finger 4 is over the upper G. As Middle C is played by the thumb in the next measure, the hand extends so that 3 can play E. That new position prepares for all notes until the octave extension in the last measure.

Through such silent practice the hand learns the music and becomes comfortable moving from position to position. Student and teacher alike will rejoice in the ease and accuracy such practice provides. *(January 1989)*

Students who don't follow a practice outline. *I am doing everything I can think of to get my students to follow a practice outline, but to no avail. I tell them week after week that they could learn their pieces in much less time if they would follow the practice steps I give them, but the only students with whom I am successful are two girls whose mother practices with them. Do you have any suggestions?*

Instead of telling your students how successful they will be if they follow the practice outline, show them. Take a new piece at the next lesson and work it out with the students, following your practice steps, then share their amazement and pleasure at how well they can learn a new piece in a short time. You may need to do this for several successive weeks. When you think the students are really convinced that it works, ask them to outline the steps you have been using. Students are much more likely to use a practice outline if they have successfully experienced it and have written it down.

You may be hurting your cause by outlining in detail every aspect of the assignment. This relieves students of any responsibility and discourages them from using their own judgment. Too much detail is as bad as too little.

For the two girls whose mother supervises their practice, I'd suggest that you encourage the mother to gradually step out of the picture. First suggest that she supervise only a portion of the assignment, leaving the rest of the lesson as the students' responsibility. When you find that they are as well prepared on the portion of the assignment they did on their own, make a big point of their ability to work independently, and gradually encourage them to do more and more of their practicing without supervision. (June 1980)

Motivating practice. *I am teaching an intelligent ten-year-old girl who has been studying piano for two years. She can read music easily and spends most of her practice time playing the pop and rock music her older brother brings home. I am having problems teaching her because her only interest seems to lie in playing her brother's music. She lacks knowledge of basic rhythm patterns, ignores accidentals and plays in a monotone manner, ignoring the dynamics, and her touch is very poor. Despite my efforts to improve her technique and increase her musical knowledge, she returns week after week with the same mistakes. She simply does not want to put forth the effort to play correctly, and would love to stop lessons, but her mother refuses to let her do this. How can I motivate such a student?*

You are beginning with two strikes against you — first, your student's interests and your interests do not seem to coincide. Second, the problem was not confronted immediately, so it will be more difficult to solve now. To begin with, nothing can be accomplished until your interests and the student's become one. You've been losing weekly skirmishes in the vain hope that eventually you might win, but all too often this approach simply contributes to and increases the problem. There must be at the very least the appearance of mutual interest in order to build mutual trust and cooperative effort.

There is nothing more discouraging to a student than to be assigned the same music week after week, and week after week to have the same mistakes corrected. This is demoralizing. It tells her she can't (or won't) do what you are assigning, so she feels bad about herself. It also gives her the negative and frustrating satisfaction of knowing that she is winning while you are losing. It is imperative that something positive happen at the very next lesson, something dramatic that makes the student feel really successful, something that you can honestly praise. Have a talk with her mother — explain exactly what has been happening, how you feel about it, and how you think her daughter feels about it. Gain her trust and cooperation, then choose a special time for the girl's next lesson, one in which is no time limit, either for you or for her. Ask the mother to observe. At this special lesson give the student a single, short piece, preferably not more than a page in length, and one carefully selected for two qualities: you think she will enjoy it, and you think she can learn it securely with your help in one sitting. Your goal for the lesson will be that she leaves the studio having worked the piece out perfectly. The side benefit will be that you have demonstrated what practice really is, both to the student and to her mother. Possible steps for the lesson are to play the piece for her, as excitingly as possible, to get her interested in the sound. Together, mark the form and divide it into sections for practice, indicating how little has to be mastered to be able to play the entire composition. For example, if the form is A, B, A^1, B^1, bracket for practice only A and B plus the parts of A^1 and B^1 that are different. Take the A section and master it. Make the rhythm secure by swinging and counting, pointing and counting, or tapping and counting. Play silently, tracing the route the hand must take in playing the piece (with careful attention to fingering), hands separately and hands together. Repeat the silent playing until the student feels secure. Play with sound (with careful attention to dynamics, phrasing, etc.) until the student feels secure with hands separately (if needed) and hands together.

Then, take the B section and master it — same steps as A. Play sections A and B together until the student feels completely secure. Master the bracketed part of the A^1 section. Then play the entire A^1, section. Master the bracketed part of the B^1 section, then play the entire B^1 section. Play sections A^1 and B^1 together until secure and then play the whole piece.

At the next lesson, hear the piece and praise the student for any ways in which her performance is more accurate, more secure, or more musical than her lessons have been in the past, then spend the rest of that lesson going through exactly the same steps with another piece, one you have chosen as carefully as you did the first. Continue this process until you have developed a real student. This does work in the long run. There is no greater motivation than a feeling of success, and the bonus of honest praise is invaluable in changing negative attitudes into positive ones. *(October 1977)*

Motivating practice. *My biggest problem is how to motivate my students to practice. They practice hard on their recital and contest pieces but neglect everything else. What can I do to help?*

This question is one that comes up frequently and I'm happy to share the insights I've gleaned in talking with hundreds of teachers who are in the same boat. I believe we have to differentiate between two kinds of motivation: extrinsic and intrinsic. Extrinsic motivation comes from outside the student, including rewards ranging all the way from the gold star on a piece well played to a large cash prize in a national competition.

Well-meaning parents offer all kinds of non-musical rewards for faithful practice, some of them better than others. The worst motivator is the threat of punishment for not practicing: things like getting grounded, taking a cut in allowance, or being given extra household chores. I knew a parent who actually threatened her child with having to attend a Sunday afternoon symphony concert if he didn't practice regularly that week. Only slightly better than the punishment system is the reward system: a penny-a-minute-for practice, candy at the end of the practice period, or permission to watch an extra television show. Usually these rewards are tied to minutes spent at the piano, rather than to accomplishment while there. Whether parents offer punishments or rewards, they are actually bribing their children. What makes these parental incentives extrinsic is that they have nothing to do with music itself. Of course, parents can also provide musically-oriented extrinsic motivation, such as the chance to attend a concert (better a reward than a punishment), have longer lessons, or get a better instrument, as an encouragement toward more intelligent practice and greater progress. These incentives are fine but are usually offered to students who are doing well already.

There is another type of musically-oriented extrinsic motivation, offered by piano teachers themselves, the auditions, festivals, and competitions sponsored by music clubs and national organizations to which they belong. We're a little closer to real motivation here, because the reward relates to a musical experience, but even such musical motivation has three limitations. The reward often comes after a long period of study, sometimes only at the end of the season. It is measured in terms of applause or a judge's rating sheet and comments. Lastly, the achievement is too often measured in terms of comparison between students, one of the least constructive value systems yet devised.

It is easy to discuss extrinsic motivation and point out its shortcomings. Intrinsic motivation, on the other hand, is subtle, elusive, highly individual, and difficult to describe. Intrinsic motivation is anything that happens inside students that makes them want to play the piano, to practice, to study a given composition, to master it, and to perform it, both for their own enjoyment and for the joy of sharing it with others. Again, the gamut is wide. Intrinsic motivation starts with the beginner's excitement about learning something new; the young student's natural desire to work at and master new concepts and skills just for the fun of mastering them; the sheer pleasure in creating a variety of sounds; the physical release of getting into a rhythmic swing; and the delight of learning a new language and finding you can use it to say something meaningful of your own.

The adventure and newness usually provide ample motivation through the first year of study, especially for those fortunate students whose teachers are able to maintain a balance between romance and precision. New concepts and skills are introduced, then drilled and refined through constant reinforcement and follow-through. How does intrinsic motivation continue as the newness of piano study gives way to familiarity in the second year and all the years to follow? How can we maintain that balance between precision and romance, so essential to developing the necessary skills, without losing the spirit of adventure? A student is almost always motivated to practice if he leaves his lesson feeling capable. As teachers, one of our main jobs is to see that our students never take something home to practice that will puzzle or frustrate them when they work on it alone. There are many ways to assure this, but two of the best should be immutable teaching laws:

- never send students home with a piece that contains any element or skill they have not already mastered
- never send students home with a piece without capturing their interest and excitement in the piece, and giving them a sense that they can master it easily.

If students always leave the lesson with a sense of excitement about new music (or rekindled excitement about music they are already studying), plus a sense that they can master the piece, a desire to practice will almost always follow.

Intrinsic motivation comes from the music itself, and from a student's direct and personal involvement with it. Such motivation has tremendous advantages: the reward is immediate, and it is measured in terms of a student's own feelings of success and delight, his own needs, abilities and goals. *(January 1978)*

Stopping and starting over. *I have good intermediate students who, no matter what I say, go back to the beginning of the piece every time they make a mistake. I have told them they are wasting their time (and mine), and I have tried to point out that to practice the beginning (which they know) instead of the problem spot is inefficient. Even so, back to the beginning they go, in spite of me.*

Actually, these students have two bad habits. They stop when they make a mistake, and they go back to the beginning instead of working on the Spot where the problem occurs. Both are natural forms of human behavior. Such habits develop easily and are difficult to uproot, but they can be corrected.

Begin by admitting these bad habits developed because we allowed them to, and that it is our responsibility and privilege to correct them. Instead of preaching, get into the act. First, uproot the habit of stopping when mistakes occur. Playing through the piece (or a section of the piece) is important for several reasons: momentum carries us along, a mistake in the first appearance of an idea may be self-correcting in its second appearance, and, most important, we need to evaluate the condition of the musical whole before going to work on it. As the teacher, you are in control of stopping or going on. "Keep going!" should be a frequent and cheerful command. Sing through the mistake, play with students at a second piano or in a different octave, and if necessary hold their hands on the keys to prevent that inevitable return to the beginning.

Once this first habit is corrected, it is easy to correct the second. At the end of a piece (or a section), stop and evaluate with your students where the trouble spots occurred and why, then isolate them for slow, careful practice. When they master any given Spot, put it back into the piece by starting just before it and playing to it; by starting just before it and playing through it; then by starting farther and farther back, and playing farther and farther along, until the mastered spot is absorbed into the fabric of the piece.

Curing bad habits means developing new ones. In the process of developing new habits, we have to be vigilant about never allowing an exception to occur. Because we are copiers of our past selves, one exception can undo in an instant all the good so carefully undertaken. Remember that not only are students rooting out old habits and replacing them with new ones, we are too. Our habit has been to allow stopping and starting over. The most difficult task will be never to allow an exception in ourselves. After that, helping students learn new habits will be relatively easy. *(January 1985)*

How long should students practice? *Do you require your students to practice a certain amount of time? If so, how long must a first-year student practice? How long for third-year and fifth-year students?*

Do not require any student to practice a certain amount of time. Try persuade parents that the clock enters into practice in just one way: the time to begin practicing. Practice is much more apt to be regular if it always begins at the same time. Once a student has started to practice, his job is to follow every step on his lesson assignment. Whenever he has completed the entire assignment he is through with his practice for that day. Obviously it takes longer to finish the assignment as he grows older and the repertoire gets harder, but always try to put the emphasis on practicing the entire assignment efficiently and carefully rather than on how long it takes. Periodically ask a student to keep a record of how long it takes him to complete the assignment, letting him understand that this information is necessary to judge how wisely he is using his practice time. One primary job as a teacher is to help students learn how to make the best use of whatever practice time they have. It never ceases to amaze me that the more a student learns about wise use of his practice time, the more time he seems to find for practice. In piano study, as in all of life, accomplishment is the strongest motivation for further endeavor. *(October 1970)*

Slow practice. *Do you always insist that a student practice a new piece slowly for a while before he plays it up to tempo?*

Before attempting to answer your question, let me challenge your premise: I don't believe that a teacher's insisting on slow practice necessarily results in slow practice at home. We can control the tempo of any piece that the student plays at his lesson, but what happens at home is probably quite different. I can't imagine anything more illuminating than for a teacher to be able to observe his student's home practice.

Now to the question of slow practice. There are two points of view on when slow practice should occur. Either viewpoint, carried to an extreme, seems to me to be wrong. One point of view is that a piece must be worked out very slowly and carefully to avoid any possibility of error. This is based on the belief that only slow, controlled practice can be 100 percent accurate. The other point of view is that a piece should be worked out first somewhere near tempo, since it exists as a piece only in the tempo the composer chose. According to this viewpoint, the piece is first learned in context — perhaps RH alone, LH alone, hands together in short sections, etc., then slow practice follows for control. It is really not a question of whether or not to do slow practice, but whether slow practice is the first or second step. There are merits in both viewpoints, and the wise teacher uses both approaches, basing his decision in every case on the nature of the piece and the practice skill of the student. Slow, controlled practice is an absolute necessity at some point in the practice. I have however, observed some disastrous results with students who have been asked to practice very slowly over a long period of time, playing note by note rather than feeling the length and movement of the phrases. Keep in mind that accuracy is not the only ultimate goal. *(January 1971)*

Hands separately. *Do you ask your students to practice their new pieces hands separately for a week before they play them hands together?*

I make such an assignment only occasionally. Some music needs to be worked out hands separately, but it is usually neither necessary nor desirable to continue to practice it that way. Hands-separate practice does not give the sound of the musical whole, and it skirts the difficulties of coordinating the hands. Sometimes technical or rhythm problems seem to solve themselves when hands are played together.

When we discover sections that need further practice with hands separate, review is always linked to practice with hands together. Of course, there are exceptions. For example, I am currently working with a student on Czerny's *Etudes for the Left Hand*, Op. 718. In these etudes the whole technical point is in the left hand, and there are no real coordination problems between the hands. Consequently I assign each etude to be practiced left-hand only for at least the first week.

In summary, much music needs to be studied hands separately, but most music that needs to be practiced separately for an entire week is probably too difficult for the student. *(April 1978)*

What students have learned about practice and performance. *At The New School's four study courses this past summer, there was a simultaneous program for students who attended with their teachers. The program included separate classes each morning in practice skills and performance techniques, plus a combined class each afternoon in which the students played for the teachers in a demonstration repertoire class. As part of the final day's activities at each course, the students were asked to prepare written summaries of what they had learned that would help them in their practice and performance this coming year. In reply to many requests from the teachers, we are devoting the column this month to a selection of the students' wise conclusions. We have corrected only the spelling, leaving everything else exactly the way the students themselves expressed it.*

About practice

> Study the form of the piece before you begin to practice. That will musical understanding and also tell you how much or how is to work out.
> Practice slow enough to be accurate.
> Slow practice really pays off.
> Be able to begin at any part of a piece, at any phrase. If you can't, you really know the piece.
> If you make a mistake in practicing, don't go back to the beginning unless that's where you made the mistake.
> When you are practicing, you are the audience. Do you really like what you hear?
> The height of the bench I use for practice is very important – I'll check on this when I get home.
> My weight should be divided, with more weight on my feet than on my seat.
> My feet are my anchor. I must feel that my weight is there (not just that my feet are on the floor wandering around).
> Don't settle wav back on the bench, sit forward, ready to play.
> You'll feel more ready to play if your right foot is forward, ready for damper pedal and your left foot is back with your weight on the ball of that foot.
> Correct fingering is very important. Wrong fingering gets you into all kinds of trouble.
> Be sure you know the accompaniment. Just because it's played by the left hand and isn't melody doesn't mean it isn't important.
> Practice makes perfect only if the practice is perfect.

About rhythm

If you can't play a fast piece at a slow tempo, you can't really control it at a fast tempo.

Rhythm is first — you can't put rhythm on notes. It's always the other way around.

Set the tempo before you begin the piece, not in the fourth or fifth measure.

Rhythm is something you feel from top to toe.

If you still have to count to play a piece rhythmically, it isn't ready to play in public.

Set the tempo, then keep that tempo throughout the piece unless the composer tells you to change it.

About performance

The piece starts on the first note, not after you've been going awhile.

Play a piece the way the composer wrote it. Follow every sign and symbol.

A slur seldom ends with a staccato.

Budget your dynamics. If the range is from *pp* to *p* to *f* to *ff*, know what your own *pp* and *ff* are and then decide what your *p* and *f* can be.

Budget your *crescendo* and *diminuendo*. If you begin a *crescendo* too loud or a *diminuendo* too soft, you'll run out of *crescendo* and *diminuendo* and ruin the effect. The same is true of *ritards* and *accelerandos*.

An *f* means to continue *f* until another sign occurs. If the next phrase is marked *p*, begin playing *p* on the first note of that phrase not on the second or third note.

If the music changes from loud to soft, it doesn't mean to get slower. If it changes from soft to loud, it doesn't mean to get faster; lots of pianists don't seem to understand this.

Some music is full of extreme contrasts where some measures are *ff*, followed by measures marked *pp*. These changes must be sudden, not gradual.

Your hands need to know the notes and your body should know the rhythm, so your thought and ears can be on the musical content of the piece.

If you accent everything, you have not accented anything.

It helps to know a lot about the composer.

Music must be clear in your ear. Don't put up with muddy playing.

A piece has to breathe.

I'm beginning to understand phrases and how they fit together to make musical sense.

Phrases have interesting shapes.

You have to know what note a phrase is moving to.

Be aware of phrase lengths and subordinate groupings within a phrase.

We create the tone, the piano does not. So first we need to know what kind of tone we want to hear.

Listen to your own playing. You are your most important audience.

Fortissimo doesn't mean harsh.

Hear everything in a piece. If you don't you are being gypped.

Play through the end of a piece, not just to the end.

The bass line tells you a lot about a piece, sometimes how to pedal, sometimes how to phrase.

Don't accent the first note of each measure. It ruins Mozart and Bach and many others.

Enjoy a piece to its full extent.

Live piece of music, don't just play it.

When you speak, you have to mean what you say. When you speak music, you have to mean what you play. *(October 1968)*

Phrasing

Melodic contour and rhythmic shape. *I heard you say that a phrase has both melodic contour and rhythmic shape. Is there a quick and simple way to teach this?*

Yes, but you may consider this too quick and too simple. The best way to teach the melodic contour of a phrase is to ask students to sing it. The best way to understand the rhythmic shape of a phrase is to ask students to conduct or dance it. Keep in mind that each complements the other. *(May-June 1974)*

Students who refuse to sing. *Ever since I heard you lecture on the use of singing to help students develop musical phrasing, I have made singing a high priority in my piano lessons and feel I have achieved greater success as a result. I still have some students who refuse to sing. What next?*

First, be patient, they may sing some day. With elementary students who are reluctant singers, encourage chanting the words instead of singing on pitch. The teacher sings while playing the accompaniment to the duets, and both the accompaniment itself and the teacher's voice help non-singing students experience phrasing. Chanting is just another way to feel and breathe phrases.

A group in which everyone else is singing is the greatest help to students who don't like to sing. Before long most students join in. With uncertain singers, sing softly but directly into their ear to reinforce the pitch. Often they can match melodic lines with this extra help. Work every week on matching pitches, singly and in phrases. One of the students' favorite activities is what we call sing-backs, in which we sing a phrase to them and they sing it back to us in the same rhythm and dynamics.

Older students who don't want to sing are encouraged to count out loud, with strong rhythmic and metrical inflection, experiencing the phrasing with their voices. Equally important is the experience of conducting. First we conduct while they play, then they conduct while we play; and finally we encourage conducting at home alone as a preparatory step to playing. Conducting is a way to experience both rhythm and phrasing, and is a great help to pianists as well as to singers. (*April 1981*)

Transfer students who can't phrase. *This fall I accepted four transfer students, all at early intermediate levels, none of whom has any idea of phrasing. They are diligent students, practice regularly, and play their assignments with amazing accuracy, but their playing makes no musical sense. It's just a series of notes with no shape, inflection, or musical meaning.*

As a starting point, why not try an analogy to language, so simple and dramatic that they can hardly fail to get the point. For example, write out a sentence such as this: It *was and* I *said* not *or.* Obviously it makes no sense at first, and they are puzzled as they struggle to extract some meaning from the words. Have them watch as you add punctuation marks: It *was "and"* I *said, not "or."* Suddenly the meaning is clear. When they see what punctuation did for the meaning of those words, you can make your point about what phrasing does for music, then make immediate musical applications. For example, write simple melodies without any phrasing marks. Play them for the student with phrasing and ask the student to mark your phrasing into the score. This takes real concentration — first hearing how it was phrased, then remembering the details long enough to write them. Another suggestion is to play pieces with a student, alternating phrases — teacher plays the first phrase, student the second, or vice versa. It is wise to start with melodies where the phrasing is regular: two measures, two measures, two measures throughout the piece. Then perhaps a piece in which the phrasing is two measures, two measures, four measures; or four measures, two measures, two measures, and so on. Later, use pieces with irregular phrases, like "Whippoorwill."

Whippoorwill

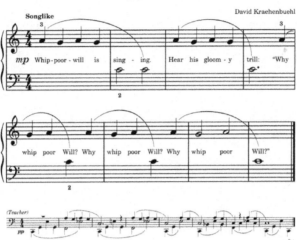

Finally, and perhaps most effective, play one of the student's pieces while he sings and conducts the melodic line, attempting to affect your phrasing by the physical gestures. When students conduct and sing, they are commanding themselves to phrase — a physiological and psychological process that is most apt to carry through into the actual performance. *(February 1984)*

Singing to experience phrasing. *My students' phrasing has improved since I began having them sing the melody to experience the phrasing, This technique has worked well with music in which there is melody divided between the hands or a melody in one hand and a simple accompaniment in the other, but how can I apply the technique to music with two voices?*

As soon as students are ready for the easier classics and their first contrapuntal pieces, ask them to learn each voice by playing it and singing it. For a right-hand part, this often means singing an octave lower than written to bring the score into a student's vocal range; for a left-hand part, singing an octave higher than written. Singing the left hand is especially important to help a student realize that a left-hand part can be just as melodic and singable as a right-hand part. When students are able to sing either part securely, ask them to play one hand while singing the other, again transposing an octave higher or lower if needed. Students who have difficulty with this are helped enormously when the whole class joins in with the singing. It is best to begin one phrase at a time, perhaps mastering only one phrase in a lesson. Mastering even a single phrase with this singing technique can improve the performance of the whole piece. When, through singing, students learn to listen to two melodic lines moving horizontally, their playing changes and each hand begins to sing.

Following are excerpts from three pieces that lend themselves well to this kind of practice: *(May-June 1979)*

Canon

Minuet

Bourrée
From the *Suite in F Major*, BWV 820

Pieces that begin three times. *At a recent lecture, I heard some discussion about compositions that begin three times or, as the lecturer expressed it, "begin three times in order to get going." That may not be an exact quote, but that's what I remember of what he said. Can you tell me exactly what this means, and perhaps give some examples?*

175

Your quotation of what the lecturer said is perhaps more picturesque than scholarly, but I believe I understand what he may have been getting at. A fairly common compositional technique is the introduction of a short motif or theme, which is repeated one or more times, and then lengthened as it grows to the end of the phrase. The repetition may be exact or somewhat modified, but the characteristic, in terms of phrase lengths, is short-short-long.

One of the teaching pieces that comes to mind is "The Mechanical Doll" from *Six Children's Pieces* by Dmitri Shostakovich. At the beginning there is a two-measure motif, which is immediately repeated, then doubled in length to form the first complete phrase.

The Mechanical Doll
From *"Six Children's Pieces"*

Following are other examples of a similar technique with the applicable passages marked. Awareness of this device is one of the essential ingredients in a meaningful performance of the piece, for the repetition and extension contain a growing tension followed by a release which is one of the chief musical dynamics of the passage. *(December 1975)*

Novelette
DMITRI KABALEVSKY

A Cozy Waltz
From *"24 Little Pieces,"* Op. 39

Dmitri Kabalevsky

Minuet
K. 94

Wolfgang Amadeus Mozart

Performing

Performer's role. *I would like to hear someone state exactly what the performer's role is in the chain of communication. Would you be willing to write on this in your* Clavier *column?*

You have really asked for something! Sometime I would like to explore this issue in real depth, in an article long enough to do it justice. To answer it here will mean a brief and, I'm afraid, cursory statement. I assume from your question that you mean a performer's responsibility, both to a composer and to an audience. My view of this chain is composer-performer-audience. An audience and a performer get together and communicate through a performer's recreation of a composer's intent. This places a heavy burden of responsibility on a performer. I believe a performer's sense of the size and scope of this responsibility increases constantly as he matures and as his study of the work in question goes deeper and deeper. However, I think this same sense of responsibility can be instilled in a young student from the very beginning. It not only can be, it must be, and the extent to which it is instilled will play a large part in his maturing process.

As I see it, a performer must be concerned at all times throughout his performance with three people: the person who created the work of art; himself, as he makes a dedicated study of the work and its recreation; and the mind of the receiver, his audience. Taken seriously, this is an enormous job, and the performer feels an overwhelming sense of responsibility. A performer's role, then, is to study what the composer intended to convey (composer-performer) and then constantly question whether his performance is really conveying to the receiver what the composer intended (composer-performer-audience). The skill and refinement with which a performer plays these three roles is, to a large extent, the measure of his artistry; and it is the ability to play these three roles that every teacher must try to develop in his students from the start. (*December 1971*)

Coaching. *I am at sea about the role of coaching in the piano lesson. Please explain exactly what coaching is and what part it plays in piano teaching.*

When pianists who are not my students come to me for help in preparing a recital, I consider my role to be that of a coach, helping them project, at a still higher level, music that is nearly ready for public performance. This usually includes some analysis and often some technical work, but basically it is a matter of deepening their understanding and mastery of the music and inspiring them to project that fuller understanding to the audience.

In contrast, I view teaching as a developmental process, taking students from the first introduction of a new piece to the point at which it comes to full life in sound. Teaching includes preparing a student for new concepts or skills, presenting them, drilling on them, and finally using them in music. When we work with a student on bringing a piece to finished performance, we are both teaching and coaching.

I believe that coaching is valid unless it is dead-end. Dead-end coaching affects only a one-time performance of a particular piece and has no carry-over to other music a student is studying. Valid coaching, on the other hand, leads a student beyond the momentary inspiration and affects the performance of other pieces. If there is carry-over, our coaching has had elements of true teaching. If not, students may revert to old habits as soon as the coach disappears. (*December 1979*)

The role of coaching. *I hear conflicting opinions on the role coaching should play in piano teaching, At one extreme are those who feel it has no place at all, while at the other end are those who believe it is one of the most important things a piano teacher does. I am certain many teachers would appreciate your thoughts on this matter.*

In order to have some common ground for discussion, let's establish an arbitrary definition of coaching as it applies to piano teaching: after a student has learned a piece and is ready to perform it, we coach. We demonstrate, sing, conduct, play along, act, move, dance, invent verbal images, and anything else we can think of, to help students project a piece over the footlights and involve the audience in a musical experience. Coaching comes after teaching, after a student has studied the piece and prepared it technically and intellectually. When we coach, we are helping students seek a balance between all the parts of the learning process and put those parts together into a musical whole that is compelling both to performer and audience.

If coaching has fallen into disrepute with some teachers, it may be because it has preceded teaching or been used as a substitute for a careful learning process. It can never substitute for any earlier stage in learning.

Coaching is necessary, especially with young students, because most young musicians are not ready yet to see the parts of a piece as they relate to the whole, or to judge the amount of projection necessary to reach the audience. Even more advanced students often imagine they are projecting phrasing, dynamic contrast, contrast in touches, accentuation, balance between parts, voicing, and so on, when in reality they are not projecting with sufficient drama. To help a student reach the desired level of involvement and projection, we coach. The performance of a piece of music should be a memorable experience, for the performer as well as for the audience. To arrive at this level of performance, most students need good coaching as well as good teaching. *(February 1985)*

Performing a single piece from a group. *In a formal concert, such as a university faculty recital, is it acceptable to perform just one piece from a group such as Debussy's* Estampes *or* Images, *or Ravel's* Miroirs, *or is it considered "less than professional" unless one plays the entire group? Similarly, could one perform three of the six* Klavierstücke *in Brahms' Opus 118?*

It is quite acceptable professionally to play one piece from the Debussy and Ravel groups you mention, or three of the six Brahms pieces, if you base your decision upon the practice common among professional concert pianists. Your question interested me enough to look through programs accumulated over the years. I find that in my concert-going experience even the greatest artists frequently perform only part of a group of pieces.

Your question relates to another that I am often asked: is it proper for a college piano major to program one movement of a Sonata? To this question the answer would be no. *(February 1970)*

Keeping a piece up to high performance standards. *My high school students are utter failures at keeping a piece up to high musical standards once they have learned it reasonably well and have it up to tempo. At that point they just play it without thinking, without* *remembering my various instructions or all the interpretive work we have done. I ask them to return to a slow tempo, and they can't even read the music any longer. The result is frustration on their part and mine. How can I remedy this situation?*

From the beginning assign slow practice in every phase of learning a piece, and hear the slow tempo (as well as the faster tempo) at every lesson. Assigning a practice step which we never hear is self-defeating, for it tells a student we aren't taking that step very seriously. This does not mean that we should hear the whole piece at a slow tempo each week. Asking to hear a phrase here, a section there will emphasize the fact that they should be able not only to play the piece securely at a slow tempo, but that they should be able to begin anywhere in the piece. *(July-August 1983)*

Playing an effective crescendo. *I have difficulty helping my students play an effective crescendo. Often, instead of reaching a climax, the sound tapers off and the effect is ruined. Do you have any suggestions?*

I establish the dynamic level before the crescendo, then establish the level at which the crescendo is fulfilled. Do this several times, until the two levels are secure, both in a student's hands and ears. Then budget the dynamic level for each successive note, from the beginning of the crescendo to the climax. Do this several times until there is a clear and audible crescendo throughout the entire passage.

Another helpful device is to diagram a student's dynamics. For example perhaps the crescendo began suddenly and at a level louder than the preceding notes; or perhaps the climax occurred too soon and had to be maintained to the end; or perhaps the climax occurred too soon and, as you suggest, tapered off, ruining the effect. Often it is even more dramatic if you play the passage a variety of ways, asking a student to draw diagrams of your dynamic levels. A student who truly fulfills a crescendo for the first time has a musical experience he will never forget. *(December 1980)*

Emphasizing a shift from major to minor. *In Kabalevsky's* The Clown, *do you agree that it helps project the humor of the piece to emphasize the constant shift from major to minor in the right hand? If so, why doesn't this same emphasis work in his* Little Joke?

The Clown

From "24 Little Pieces," Op. 39

Dmitri Kabalevsky

In *The Clown*, the rapid changes from major to parallel minor definitely make it a funny and clever piece. Students who are willing to play with this idea, projecting the constant mood changes ("first a smile, then a frown, then a smile, and then a frown") are able to bring down the house when they play this piece.

A Little Joke

DMITRI KABALEVSKY

The humor in "Little Joke" comes about differently. While it is true that the one-measure musical gesture is made of two white-key triads (one major, one minor), the ear doesn't pick this up because the key is constantly changing, and the change does not occur between parallel major and minor triads. Instead the composer sets up our expectation through seven measures of this basic musical gesture.

The joke here occurs through the sudden, dramatic interruption of the gesture, which comes to a halt in two accented quarter-note pulses played: *(December 1980)*

Contest pieces sound like recitations. *In judging piano students over the years, I see real progress in performance in terms of accurate notes and rhythm, but there is still a long way to go in the choice of music. Much of it beyond a student's understanding, and as a result sounds like a recitation instead of a performance.*

The cause of your concern is teachers, not students, because it is almost always teachers who make repertoire selections for auditions and competitions. Perhaps some teachers do not understand the true musical content of the repertoire they have chosen, or perhaps they misjudge the maturity required from their students to produce an expressive performance. Or perhaps they simply are not skillful in developing musical understanding in their students.

However, there are two other areas which contribute to the problem, and they are more easily improved. The first is the music lists from which repertoire for auditions and competitions must be selected. I especially question some of the compositions included in lists for students 10-12 years of age. So often these lists include music that only the rarest and most gifted children can play with any degree of understanding or personal involvement. Emotionally and intellectually, such music is simply beyond the comprehension of the average 10-12-year-old. Quantities of beautiful and expressive music exist that young students can enjoy and play with full musical understanding. but the contest lists won't change unless concerned teachers get busy and lobby against them. Too often we complain, but do nothing. The pleasant, firm, consistent expression of an opposing view is often the first step toward healthy change. I recommend making your views known whenever and wherever you can.

The second problem area is that of judging. Many contest rating sheets and written evaluations are too high. Over the years I have come to believe that unrealistically high ratings are one of the great problems on the whole audition/competition scene. Let me describe a recent experience. I interviewed a 12-year-old girl who came highly recommended by her former teacher. She had received superlative ratings in each of four preceding years. In the interview she played four pieces for me that she had recently performed for a judge: a piece from Burgmüller, Op. 100; a more difficult piece from Heller's *Melodious Studies*, Op. 25; a Bach Invention; and the Mozart *Fantasie* in D minor. She played the Burgmüller and Heller pieces competently and with style; I was delighted and impressed. She then played the Bach Invention in Bb Major accurately and securely, but with no understanding of Bach or of an Invention. Finally she played the Mozart *Fantasie*. Musically speaking, the performance was a monotonous series of accurate pitches and rhythms. When all four pieces had been played, I asked her which she liked best. She replied that she really liked only the Burgmüller and Heller, the two that obviously were meaningful to her. Then I read the judge's report. All four compositions had received equal superlatives. This student was wiser than her judge. Of course we have many wise contest judges, but I have read so many superlative reports on mediocre performances that I have come to believe that over-rating is a serious national problem. Again, it's one we can do something about, by making our views heard and by encouraging local audition committees to select judges who stick to high standards. *(December 1980)*

Chapter Five
Teaching Methods

Group and Private

Relative advantages of group and private teaching. *I know that you have been interested in group teaching for a long time and that you believe in it and are enthusiastic about it. Under what conditions do you prefer group lessons to private lessons? Also, do you think that group lessons are the best way to find out if a student is musical?*

You are right, I have been interested in group teaching for a long time (40 years!). My belief in it and enthusiasm for it increase each year. A group method is a natural way to teach any subject, and it is possible to apply group teaching techniques most artfully and effectively to piano teaching, yet it would be impossible for me to state that I prefer group lessons to private lessons. I prefer both, and I believe strongly in combining both study plans for every student. Following are the conditions that, in my opinion, produce successful teaching:

- The teacher believes that the group learning situation is best for every student in the group.
- The teacher knows how to keep every student learning during every minute of the group lesson; this depends on the teacher's ability to use the interaction between students.
- The teacher is alert to the pitfalls of group teaching and is able to avoid them. The worst of these is that the lesson becomes a routine of extramusical drill. The group lesson must be a music lesson with the emphasis on musical listening, musical thinking, and musical performance,
- The teacher is alert at all times to the possibility that a student may be held back or unduly pressured by the group situation, and makes a change at once. This adjustment might be either to a different group or to a different study plan.

As to whether group learning is the best way to discover if a child is musical, I state again my basic belief that all children are musical. What we need to find out is whether this particular child is ready for lessons at this particular time. Piano lessons, either group or private, are not the way to make this discovery. You need to determine the child's readiness before he begins lessons. Some teachers use interview to make this decision. Others use a piano readiness class to help prepare the child and to determine the extent of his readiness. Not all children who complete such a readiness program are ready for formal lessons, and it is sometimes necessary to encourage parents to wait a year or two to begin study after the child has developed and matured. There is a hurry to begin musical experiences, musical awareness, and musical learning; children should be exposed to some introduction to music early in life, yet there should be no hurry to start piano lessons, regardless of the artificial anxieties many parents reveal on this score. Lessons begun too soon can be more damaging than no lessons at all. *(February 1988)*

Group study versus private. *At a recent convention, a group of us were discussing group teaching versus private teaching. You were quoted by a number of teachers, but they disagreed among themselves as to your personal opinion of the relative value of each. We would greatly appreciate your answering the following questions:*

> *Do all the students at your school have both group and private lessons?*
> *Where is the assignment made, in the group lesson or the private lesson?*
> *If you were in a position where you could not give both group and private lessons, would you choose to teach group only or private only?*

All students in our school have a combined program that includes private lessons and group study. In the elementary department, for example, there are two study plans. Most students are on Plan 1, an hour group lesson each week plus a 30-minute private lesson each week (scheduled on a different day). On this plan, the assignment stems from the group lesson. The private lesson allows time for the personal relationship so necessary between teacher and student, and for attention to the student's individual needs, especially his personal technical development. A smaller group of students is on Plan 2, a 45-minute private lesson each week plus a repertoire class once each month. On this plan, the assignment stems from the private lesson, and the monthly class is devoted to analysis and performance of the repertoire the students are studying.

In answer to your third question, I really cannot imagine being in a situation where I would have to choose between group or private study. I believe whole-heartedly in the benefits of both and that by far the best study program for any student combines the advantages of both. However, if I were forced to choose between group lessons with no private study or private lessons with no repertoire class, I would unhesitatingly choose private only. *(January 1972)*

Must an up-to-date piano teacher do group teaching? *Do you consider it absolutely essential that an up-to-date piano teacher begin to do class teaching? I am sure there are many teachers in the country who would welcome your opinion on this.*

There is plenty of room in this world for both good private instruction and good group instruction. Even though group instruction is in the forefront of our profession at present, there are certainly progressive and up-to-date teachers who do not teach in groups. So much depends on the teacher himself, as well as on the particular student involved.

My advice is to begin experimenting with group instruction on a limited basis. Only in this way will you be able to determine the advantages (or disadvantages) of group instruction as well as your own capabilities as a group teacher. Group teaching is a very special skill and cannot be learned overnight, but all of the teachers I know who have begun to experiment with it have found that the more they did, the more enthusiastic they became about it, and the more skillful they became as group teachers.

We have been developing a course in group instruction for over two decades, and believe in it whole-heartedly, but our group study plan also includes private instruction. The students come one day for an hour group lesson (7-8 students in a class) and another day for a 30-minute private lesson. In this way they enjoy all the benefits of group study for their major lesson, yet have the added benefit of private instruction for areas that are entirely individual: technique and interpretation, for example. Our private students have group experience, too. These students have a 45 or 60-minute private lesson once each week, and an hour repertoire class every other week. In other words, all our students have some group and some private experience, and we are convinced that this is the ideal combination for all piano students. If you begin to experiment with group instruction you will soon find that its benefits are too great to be ignored. (January 1969)

The Disruptive Student. *What do you do when one of the students in a class is so disruptive that the teacher and the other students are unable to work effectively?*

A group lesson should be a happy and creative time. If you have tried everything you can think of and are still unsuccessful, I'd suggest taking the student out of the class and having him study privately for a few months. Sometimes dramatic improvement or maturation occurs in a relatively short span of time.

I wonder, though, if you have truly tried everything, and whether you might have avoided the problem had you recognized it early enough. Two types of problem students who may not cause a problem if we are sensitive to their difficulties early enough are the hyperactive child, who can't sit still or refrain from talking, and the self-centered child, who behaves well only when he is the center of attention. With children like this, consider these possible approaches:

Never begin any activity until the room is absolutely quiet. This means showing the children what a truly quiet room is like. Waiting for quiet can be an impressive experience for a child. As teachers we have to be gutsy enough to wait, and wait, and wait. If we take that time, though, the quiet will always come. To carry this a step further, use the name of the disruptive child: "We'll begin as soon as Harry is ready." This instantly quiets the other children, who watch with fascination to see if Harry will settle down. Left out on a limb, Harry will almost always calm down as well.

Occasionally it is necessary to have a private talk with the child, explaining your problem with his behavior and asking for his help. It's a difficult child indeed who can resist the opportunity to help the teacher who requests it in this direct way. Failing all else, talk privately with the child and his mother, explaining the problem to them both and asking for their help in solving it.

All of these tactics work only if you use a quiet, good-natured voice, with a pleasant face and a patient, supportive manner. Lecturing, scolding, or showing that you are upset are counterproductive. I am almost always amazed at how basically decent even the most obstreperous children are, and how gallantly they cooperate if approached in the right spirit. *(September 1989)*

Special sessions before the fall term. *I would like to know more about the special sessions that some teachers give their students before the beginning of the fall term. Are these sessions for beginners, for transfer students whose introduction to piano study was inadequate, or for students who have specific problems in an area such as reading or rhythm? Are the sessions given privately or in groups? How many weeks do they last and what is the length of each session? I plan to start similar sessions this summer and would appreciate all the information you can give me.*

I am delighted to learn of your interest in offering pre-study sessions. You will find them beneficial to your students and helpful to you as you make plans for the fall term. The following are some ideas from other teachers.

A teacher in Michigan schedules special classes for her new beginners during the last two weeks of August. She meets the students in a group for 45 minutes, five days a week, for two weeks. Students do all their work with her; there are no assignments and no home practice. This teacher's goal is to prepare her young beginners so that when they start formal lessons in September they are rhythmically free, have hands that are ready to play the piano, and have begun to good practice habits. The teacher has been doing this for many years and is increasingly enthusiastic about the results. She says she has proved to her own satisfaction that an ounce of prevention is worth a pound of cure.

A teacher in North Carolina offers pre-lesson sessions for new transfer students whose previous training has been spotty. One group for whom rhythm was the overriding problem met for an hour, three mornings a week, for two weeks. They spent the entire time moving to music: walking, dancing, swinging, conducting, clapping, and playing rhythm instruments. By the end of the sixth session the students were much more aware of how wonderful it feels to move freely to music, and they were a step closer to understanding the need for adequate rhythmic preparation before beginning to practice a new piece.

Several teachers I know offer pre-lesson practice clinics to help their students prepare for the fall term by refreshing their practice habits after a summer vacation from piano lessons. The teachers work with their students in four areas: learning to concentrate when they practice; discovering the simplest, most direct way to learn a new piece; criticizing and evaluating their own performance; and setting goals for the next day's practice.

A California teacher sent me a report on some sessions he conducted to raise his students' performance standards. This experiment involved a group of junior high boys and girls whose notion of a big piece was one that was fast, loud, long, or preferably all three. By selecting only music that was well within the students' technical ability and musical comprehension, and by asking all the students to work on the same music day after day, this teacher helped students to see beauty in music that was slow, soft, and as brief as 16 measures. He attributes the success of this project to the fact that the students worked in a peer group, enabling them to experience a feeling of confidence and enjoyment in their own performance.

Any teacher who offers such sessions will learn how to help students break old, negative habits and replace them with new, positive ones. During the regular teaching year, only constant emphasis day after day, with no exceptions, creates the miracle of this kind of improvement. (October 1985)

Repertoire Classes

Helping students make worthwhile criticisms. *I have divided my class into four groups, each of which meets once a month. I am surprised and delighted with the students' response and with the difference these classes seem to be making in their motivation. I have not yet succeeded, however, in getting the students to make worthwhile suggestions or criticisms of one another's performances. When I ask for comments I get either silence or a superficial comment. Please advise.*

Children for whom piano classes are new need guidance in how to make meaningful suggestions and contribute something of value to a class discussion. At first they need a structure in which to listen and think. There are two ways to provide such structure: by suggesting things to listen for before the performance begins, and by asking leading questions when the performance is over. Probably a combination of both will be most helpful to your students.

Before the performance draw the students' attention to the form of the piece, to the title and mood, to special dynamic or articulation marks, to details of phrasing, or to technical or interpretive problems that may give trouble. If another student has studied this same piece, you might ask what particular problems this piece presented. In other words, set performance goals for the student who is about to play and listening goals for the rest of the class.

After the performance begin by asking what the class thought was especially well done. Once the praising is over, it is time for specific suggestions that might help the performer improve the piece. Instead of leaving inexperienced students on their own without guidance, lead them to focus on specific aspects of the performance. For example:

"This piece is marked *giocoso*. Did Fred's performance of it really make you want to laugh?"
"The dynamic contrast between lines one and two was excellent, wasn't it, but did you think Mary's crescendo reached *fortissimo* in line three?"
"How many accents are there in line four? How many did you hear? Which one did you feel Susie could bring out even more?"
"Was there one line where the pedaling wasn't clear? What could Peter do to make that passage sound less muddy?"

Perhaps an even easier way to guide the students' attention is to make a single point about all performances in a given class. You could announce:

"This week we're going to listen for contrast in all our pieces — contrast between loud and soft, legato and staccato, happy and sad, march-like and song-like, accented and cantabile, and so on."

Another week the focus might be on articulation and phrasing:

"Were all the phrasing marks carefully observed?"
"Were the little articulation marks within longer phrases clear?"
"Was there a real difference between notes marked staccato and those marked legato?"
"Was the last note in a staccato passage as short as the other staccato notes?", etc. *(April 1984)*

When teachers join together for repertoire classes. *I began repertoire classes with my students a year and a half ago, and am sold on them. I talked another teacher into going into the project with me. We divided our students by level and age. The classes meet once a month: the elementary come on the first Saturday of each month, the intermediate students on the second Saturday, the advanced students on the third, and the last Saturday is a free-for-all for any students who are ready to play. This last class is getting out of hand because more and more of the students want the extra session on the fourth Saturday of the month. We both attend all the classes, and take turns teaching them. These classes have been the* greatest thing that has happened to us as teachers, and they provide tremendous motivation for the students. The parents, also, are impressed with the students' enthusiasm and the improvement in practice and performance. Now another teacher wants to join us. She has just graduated from college and is beginning to teach. I have helped her by going over materials, but she really knows very little about teaching music to children. My question is: should we take on a third teacher when our sessions are already crowded, and when the teacher has so much to learn?

Before attempting to answer your question, I'd like to offer my congratulations for giving your students this fine opportunity, and for your imagination in doing it with another teacher. It is impossible to recommend whether or not to take on the new teacher when I know neither you nor her. It seems that your basic decision in this case is whether or not you want to get into the teacher-training field and, if you do, on what basis? It might be sensible to suggest to your young colleague that she study piano teaching methods and materials with you on a weekly basis, with an appropriate fee. If she is interested in doing this, you might include an opportunity for her to watch you teach, and for you to watch her teach. This mutual observation could be the healthiest and most productive basis for your weekly sessions together. Your teaching and learning roles should be clearly defined, and there should be some financial remuneration to you for the hours of effort you are devoting to helping her become a good teacher.

As her teaching skills develop and she produces students who could profit from the repertoire classes, you could add them to the successful venture already under way. A word of warning: you and your present colleague already seem to have a time problem; more and more students are asking for the extra session each month. Before you add the students of a third teacher, perhaps you need to face how you will handle still larger classes. One solution might be to schedule two classes for each of the Saturdays in the month; this would require more of your time and energy, but might be well worth it. Good things like this have a way of snowballing, and before you know it other teachers will want to join you, too. (October 1976)

Recitals and Festivals

Preparing students for recitals. I graduated from college three years ago and have been teaching piano ever since. I have attended recitals of many of the teachers in this area to try to learn more about teaching repertoire and what performance standards I can expect from my own students. Two of the teachers have recitals that are really enjoyable and bring good audiences. Their students seem to enjoy what they are playing and sound secure; their poise is almost like artists. So far I have not been able to arrive at these standards for my own recitals. Could you give me some suggestions for how better to prepare students for recitals?

I think the real source of the students' poise, musicianship, and enjoyment can be found in the week-to-week instruction by those teachers whose student recitals you most admired. Perhaps your concern with recitals should change to a concern for every lesson. A student plays in public the way he's been taught to play week-by-week, not the way he is taught to play his recital piece. I know of no better way to improve recital performances than the self-evident one — better teaching all through the year.

Once your students' performances of their recital pieces satisfy you at the lesson, there are some legitimate tricks of the trade to help insure each student's best performance in public. The only real difference between performance at the lesson and performance in a recital is that in the recital he has only one chance, and he has this one chance in front of the people he cares most about, his parents and friends. This spells pressure. Preparation for the pressure aspect of public performance is very important. As we have often said, "A student learns to play in public by playing in public." Our job is to make this happen as often as possible.

One of the best vehicles for frequent public performance is the monthly or bi-weekly repertoire class, which so many teachers include in their students' study program. In repertoire class the students can have a public one-chance experience in an informal setting, where there is less at stake. Periodic opportunities for more formal 'Public performance, too, should be accepted eagerly, both by the student and his teacher. If they don't happen spontaneously in the course of his school, church, or social activities, they can often be recreated by the teacher who is willing to take the necessary time.

Much of what appears to be poise in public performance can also be achieved by rehearsing every small but vital aspect at the lesson. For example, the student needs to learn how to walk to the piano and adjust the bench (to the right distance from the piano and to the right height). He needs to know how much time he can take to think through rhythm, mood and dynamics before putting his hands on the keyboard. He needs to learn how to really finish the piece before putting his hands back in his lap, how to take two or three steps forward from the piano before bowing, how to make a professional bow, how to walk purposefully away from the piano, etc. The student who does this often learns to do it naturally and this makes his appearance seem more professional and artistic. How he looks and feels before he plays and after he plays even affects how he plays.

If your recitals take place in a location other than your own studio, be sure to have rehearsals there. A student must feel comfortably at home with the instrument and with the hall in which he is to play. This is even more important for young students than for more advanced ones, but it is necessary for all students. At these rehearsals be sure to listen to each student from the back of the hall to make sure he projects

192

well. *(February 1972)*

Recital nerves. *Should we expect our students to play their best in public? I have a big recital each spring. My students work hard for this occasion and play their recital pieces very well for me at their lessons. But in the actual recital, very few play their best. They seem to feel nervous or frightened, and occasionally a student will ask not to play at all.*

Unfortunately, the situation you describe is not an uncommon one. When we fall into this trap, it seems to me there are probably four reasons for it.

The music we have chosen may be too difficult, technically or musically. There is a marked difference between the level of difficulty a student can handle in his own practice or at his lesson and what he can handle securely in a public recital. The recital piece should not be the hardest thing he has worked on all year, his big reaching out piece. It must be something he feels completely confident with, in which he can begin securely at any part, play at half tempo, keep going despite annoying interruptions in the room, etc.

Perhaps we have played up the event as a test of the students' prowess, instead of just an opportunity to play for their family and friends. Often our own undue emphasis on the state occasion is what makes the students nervous. If we feel a public recital puts us on trial, at least we must be very careful not to communicate the trial quality of the event to our students. I would never want a student who flubbed in recital to feel he had let me down. The most positive feeling he can have is one of natural disappointment that he did not play his best for his friends.

Some teachers place too much emphasis on the recital piece instead of continuing, right up to recital time, to learn many beautiful pieces of music, each one of which an audience would thoroughly enjoy hearing. It's wrong to consider a recital piece as something different from other music a student is studying.

Perhaps the greatest mistake we can make, and the most common one, is the event of the yearly recital, without giving our students many more opportunities to play in public all through the year. A student learns to play in public by playing in public, and no one learns anything by doing it once a year. If your students are not already having some group learning experience, you would find it well worth the time and effort to divide them into several groups (either by age or level of achievement) and give each group at least one repertoire class monthly. Such a repertoire class, at which each student plays for his peers and you, is the one time students want to do their best. You might even consider a few of these monthly classes as informal recitals, inviting the students to bring family or friends. Most of the time have just the students themselves, and make the repertoire class a time when they can evaluate each other's performances and learn enormously from that experience. Then from the group of pieces that each student has played beautifully in these repertoire classes, you and he together can choose something to be played at the recital. *(November 1970)*

Playing memorized pieces in public. *I have just completed my umpteenth piano recital, and somehow I must be able to teach my students more about memorization. I realize it is an individual ability, but so many times just one fingering flaw or missed note will throw them off completely. They all have points of reference to go back to, but at an initial mishap, they become flustered and panic. What can I do to prevent this? More playing before an audience is definitely on my agenda for next year.*

Perhaps you can take your best cue to the answer from "just one fingering flaw or missed note will throw them off completely." Of course we work for no fingering flaws or missed notes, but since most students occasionally suffer such mishaps in public performance, I suggest you begin by teaching what I call the art of recovery: what to do if a mishap occurs.

The first thing is to learn to keep playing no matter what happens. A regular part of recital preparation should be the step that requires students to play a piece through from beginning to end with no stopping or hesitating allowed. If there's a slip, the student continues to play whether by returning to the beginning of the preceding phrase, jumping ahead to the beginning of the next phrase, or improvising. The playing must go on without interruption. This method is not easy If you aren't used to it, but it can be started at any point in a student's career, and the sooner the better. Once students know they can't stop, they're not as apt to. Always congratulate them enthusiastically on a good recovery.

Some students are more easily distracted than others and may be disturbed by the rattle of a program, the movement of a child in the audience, or even a cough. Such situations occur in every public performance and students must learn to cope with them. Those with advance concentration problems need extra practice. Warn them in advance that you are going to simulate the disturbances of a normal public performance and that their job is to concentrate no matter what you do to distract them. Then while they play, cough, rattle a program, drop a book, or slam a door. This can become a game, but it will be invaluable when the chips are down. (Warning: use it cautiously in group situations — a class is apt to get carried away with providing the disturbance.)

The best solution is one you have already suggested: more playing for an audience prior to a recital. The only way we learn to play in public is by playing in public. To expect youngsters to master this art on a once-a-year basis is asking for the moon. *(October 1984)*

Using music in recitals. *I have heard that you advocate letting students perform with their music at recitals. Is this true and, if so, why? Am I wrong in insisting that my students always play from memory?*

For years it was a must with me to have all my students play from memory in recital, but at that time I had recitals only once or twice a year. Over the years it has become increasingly clear to me that students learn to play comfortably and securely by performing often. Now our students play for others, either formally or informally, many times each season.

The students may choose to play with or without their music. In a recent series of informal programs here, about 50 percent of the students chose to play without music. Since successful public performance is our number one recital goal, we encourage them to do whatever makes them comfortable for a given occasion. This does not diminish the importance of memorizing as a skill and discipline. When the student performs in public we are not testing his memory, but his ability to pull all his resources together and make a piece go under the stress of playing for an audience. Let's do everything we can to help bring this off triumphantly. *(April 1971)*

Ensemble music helps recital nerves. *One of my students, a junior in college who has been studying with me for four years, is too nervous to perform in public. At present we have reluctantly abandoned all public performance for her because it is such an agony, and neither of us is ever satisfied with the results. She has performed successfully in a drum and bugle corps and in her college band, but in neither case is she a solo performer. She enjoys piano and her lessons but is frustrated because she really wants to play in recitals yet never has a successful recital experience. I think that if she had started studying at an earlier age, she would not have developed the problem of paralyzing nerves, but perhaps I am wrong. I would appreciate your thoughts and suggestions because I have run out of ideas.*

When you speak of your student's successful ensemble experiences, you may have answered your own question. Even in piano study it is not necessary always to perform alone. There is a large and rich repertoire of piano ensemble literature at almost every level, and your student could study and perform such works with you or other students. In addition to all the musical benefits of working in an ensemble, a student who is unusually anxious about performance receives the support and confidence of playing with others. After many successful ensemble performances, some of your student's performance anxiety will disappear. *(September 1980)*

Preparation for a recital. *I feel I need some help in planning my spring recital. How early do you begin preparing for a recital? What special steps do you use with students in preparing recital pieces? What about the student whose memory seems secure in the studio but who* *breaks down in public? Do you have a rehearsal the day of the recital? How do you avoid student anxiety?*

Preparation for a recital occurs in every lesson throughout the year. The recital piece is nothing more than the culmination of the student's work on dozens of pieces throughout the year, for a recital is not an end in itself but one step in the whole learning process. Following are some suggestions for preparing students for recitals.

Play in public as often as possible. Teachers who use group lessons give their students a public-performance experience every time the group meets. Those who include no group teaching can nonetheless provide students with experience in playing for others by letting each student play for the one who precedes or follows him in the lesson schedule. All of us should encourage our students to play for school and church events, for relatives at home, and for friends at parties. With enough public performance during the year, a recital will not be and frightening experience.

Feel confident and comfortable with every aspect of public performance. This includes not only secure preparation of the music, but also such details as walking comfortably to the piano, adjusting the position and height of the bench, sitting quietly (hands in lap) long enough to think through the mood and tempo of the piece, and, at the end of the performance, finishing the piece with a gesture that sustains its final mood, putting hands back in lap until the applause begins, standing, bowing, and walking off the stage. All these experiences need to be part of students' lessons throughout the year. A piece of music, like a picture, needs a frame. Experiencing this frame, over and over again, will contribute immeasurably to a student's comfort and ease public performance.

Play recital pieces from memory only if many other pieces have been played from memory in public throughout the year. The minimum tests for memory on any public performance piece should include playing the piece through securely from memory on the first try; beginning securely from memory at any major section or, in some cases, at any phrase; playing the piece from memory at half tempo; and playing the piece, reading from the score (the student must never stop practicing a memorized piece with the music, no matter how well he thinks he has it memorized).

Remember, these memory checks should not be used just for recital music but for any piece a student plays from memory throughout the year.

No rehearsal on the day of the recital. Recital rehearsals are important under any circumstances, and they are essential if the recital is to take place on an unfamiliar piano. A rehearsal on the instrument and in the room where the recital will take place should be scheduled several days ahead of the main event to avoid a feeling of last-minute pressure.

On the day of the program students should practice their regular assignment and play their recital piece once only and at half tempo. They need to save their total involvement in the piece for that all-important, one-time projection in the recital itself. Young students often run a piece into the ground by playing it over and over just before the program. If you can convince them that this is both unnecessary and unwise, you are more apt to be pleased with the final performance. I believe that if the four steps suggested above are followed carefully throughout the year, recital anxiety should diminish or disappear. In this way the program can be a joyful occasion representing the fruition of the year's study. (*March 1979*)

When to start the recital piece. *After years and years of teaching I still don't seem to make a wise judgment about when to begin work on my students' recital pieces. If we start too soon, the students grow tired of the piece, and if we begin too late, they are not secure and comfortable by the time the recital arrives. I have tried your suggestion of choosing a recital piece from a list of pieces the students have studied and performed well during the year, but I haven't been able to arouse their enthusiasm for music they have already played – they feel it is going backwards. In fact, I have a problem in building repertoire with all my students (elementary to advanced), perhaps for this same reason.*

Progress for elementary students is so dramatic that it's easy to understand why they aren't excited about reviewing music they learned a few months ago. Their current pieces are conspicuously more advanced, and it's natural for them to lose interest in former repertoire when the new pieces are more exciting. With intermediate and advanced students, however, this need not be the case. The art of keeping repertoire should begin early, so that students will learn to enjoy reviewing music for its own sake, not just for recital.

With elementary students, as any book is completed, we continue to review the students' favorite pieces from it, even though the major portion of the lesson is devoted to new material. Students develop lists of special pieces that they keep in performance condition. In the process of this review, students discover that there is still more to learn about pieces they have already studied. With their improved technical and tonal control they feel more secure and have more fun performing pieces they studied earlier.

If we don't continue to work on review pieces, music study is limited to the challenge of mastering new material. In reality the greatest joy, and perhaps the greatest benefit, comes from performing music already learned in an increasingly more sensitive and secure manner. As we continue to study and review former music, our students grow in the knowledge that music is never finished and that any book of good music is worth returning to again and again. This is the best possible recital preparation, and in a larger sense it is the best possible route to musical growth.

Teacher and student share in the joy of new discoveries in old pieces — new sounds to hear, new ways to feel, phrases that suddenly shape themselves naturally, a crescendo truly fulfilled, discovering a passage that now sounds more authoritative, sophisticated, or imaginative. Such new musical insights and new physical security make boredom with former repertoire unlikely — providing, of course, the piece is worthy of further study. *(July-August 1985)*

Planning an audience-friendly recital. *Every spring I have a recital in which all of my 42 students perform, beginning with the very youngest and ending with the most advanced. I felt the students played well in the recital this past spring, but I did not feel a warm response from the audience. The students and their parents have become concerned about where they appear on the program. One mother said that her son was 14th on the program last year and only 12th on this year's program, and wondered if he were making satisfactory progress! Would you give me some ideas for successful recitals?*

In my opinion a student recital should last a maximum of an hour and ten minutes, preferably slightly under an hour. The audience should be left wanting more, not looking at their watches. Therefore my first suggestion is to have two recitals instead of one.

Probably the best way to program is for musical reasons, not because of age or achievement. A short piece of music played beautifully by a first-year student is as memorable and meaningful an experience for the audience as the most brilliant piece by an advanced student. In planning a program be sure to consider variety in style, key, and tempo, and contrast between pieces that are brilliant or lyric, poetic, or dramatic.

Since a piano recital is limited to the sound of one instrument, it's helpful to include ensemble music for one and/or two pianos. Other ways to spice up your program might be to have an all-boy recital, an all-ensemble program, or a program made up entirely of elementary students with a few of your intermediate and advanced students appearing as guest artists. Above all, keep your audience wondering from year to year what surprises your next recital will have in store for them! *(November 1977)*

Planning an all-Tcherepnin recital. *My first recital for this year is going to be divided by periods in music history, beginning with pre-Bach and coming right up to today. For my second recital we have decided to do an all-Tcherepnin program, providing we can find enough music of the right levels of difficulty for all of my students. We will use the pieces in your six* Contemporary Piano Literature *books, but we do need more, both at the intermediate and more advanced levels. Could you give us some additional suggestions?*

Tcherepnin is a good choice, for he has written a vast amount of piano music. You'll find a complete list of his piano works on page 20 of the March 1968 issue of *Clavier*.

For intermediate students I suggest you use the *Chinese Bagatelles*, Op, 51. No.3, published in Paris but available here through Mercury Music Corp. For your more advanced students you might consider the *Bagatelles*, Op. 5, published by Leeds (and other publishers). This set of ten pieces makes a good program. *Expressions*, Op, 81, published by M.P. Belaieff (Paris) and available in this country through CF. Peters, is another set of ten programmatic pieces, each with a descriptive title. Most of the pieces in this group are one or two pages in length. *Songs Without Words* is a group of five rather short pieces, published by Peters. The *Rondo*, also published by Peters, is a stunning piece for two pianos, four hands; it would make a very exciting conclusion to your program. *(February 1972)*

Students who practice nothing but their festival or recital pieces. *I have some students who practice nothing but their festival pieces as soon as I tell them what they are. From then on, they neglect the rest of their assignment. What can I do to overcome this problem?*

If you are free to choose the student's festival music, I wouldn't tell him what specific pieces he will play until very near the date. You will have decided well ahead of time, of course, and will be working on it at his lesson, along with the rest of his assignment. But if he doesn't know, there can be no problem of his concentrating on that music to the exclusion of all else. This solution doesn't work, of course, if the music is predetermined by a festival committee, or if this is multiple-piano ensemble music where rehearsals would have to begin long in advance.

I have had similar questions from teachers who say their students practice only their spring recital pieces, letting the rest of their assignment slide. Students can't do this if the teacher doesn't tell them what they are to play for the recital until near the time. Except in the case of quite advanced students, don't make a final decision on what each student will play until two or three weeks before a program. Choose from the many pieces he has on his current repertoire list — pieces he has played up to recital standards, and which he likes well enough to keep in recital condition. Near the time of the program choose from each student's special pieces those that will fit together to make the best balanced and most colorful program for the audience. Always be careful to select music that shows the student's strong points and best demonstrates his growth since the last program. *(February 1977)*

Planning a festival. *I am on a committee whose purpose is to try to raise the standards of piano teaching in our out-of-the-way area. Teaching here is pretty bad, and some of us are* *hoping to be able to do something to improve the situation. The plan discussed to date is to have a piano festival where all the students of at least 30 teachers (possibly 400-500 students) will come play for judges who will be leading teachers from other areas. Our committee thinks this would be a good first step, but getting it organized, securing the judges, etc. looks too big to me for the first step. Could you suggest a simpler idea that I could present to the committee for its consideration!*

I have one suggestion for you to consider. From the description of teaching in your area, it seems to me that long before you bring in a judge you need a situation in which the area teachers are encouraged to bring their students to play for an audience of the other area teachers and their students — in other words a real festival instead of competition, A grading or commentary by an outside judge would be less meaningful at this point than for each teacher in your area to hear his students in a situation where he can compare them with the students of other area teachers. This will work wonders providing your committee sets up a situation that includes the students of your very best teachers as well as those whose teaching is not as successful. This could mean the following steps

Set dates for a series of area recitals, each recital in a different town, (schools and colleges will offer their facilities, I am sure).

Send an attractive announcement about the event to all area teachers, inviting them to enter their students and describing the advantages to their students of such participation. (Include in such an announcement the dates and places of the various programs, and the procedure for entering students).

You might want to limit each program to 15-20 students on a first-come, first-served basis, and limit each student to 3-4 minutes of performance time. Perhaps each teacher should be limited to entering just two students to make room for as many teachers as possible.

The results of such an event would include widespread interest in piano study and piano performance; teachers would have an opportunity to meet other teachers and to hear the students of other teachers; and students would meet and hear other students. Inevitably each student and his teacher will do some self-evaluating in the light of this wider listening experience. Out of such soul-searching many positive benefits could come. *(September 1974)*

Students

Transfer Students

What to do with transfer students. *I feel that I can count on a fair degree of success with students I start from their very first lesson, but I need help with students who transfer to me from other teachers. Many of them are poor readers, careless musicians, and have little or no technique; but most important, they are playing music way over their heads, and don't know it. What do you do with them?*

This question, worded in a variety of ways, has been asked of me more than any other single question. I have postponed answering it because there are as many answers as there are transfer students, but because of the persistence with which it continues to arise, I have decided to take a stab at it.

A real study of the transfer student begins with careful consideration of our own successes and failures. This makes it easier to analyze mistakes the former teacher of our transfer student may have made, and the steps we in turn must take to remedy his present condition. Even more important than a careful analysis of what he needs, and the order in which to present it, is the intelligent and sympathetic understanding we must have for the student's emotional and psychological problems in making the transfer to us. Here are some general suggestions:

First, plan time in your schedule for an unhurried interview with the student (and, if he's young, with his parents) before his first lesson. The purpose of the interview is three-fold: to begin to know him, to let him talk; to discover, through hearing him play music he studied previously, as well as music you give him to sightread, and what it is that he knows, and can do on his own; and to find out as much as possible about the music he has studied in the past, and determine your best point of departure for him.

In addition to these "dos" for the interview, there are some equally important "don'ts". Don't imply, either by what you say or don't say, that his former teaching was poor. The reason for this is far more than an ethical one. What good would it do him to be told he had been badly taught? Further, what good would it do you? Let him make that discovery for himself later on, when he discovers (for himself) that you are a good teacher.

Don't blame his lack of success on his previous study materials (method books or music), either to him or to yourself. I know no printed material so bad that it can be considered the cause of poor teaching.

A second general suggestion is to include in the student's first assignments at least some of the music he was already studying, even if you don't like or approve of it. There must be some pieces somewhere in that music he brought to the interview that you can use, and from which he can learn. He must feel that he is going on where he is, not going back.

If this transfer student is a poor reader, if he's careless, if his standards for performance are low, and if his rhythm is insecure, of course he can't go forward until these gaps in his background are in. So our job is to go on, and to fill in, all at the same time. The filling in must be done under headings which he will understand, and which will appeal to him as reasonable. For example:

Review is a word generally accepted as part of the educational pro. This student, indeed all students, will recognize the need for review, But don't do your review with the music he has studied before. In this case, since you have serious gaps to fill in, assign a book at a much easier level, call it "review," but actually use it as your opportunity for real teaching.

Sight-reading, too, is a generally accepted term, and most piano students recognize the need to increase their skill in sight-reading. Again, sight-reading can be used as an excuse to assign easier material, in which you can work at real teaching, filling in those gaps.

Getting a broader background is a third category which our transfer student will probably accept as necessary and desirable. Let's say, for example, that one of the things he played at his interview was a Schubert *Impromptu,* The way he played it may have been unbelievably distorted, but amazingly enough, he likes it. Here's your chance to fill in his background, at the same time assigning easier material in which to do some real teaching. You might ask him what other Schubert he has studied, and if it isn't much, suggest that to increase his understanding and enjoyment of this *Impromptu,* he needs much more experience with the music Schubert wrote. Of course, in order to play lots of Schubert, it will have to be at an easier level. Again, this reasoning will make sense to him. You might assign a whole group of the easiest waltzes, or German dances, later some Ecossaises. With this much simpler Schubert, it is possible to teach, to hold him to higher performance standards, and to create a situation in which he has the experience of playing music he can really master, and playing it beautifully. One taste of that, and he'll want more and more.

New areas of study can also become a place to start. Using what you learned at the interview about what he has studied, find an area, a period, or even a composer, with which he is totally unfamiliar. For example, he may never have studied any contemporary music, or any technical studies, or any ensemble music. Any unexplored area will be readily accepted as a hole in his background, and one he will be ready and willing to fill in. All students recognize that when you begin a new subject you start at the beginning; so again you have a built-in opportunity to assign music at a much easier level.

In summary, it has always been my experience that getting a student to his proper level, by hook or crook, was worth it. Once he has experienced playing really well, with complete accuracy, control, and security, and has had a real musical experience, he will never be content with anything less. The result is a gradual willingness to study music at a level commensurate with his ability. And when this has been accomplished, the student may be said to be truly transferred. *(March-April 1966)*

Why interview transfer students? *My question refers to interviewing transfer students. I do not have time in my busy schedule for an interview prior to the first lesson, so I use some of the lesson for getting acquainted and find it works very well. What advantages do you see in interviewing students before they have their first lesson with you?*

There are two definite advantages to interviewing students before committing either side to the arrangement. The first concerns the mutual understanding that is necessary before we accept new students or before they accept us as their new teacher. This understanding includes everything from practical business matters (fees, schedule, policies, and so on) to our educational and musical goals, what we expect of our students, the parents' role, and what they can expect of us.

An interview that precedes registering for lessons allows the teacher to evaluate the student, and gives parents and student an opportunity to reconsider their commitment. An interview almost always ends with a meeting of minds and with an enthusiastic feeling about getting started. At the same time, it makes it easy for parents and student to change their minds if they are looking for a different type of piano study experience.

The second advantage concerns selecting repertoire for a new student. When we interview, we hear students play repertoire they have been studying, so that we can begin to determine where they are musically, technically, and intellectually. After the interview we need lead time for planning what the first assignment should include, what new repertoire is appropriate, and what emphases we should give priority. Such decisions can't be made on the spur of the moment. For these two reasons we consider it essential to interview transfer students before accepting them or giving the first lesson. *(January 1985)*

Interviewing transfer students. *In interviewing a student who has studied with another teacher for five or six years, what would you do if you had only a limited amount of time?*

I would:

Hear the student play 2 or 3 pieces from his current repertoire, watching and listening carefully. This will help you judge the level of his musicianship, technique, and standards of performance.

Select a passage from one of the pieces he played for you and work on it. This will help you determine how flexible he is, how quickly he learns, and his response to your teaching.

Ask him to sight-read, beginning with music much easier than the repertoire he has played for you, gradually increasing the level of difficulty until you discover the upper limits of his sight-reading ability.

However, my first response to your question is to suggest postponing the interview until you have an adequate amount of time to spend with the new student. What you learn at the interview will save endless time, both for you and the student, in the future. *(October 1981)*

Evaluations from former teacher. *Do you require any sort of written evaluation from a former teacher when a student transfers to you? If so, should it list the student's strong points and weak points? Is there a questionnaire you ask the former teacher to fill out?*

We do not require a written evaluation from the transfer student's former teacher. Instead, we ask the student to bring to his interview all of the music he has been studying. During the interview we find out for ourselves all we can about the student himself, his practice habits (by watching him work out a new piece of music), and where he is musically, technically, theoretically, and intellectually.

A written evaluation is occasionally furnished by the former teacher. We sometimes find it helpful but as often as not find it misleading. Why inherit the former teacher's attitudes and possible prejudices? There is something very healthy about seeing a new student for the first time through your own eyes. *(May-June 1976)*

Adult Beginners

Comparing adult beginners with children. *I have never taught adult beginners and have always thought I would not want to. This year I have had so many requests for lessons from adults who never studied as children but now desperately want lessons, that I'm beginning to change my mind. Could you give me some idea of the ways in which working with adults would be different from working with young children? I have no way to know whether or not I could be successful with this age group.*

I think most of us are sharing your experience. The adult population does seem to be growing more and more interested in learning to play the piano, and an ever larger percentage of our adult applicants are real beginners, people who never had lessons, even in early childhood. The adult students we have are eager and conscientious, and a joy to teach.

Working with adult students is different from working with children. The most important thing to keep in mind is that the older beginner needs to learn the very same things as the younger student and, for the most part, in the same order; but the areas in which the two age groups differ are equally important. Because the child's concepts develop slowly, his technical development and physical control can keep pace with them easily — there is plenty of time for his muscular skills and coordination to develop at their own natural rate. The older student, however, can grasp concepts more easily and rapidly; but unless we are skillful, this asset can become a liability. Adults expect their ability to play the piano to keep pace with their grasp of new knowledge and unfortunately this rarely happens. The physical and technical control of the older student develops more slowly than does his understanding, and this can be the point at which frustration and dissatisfaction set in. For this reason, adults need almost twice as much work in the area of technical development, and at least twice as many pieces to play at every step of the way. More lesson time needs to be spent on developing technical facility and on the ability to project a meaningful musical idea in a fulfilling way. It is regrettable, but true, that most books designed for the older beginner fail to take into consideration these important differences, both in learning speed and in the amount and type of music required for the more mature student.

I hope you will accept the challenge of working with this age group, not only because it renders an important service, but because it holds its own special challenges and satisfaction for the teacher. (January 1976)

Private or group study? *I am becoming interested in teaching adults because more are inquiring about lessons. Some of the requests are from adults who have had previous study, but a surprising number are from those who claim to be absolute beginners. Do you recommend teaching them privately or in groups?*

We recommend private lessons for all adults who have had previous study. Prior experiences are so different that a meaningful group-study experience for adults with previous study is almost impossible, except for an occasional informal repertoire class where they play for one another. For adults who are real beginners, our first preference is for a study plan that combines private and group work. This can sometimes be arranged on a weekly basis (one group lesson and one private lesson each week), but we have also found it successful to schedule a group lesson one week and a private lesson the next. We also have had considerable success with adult beginners in group only, never seeing them for a private lesson. Most adults find it easier to accept their role as beginners when they are working with a group of peers, so we favor a plan that includes at least some group experience. *(May-June 1976)*

How should adult beginners count? *What method of counting do you recommend for the adults who are just beginning piano study — metrical counting or counting notes for their value?*

I think you should use the method with which the student feels most comfortable. My own experience has been that most adult students, even those who claim to be absolute beginners, already know a good many things about music, and have had some experience with rhythm and counting. They usually feel most comfortable with metrical counting, so that is what we use.

With younger beginners, when counting is first introduced, we count notes for their value.

It avoids ambiguity and confusion if they always count "1" for a quarter note, "1-2" for a half note, etc., regardless of where the note occurs in the measure. With older students, this confusion does not occur, so we begin with metrical counting. *(April 1976)*

Moving freely over the keyboard. *How do you get adults to feel free moving over the keyboard if they begin with music in 5-finger positions? In their practice they never hear any of the wonderful high and low sounds that the piano can make, and the moment they go to music that does move over the keyboard, they become awkward and self-conscious.*

Your question implies that there is some reason why adult students need to begin in the middle of the keyboard and stay there. I think they can and must begin by moving freely over the entire keyboard, just as the younger beginner does. This can be accomplished in many ways: assigning technical exercises to be done all over the keyboard; asking the student to play his middle-of-the keyboard pieces in different octaves; and teaching at least some music at each lesson that uses a wide range of the keyboard, and which he can learn quickly and easily by rote, without having to read. Following is one such piece:

In other words, there need be nothing limiting about playing entirely in 5-five-finger positions, so long as the music is designed to use the whole piano. (*April 1976*)

Early Childhood

"Songs for Our Small World." *Is Lynn Olson's* Songs for Our Small World *written for piano teachers, or for public school music teachers?*

Songs for Our Small World was created by Georgia Garlid and Lynn Freeman Olson for use in early childhood classrooms (Kindergarten, first and second grades). It was designed to provide new songs as well as reading readiness activities. Since its publication, private music teachers, including piano teachers, have found it useful as a source in their studios for "pre-piano" groups and as reinforcement for piano classes or young private students. The book offers a wealth of unusually appealing children's songs, easy to remember and great fun to sing. In the Teacher's Book, there is a page of suggestions for each song, involving children in aural, physical, and visual activities that help promote musical awareness and reading readiness. Like the songs themselves, the activities are direct, enjoyable, and easy to remember.

Songs for Our Small World is available in a package that consists of:

Teacher's Book (64 pp)
— 33 songs with easy-to read piano accompaniments
— full page of teaching suggestions for each of the songs, divided into readiness activities for rhythm, melody and form

Child's Book (24 pp)
— a set of visuals related to song material in the Teacher's Book and geared to link the look of musical notation to previous rote discoveries about rhythm, melody and form

Recording (2 LP records in one set)
— every song in the Teacher's Book is recorded with children singing to charming instrumental backgrounds.

All three are published by CPP/Belwin, 15800 N.W. 48th Avenue, Miami, Florida. (*May-June 1968*)

Orff and Kodaly. *I'm planning to attend your August study course in Washington, D.C., but would also like to attend a workshop in either the Orff or Kodaly method. Which would you recommend and where are such workshops being offered this summer?*

I recommend both Orff and Kodaly, and believe that all piano teachers owe it to themselves to attend workshops in both methods. Orff and Kodaly both admit a debt to the methods of Emile Jacques-Dalcroze, who pioneered in developing total musicianship from early childhood, and in the all-important field of music study through motion. I have been recommending Dalcroze to piano teachers for many years. Now that the more recent methods of Orff and Kodaly are being so widely publicized and implemented in American schools, we need to know as much as we can about each approach. The best source of information on Kodaly in America is the Kodaly Musical Training Institute in Newton, Mass. Established in 1969 by a Ford Foundation Grant, its goal is "the upgrading of music education and the affecting of musical taste in this country through the introduction of an American adaptation of the Kodaly method." It was Kodaly's belief that every child can and should learn music, that music study should be started as early as possible, and that a child should learn music daily in school, just as he learns reading or mathematics. Kodaly believed that music study begins with singing because every child has the natural gift of a voice. In addition, children learn not only to sing beautifully but to read and write music as naturally as their native tongue, and to improvise vocally. Kodaly believed that the daily music lesson stretched the child's attention span, strengthened his powers of retention, and developed his alertness and powers of observation. Studies done in the Hungarian school system demonstrate a general increase in intellectual capacity as a result of this nationwide music program. For further information, contact the Kodaly Center of America, 295 Adams Street, Newton, Mass. 02158.

Karl Orff's world-famous "Schulwerk" was also designed for music teaching in the public schools. It is widely used in Austria and Germany, just as Kodaly has been universally adopted in the composer 's native Hungary. The Orff method includes emphasis on chanting words in rhythm, singing, movement, and, especially, the use of the superb basic rhythm and melody instruments designed by Orff for children to use before they begin the study of more complex instruments. The official source of information on American Orff is the Orff Schulwerk Association, Box 391089, Cleveland, Ohio 44139-1089. *(May-June 1971)*

Kodaly. *I am interested in learning more about the Kodaly method that is used with such success in Hungary. Do you think a study of that method would help me as a piano teacher? What are the best books on the subject?*

By all means study Kodaly. The principles underlying it are musically and educationally sound. As you study the method, keep in mind that singers and instrumentalists use very different physical processes for producing sound, and that Kodaly's approach is through singing. For this reason the technical aspect of the method (and its materials) does not transfer to piano study. Outside the realm of technique, however, you will find much common ground in philosophy and methodology between what the best Kodaly exponents are doing both in Hungary and in America and what the best piano teachers are doing.

The following recommendations for study material were given to me by Denise Bacon, director of the Kodaly Center of America (all materials listed are available through the Center, 295 Adams St., Newton, Massachusetts 02158.) The best way to learn about the method is to enroll in a training program. Both short courses and full-year resident training programs are offered by the Center, and you may contact them for more information.

Books asterisked are recommended for beginning levels and as an introduction to the Kodaly concept.

Kodaly, Z., *Selected Writing of Zoltan Kodaly**
Szabo, H., *The Kodaly Concept of Music Education* (Book and three recordings).
Szonyi, E. *Kodaly's Principles in Practice*
Zernke, Sr., L. *The Kodaly Concept – Its History, Philosophy and Development.*
The following song collections may be used as supplementary and include information on various aspects of the Kodaly in their introductions:
Bacon, D., *Let's Sing Together** (Songs for 3, 4, and 5-year olds)
Erdei/Komlos, *150 American Folk Songs to Sing, Read, and Play**
Video Tapes
1978 KCA Summer Course: A Quality Teacher-Training Program (40 minutes reel-to-reel or cassette)
Film
The Children Are Singing (20 minutes, made in Hungary in the 1960s)
(December 1978)

The Music Within Us. *I am interested in preparing young children for piano study, rather than starting right off with formal lessons. Have any books on the subject been published in recent years?*

In my judgment of all the books written on early childhood music since 1975, the most significant is a little volume called *The Music Within Us (An Exploration in Creative Music Education)* by Helen Lanfer, published by Hebrew Arts Music Publications-Tara Publications 1979. In its brief 80 pages you will find a discussion of the very heart of music education. It should be required reading of all music teachers. Tzipora Jochsberger writes in the introduction, "Her students find the most primitive sounds in their own bodies or in nature around them, just as primitive people did at the dawn of mankind. And they arrive in this fashion at writing their own scores in their own musical notation, just as contemporary composers do." *(July-August 1980)*

Pedagogy Programs

Continuing education. *In a recent editorial in* The Saturday Review, *Norman Cousins writes about a "Revolution in Higher Education," and describes a shift in American colleges and universities from the education of traditional full-time students to continuing education courses for people in the community. This has caused me to wonder where continuing education courses for piano teachers are to be found. I know something of the programs offered through your school, but wonder how many colleges and universities are making similar opportunities available to teachers in their communities?*

At the National Conference on Piano Pedagogy at the University of Illinois, I took part in discussions about developing piano pedagogy curricula at undergraduate and graduate levels. The good news is that many of the pedagogy teachers present also seemed to sense their responsibility to the piano teachers in their communities and that a number of colleges and universities are offering just the sort of work you describe.

For example, each year I have the pleasure of observing the program in piano pedagogy at Columbus College in Georgia. In addition to a fine four-year undergraduate degree program, the entire pedagogy curriculum at Columbus is made available to local and area piano teachers. Such teachers may enroll as auditors or as matriculated part-time students working for credit. Approximately 20 full-time professional teachers in the community come to the campus one day each week throughout the school year. They attend lectures, observe teaching, and participate in lesson planning and critiquing. Others enroll their students in repertoire classes at the college so that they may observe a master teacher working with their students. A number of them study piano privately themselves at the college. The entire Columbus Piano Teachers Association has been drawn into a supporting role, and there seems to be no sense of rivalry between the community teachers and the teaching being done in the preparatory department at the college. This is just one example of a new spirit of cooperation between the pedagogy program of a college or university and the professional teachers in the community who look to the college for continuing education, updating, and renewal.

As another example, we offer an annual fall Seminar on six consecutive Wednesdays. In the morning, staff members present courses especially designed for local and area piano teachers. In the afternoons, some of those teachers stay to take group or private lessons in areas of particular interest to them, to observe teaching in the preparatory department and, if they wish, to participate in the planning and teaching of given lessons or classes. Throughout the season teachers may enroll for private lessons on the repertoire they are teaching or on their own performance repertoire; they may enroll students in the school's regular repertoire classes, so that they can observe a master teacher work with their students; they may bring a group of students to the school for a special one-time repertoire class, followed by a diagnostic session; and they are invited to attend both student and faculty recitals at the school.

I'm sure music schools, colleges, and universities still aren't doing enough for the local piano teacher, but I do believe that a national survey of such opportunities would be impressive. To this end, I invite college and university teachers who offer such continuing education programs to write to me about them, so that a comprehensive list can be compiled and published in a future column. (*March 1981*)

Certificate programs. *I am interested in offering courses to train piano teachers. The college where I teach is far from ready to initiate a degree program, but I do see a glimmer of hope for starting a nondegree program, and I understand that at the New School you offer both a master's degree in pedagogy and a nondegree certificate program. I would appreciate any suggestions you can offer on how I can start the ball rolling here.*

You will probably be interested to learn that the National Conference on Piano Pedagogy has a standing committee on certificate programs. At the 1984 biennial conference at Ohio State University, this committee's report included a summary by William Hughes of Indiana State University describing the process he and his university went through to start such a program. Excerpts from his report follow:

> "The idea of a certificate program came to our attention just as we were about to abandon all hope of ever being able to offer a pedagogy program. Our certificate program had to go through approval channels, but they were all within the university. I am happy to say that after all our hard and careful work, the certificate program has sailed through the approval system.

Early on, you will have to enlist support from several places. You may wish to begin with your continuing education division staff. They are usually positive in their support and may be more receptive to ideas for new course offerings and programs than are some of your more crusty colleagues. They may be of help not only as you recruit teachers in the community for the courses, but also as you register and process the fees of the young students who will be taught in the program. You will need to enlist support from your departmental colleagues and your administrative officer. The more information you have to show that these programs are the 'wave of the future,' the better your case will be. Find out early the format best suited for your information and determine the channels and the timetables involved. Perhaps the most important aspect... is the recruitment of students. The clientele will come principally from two sources. First are prospective full-time students. Every year I have a few inquiries from prospective students about the training available for a career in piano teaching. I am convinced that many more students will be interested once they know that such training is one of their options. Some students who like music come to college without a clear idea of what they want to do for a career. I have seen their eyes literally light up when I present the option of a career in pre-college piano teaching. The second source is persons from the community who are already teaching or who would like to start. Teachers in our community respond very well to our pedagogy workshops. It is necessary to take every opportunity to plant seeds of interest in these people. Emphasize the fact that your program is designed for honing and updating the skills of teachers already in service.

"In the end, the success of your program in the area of recruiting will depend upon how well and how thoroughly you spread the word. This committee offers the following suggestions:

"Personal contact is the most important means. Attend professional meetings, workshops, seminars. Get to know the teachers in your region and your state. Write letters to anyone expressing interest in the program; follow up with phone calls. Your letters and calls should contain names and addresses of people who are already in the program or who have completed it. They may be your best salespersons. Contact the public through printed matter — brochures and/or newsletters describing your program and the activities of your school. Place the brochures in music stores. Every teacher who comes in to buy music will be able to read about what you are doing. Develop a mailing list. This task takes an enormous amount of time to set up, and the maintenance of it is a never-ending job. However, once the list is made up and the system for keeping it current has been set up, the actual maintenance can be done by student assistants

or clerical staff. To begin your mailing list, secure the lists of the M.T.N.A. state chapters in your area; also contact the Guild, local teachers' groups, and anyone else you can think of as a source for names and addresses of teachers. Be greedy for names! You may have to pay for these lists, but you will find that your administration is willing if you make it clear that the purpose is for recruiting. Music stores that hold workshops are usually quite willing to supply names and addresses of people who attend."
(January 1987)

Observation guides. *I direct a new one-year pedagogy program in which we devote a 12-week trimester to each of three areas; surveying methods, observing class teaching, and practice-teaching in a class of elementary students. Our pedagogy students are motivated and enthusiastic about the first and third trimesters, but seem lost during the observation period. They say they get very little out of it and even seem bored and resentful of the time required. How can students get more out of observing teachers?*

When students begin observing, they need to watch a masterful teacher. In addition, they need a guide to observation that asks them to watch for specific things. Without such direction, students are easily lost or confused in the course of a lesson. A guide might begin with something as concrete as this:

- Outline in sequence what happened in today's class, commenting on the success of each activity. If any activity was not successful, explain why.
- In today's class keep track of the time spent on performing music already assigned, working out new music, and on activities or drills in the areas of reading, rhythm, theory, ear training, and composition.
- Next, concentrate entirely on the students, noticing whether there is a class leader, whether anyone is consistently left out, and which students were actively interested and involved during the entire class.
- For students who lost interest or let their attention wander, note when and why this occurred, how long it lasted, and what happened to reinvolve the students.
- Notice any students who stand out as being especially intelligent or musical, and if any are noticeably slower. In what ways does this slowness show itself for these children? Do any of the slower students appear to have special abilities and strengths? Is it possible to find any correlation between areas of apparent slowness and apparent ability or strength?
- Select a single student and concentrate entirely on that student throughout the lesson, writing down all observations, especially such things as:
— How well was this student prepared for the lesson?
— How often did this student volunteer?
— Describe this student's relationship to the teacher and to the rest of the class.
— How does this student feel about himself, about music, about piano study?

— What specific observations can you make about this student's posture, hand position, technical approach, tone quality, rhythmic security, ease in working out new music, confidence in performance, and natural musicianship?
— Is this student mature or immature, physically, mentally, and emotionally?

More questions to guide the student observer might include:

- Did the class seem long or short to you? to the students?
- What aspects of the lesson did the students do together?
- Was there enough emphasis on the students' posture at the piano?
- What percentage of the time were students at the piano, their seats, or the board? What percentage of the time were they sitting, standing, or moving?
- Do the students count out loud, with confident voices and musical inflection?
- When they tap rhythms, is their tapping free and musical?
- Of all the activities included in today's class, which did the students enjoy most and least? Which did they need most?
- Which students were best prepared? Which students were most responsive in class? Are these things consistently true every week? Do you see a correlation between the two?
- List examples of interaction between students.
- Was the class a stimulating experience for the teacher? for the students? for you?

These suggestions for observation guides are geared to class situations, but the same types of questions could be asked about private lesson observations. With the aid of such observation guides, pedagogy students will begin to develop critical observation skills. Ideally, they will begin to view the students they are watching as their own students, and the responsibility for what happens in class as their personal responsibility. When this happens, they are actually beginning to teach vicariously. This is the best way to turn observation periods into times for vital learning. (May-June 1985)

Observing student teachers. *I have several questions about observing pedagogy students as they teach. Do you notify them ahead of time that you plan to observe, or do you just drop in? Is the critique written or verbal? If written, does a conference follow? What are you looking for during your observations, and do the pedagogy students know which areas of their teaching you plan to critique?*

At the beginning of the year we notify our pedagogy students when we plan to observe their teaching. Later, when they have discovered that being observed is not a frightening experience, but one they welcome because they learn so much, we feel free to drop in on lessons unannounced. Of course, many times we are observing because the pedagogy student has requested help with a particular student. Every observation includes a written critique, prepared during the lesson and given to the student teacher to study. This may be followed by a conference.

The overriding issue in every observation is: what do the students know and what can they do (perform) at the end of the lesson that they didn't know or couldn't do when the lesson began? In other word, what happened, what progress did they make, and what did they learn? This issue is so broad and profound that it probably does not belong in critiques given early in the year. Instead, at the outset, we draw the student teachers' attention to their own teaching with such practical questions as these:

> "Did you remember to check the student's position and posture height of the bench at the beginning of the lesson?"
> "Did you check hand position frequently?"
> "Were you where you could see the student's face and the student yours?"
> "How many pieces did you hear from beginning to end without interruption?"
> "Did you praise where you saw improvement?"

We often find questions more effective than comments because they alert the student teacher to problems without causing him to become defensive.

Frequently we need to make suggestions or to praise improvement. We use comments that help student teachers to relive objectively what really happened (or didn't happen) at the lesson. For example:

> "I liked the upbeat way this lesson began."
> "The student was distracted at the beginning of the lesson. Would it have helped to spend a minute or two in conversation until she was with you and ready to begin?"
> "Real improvement in your voice this week — you were talking to not talking down."
> "The lesson was well paced — you got through your plan efficiently but without seeming hurried."
> "Big improvements in eye contact this week!"
> "Watch out for using 'do it for me'; our students aren't really doing this for us, are they?"
> "This assignment was better balanced than last week's — enough technique and theory and nice variety in repertoire."
> "Don't be afraid to touch. The problem with release in the crossing didn't need talk, it needed your fingertips under his palm or under his forearm."
> "Discussing a desired change and demonstrating it are only the beginning. If you want it practiced correctly, the student must experience it successfully at the lesson."
> "I doubt that the student will really make that long crescendo unless you get off

the bench and physically coach it."

"When you ask the student to play again, do you have a reason, or are you stalling?"

Midway through the year, the critiques and conference change from considering practical issues such as those above to more philosophical issues of what was learned, how, and why. Remember, we have taught only the things our students have learned. (*September 1987*)

Teaching for the critic teacher. *I have taught piano for five years and am now enrolled in an evening class in piano pedagogy. I am required to teach under observation by a college teacher. I feel successful when alone with the student but make many mistakes when the critic-teacher watches. I can't convince her that I do well when alone. What can I do?*

You do not need to convince her; any seasoned critic-teacher already understands your problem. My best advice is to remember the students of yours who have had the same problem. They play their prepared pieces at the lesson and invariably comment, "I didn't make those mistakes at home." They may have made the same errors at home, but more likely at home they were concentrating on the music while at the lesson they are concentrating on you and what you are going to say.

I believe you can teach as well under observation as in your own studio if your concentration is entirely on the student, not on the critic-teacher's reaction. In fact, you can get to the point where you forget the critic-teacher is in the room. (*July-August 1982*)

How to choose a beginning piano course. *Our Community College offers special evening courses for adults. I am enrolled in a piano methods class that meets two hours each week.*

So far we have been having general lectures on piano, piano pedagogy, and the history of piano literature. This coming semester we are going to begin to study various piano courses available.

In preparation for this, I have been assigned to lead a discussion on how to choose a method for beginning piano students. I am a pianist but have never taught and don't feel competent to lead such a discussion without some help. Are there any books written on this subject? Would you be willing to give me some advice?

I don't know of any book on this subject. I believe the only approach is to choose three or four of the best courses (your local music dealer or a leading piano teacher could help with this selection), then study those courses, making notes on what you find. As you study the various courses you might ask yourself the following questions:

- Is quality of the music good, and will it be of interest to the average beginning piano student (ages 7-9)?
- Does the order of the presentation of new ideas or new musical seem logical to you?
- Is there enough material provided for each step in the student's development to insure that he really learns each new idea or musical element? This material includes the actual presentation of the new discovery, music using the new discovery, plus other kinds of drills and activities.
- Is there adequate follow-through — that is, is there always sufficient material so that no new discovery ever begins to be unlearned?

If you ask yourself these questions about three or four of the major courses, and keep notes during your study as a guide in making your report, the result will be a valuable case history of how one inexperienced piano teacher (you!) decided which beginning piano course to use.

Incidentally, I note that you use the words "method" and "course" interchangeably, a practice shared by many teachers. In my own speaking and writing I differentiate between them, using "course" to mean an organized series of study materials and "method" to mean the way in which the teacher uses the materials in his or her own teaching. For example, you and I might choose to use the same course, but our methods could be very different, reflecting our own teaching experiences, tastes, and predilections. *(March 1974)*

Chapter Seven

Repertoire

Standard Teaching Pieces

"Galloping" by Kabalevsky. *When I teach "Galloping by Kabalevsky, I always show my students that the left hand plays exactly the same notes as the right hand, one octave lower, and that measures 9-17 are the same as measure 1-8, but with the two hands reversed. In spite of this, they often stumble at the place in the score where I have marked an "X." How can I avoid this problem?*

As you know, "Galloping" is made of two simple gestures. In the first eight measures, the left hand leads, coming in on the downbeat, while the right hand follows, coming in on the off-beat:

In the next eight measures, the right hand leads, coming in on the down-beat, while the left hand follows, coming in on the off-beat.

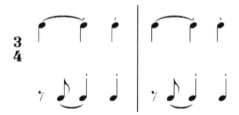

The problem arises because each gesture is repeated eight times, so that the hands have formed a habitual response which has to be changed in a split second between measures 8 and 9, and again between measures 16 and 17.

To avoid the problem, be sure that when you work out the piece with the student, you include practicing not only the two gestures, but changing from one gesture to the other. This practice should include both tapping and playing.

The only way to avoid trouble at the points of change is to practice the transitions many more times than the rest of the piece. *(October 1979)*

Galloping
DMITRI KABALEVSKY

"Sonatina" by Duncombe. *This Sonatina by Duncombe is a favorite of mine, and of those of my students who have no problem with the rhythm in the first two lines, to many stumble over the change from triplets in measures 1-2 to duplets in measures 3-4.*

What practice steps can you suggest in addition to pointing and counting, clapping and counting, and tapping and counting?

Sonatina

An important practice step for the Duncombe Sonatina, and for most music in which there is alternation in rhythmic groupings, is to walk the rhythm while counting aloud.

We do this in two distinct steps: walk and count the rhythm, taking one step for each beat; walk and count the rhythm, taking one step for each note.

Once the rhythm exists in the entire body, it is easier to change the eighth-note groupings from triplets to duplets.

An additional problem here is that measure 2 is an exact repetition of measure 1, not only in rhythm but in intervals and technique. This repetition sets up a strong prediction for the pattern to continue. However, in measure 3, the repeated note and rising 2nds suddenly change to ascending and descending 3rds.

To help the student concentrate on rhythmic change, create a practice pattern for measures 2-3, like this:

Once the student masters the change from triplets to duplets, it should be easy to master the melodic and technical changes in measure 3 itself. At this point an excellent practice pattern would be to alternate measures 2-3, like this:

Not all students need the detailed breakdown of these last two steps, but young students' techniques vary in readiness for such fast changes, and in some cases need this gentle guidance to the desired goal. *(May-June 1988)*

"A Little Joke" by Kabalevsky. *I'm having difficulty teaching Kabalevsky's delightful piece, "A Little Joke" from Ten Children's Pieces, op.27. My students love it and start out with great enthusiasm, but bog down in measures 17-34. I would appreciate some suggestions on how to teach this section.*

A Little Joke
From *Children's Pieces, Op. 27*

In assigning any new piece it is helpful to study it from the stand- point of what makes it easy and what may cause difficulties. This piece is easy because it is entirely in five-finger patterns and because the rhythm throughout is mainly:

In the first 17 measures of the piece, the thirty-second-note passages are played entirely by the right hand and, with just two exceptions, all are played on white keys. But in the section you indicated, the thirty-second notes are played by the left hand. Moreover, in measures 18-21, the black key (F#) must be played by a different finger in each measure.

In the first 17 measures the left hand consistently outlines the right hand passage an octave lower, whereas in the difficult section there is nothing consistent on which to rely.

To compound the problem, the most dramatic interpretive demands (the *forte*, accents and larger moves in the fifth score and the sudden *crescendo*, *sforzando* and *forte* in the sixth score) occur in spots that are technically the most difficult.

Here are some practice suggestions for this problem section:

- To gain security in the moves, block the positions hands together until they are secure, beginning with a slow tempo and gradually increasing it until the position changes can be made at a very fast tempo.

- Play each of the following exercises for left hand (based on 18-21) until secure, beginning slowly and gradually increasing the tempo until they can be played at the same tempo as the rest of the piece.

- If the student has difficulty with the last three scores where there is a delightful *diminuendo* from *mezzo forte* to *pianissimo* (and with no *ritard!*), that section should be played in blocked positions for security as in the example shown with the first practice suggestion. *(January 1979)*

"Game" by Bartok. *I consistently have a problem in teaching pieces that depend on strong accents, such as "Game" from For Children Vol. 1, by Bartok. My students play the notes and rhythm accurately and at a fast tempo, but are unable to add the accents. What am I doing wrong?*

Game

BÉLA BARTÓK

From "For Children," Vol. I

Fast, with energy (♩=138)

Apparently you are asking your students to add the accents after they have learned the notes. The next time you teach this piece try reversing the order — add the notes to the rhythmic accentuation the student already feels and hears — by following this procedure.

1. Count the rhythm of the piece aloud, tapping only the accented notes until the accents are clear. Do this at three different tempos — slow, moderate, and fast.
2. Count the rhythm of the piece aloud, tapping all the notes, but giving an exaggerated tap to the accents. Again, do this at three different tempos.
3. Tap as before with strong accents, differentiating between three distinct types of accentuation:

Do these steps at the lesson when you assign the piece. At the next lesson, listen to step 3 first and then back up to steps 1 and 2 only if it is necessary. Do not ask the student to play the piece until the accented tapping is beyond the stage of studied accuracy. It must feel and sound as free as if the student had just composed it!

"Solfeggietto in A Major" by C.P.E. Bach. *I have taught the enclosed Solfeggieto in A Major by C.P.E. Bach to several students. Each of them likes it very much but each has had a real problem with getting measures 5-7 up co speed. They can play it accurately once, but are just as apt co make a mistake the second time as not. We can never count on it for public performance. I have assigned every trick I know for practicing this passage, including slow practice and also impulse practice in impulses of one beat and impulses of one measure. Are there some other ways co practice I might assign?*

I think the problem with measures 5-7 has as much to do with the ears as with the fingers. Perhaps you should try emphasizing what the student is to *listen for* rather than how he is to *practice*.

These three measures are particularly difficult because they are entirely different from the rest of the piece. In most of the Solfeggietto, the right-hand melody is in sixteenth notes which are interrupted before the first and third beats of every measure. This "interruption" allows time for the right hand to release and for the piece to breathe. Suddenly, in measures 5-7, the sixteenth notes are continuous and, moreover, the melody line is played by both hands at intervals of a tenth.

The student's attention should be focused on the melody in tenths and especially on the changes in direction (parallel motion on beats 1-2, contrary on beats 3-4). A good practice device is to play just the melody line, listening for the opening leap, followed by a diatonic descent, then the change in direction as the left hand begins to ascend contrary motion. For example, measure 5 could be practiced this way:

Once the sound and feel of the melody and directional change is in the student's ear, you may find that the technical problem solves itself. If not, I would add to the impulse practice you have already assigned, beginning on the third beat of each measure and playing to the third beat of the next measure. *(January 1972)*

Solfeggietto in A Major

Carl Philipp Emanuel Bach

"Moonlight Sonata" by Beethoven. *How do you count these two measures in the third movement of Beethoven's "Moonlight Sonata"?*

Students usually find it simplest to begin counting a passage like this in 8, one pulse to each eighth note or to each group of thirty-second notes. We have written in the eighth-note pulses in the example you sent.

You may need to explain to the student that the groups of thirty-second notes are written with both downstems and upstems because each of the thirty-second notes is to be tied to the chord which follows it. The downstems show when to play each note, the upstems show how long each note lasts. In other words, Beethoven has chosen to write a very precise rhythmic notation for a chord which might normally have been marked with a simple indication for a roll. But he wished to show exactly when each thirty-second note should enter, so he used an elaborate notational picture for what is really quite a simple sound. *(January 1970)*

G Minor Concerto by Mendelssohn. *One of my college freshmen is scheduled to perform the Mendelssohn G Minor Concerto in the spring. All is going well except for the octave passages. For these, he doesn't have adequate tempo or loudness. Can you offer some practice suggestions?*

This concerto makes a variety of demands on the performer's ability to play octaves. Let's use part of the opening solo passage to illustrate some suggestions for octave practice.

Slow Practice

Play in slow tempo but produce each tone as suddenly as if you were playing a tempo. After each octave relax immediately, but keep the keys slightly depressed until you are 100 percent aware of your relaxation.

Do this slow practice hands separately, then together.

Impulse Practice

Impulse practice should be *presstissimo* and *forte*. Relax on the final octave of each impulse group (shown by ⌢), keeping the keys slightly depressed until you are 100 percent aware of your relaxation.

Do impulse practice hands separately, then together.

Practice first in impulses of two:

then in impulses of four:

then in impulses of eight:

Trill Practice (slow to fast)

Combine adjacent octaves trill fashion, like this:

Do trill practice hands separately, then together.

Excess motion creates tension and impedes the control, speed, and rhythm necessary to play these octave passages brilliantly; so throughout these practice steps, be especially aware of economical motions in relation to keyboard topography. For example, in playing octaves on D, E, and F, play *here* on the keyboard:

But, in playing octaves on D, E, and F#, play *here* instead:

(*January-February 1966*)

"Small Piano Pieces" by Kadosa. *I hope you can settle a friendly though determined argument for three teachers, each with a different rhythmic interpretation of No. 48 in Kadosa 's Small Piano Pieces, Book 2 (Boosey & Hawkes):*

- *The value of the eighth notes is constant, the accents changing from measure to measure.*
- *The eighth notes in the 3/8 measure should be treated as triplets, making them slightly faster than those in the 2/4 measure.*
- *The beat unit is constant, making the eighth notes in the 2/4 measure twice as fast as those in the 3/8 measure.*

Vivo

I have taught many pieces using this or similar changes of rhythm, but now I hesitate to assign such a piece, in case I am wrong.

Personally, I do hope you agree with number one!

Your solution (number one) wins hands down. To back up your point of view, you might want to quote to your colleagues a statement from Gardner Read's book, Music Notation: "Performers beginning their study of works in combined meters would do well to remember that the note-values are constant; only the major stresses change." You might like to read the entire section of his book dealing with combined meters, for it is very clear and helpful. *(November 1972)*

"Avalanche" by Heller. *I like to teach "Avalanche" by Stephen Heller, but am not sure of the correct articulation.*

I have always taught the piece with the articulation marked below:

Allegro vivace

but I recently heard a clinician suggest that the entire piece be articulated [♩♪♪♩] to make it consistent with the markings in the last line:

Which do you recommend?

I have three different editions, all of them showing the articulation printed in your score, and this is the one I recommend.

The change in the last line is necessitated by the repeated notes, and need not affect the rest of the piece. *(July-August 1986)*

Composers and their Works

Albeniz: Who publishes his music? *Who publishes the works of Albeniz?*

Almost all works of Albeniz can be procured through Hal Leonard, 8112 West Bluemound Drive, Milwaukee, Wisconsin. Some items can be ordered from International. *(February 1967)*

Bach: Inventions. *I use the Two-Part Inventions of Bach as preparation for the Well-Tempered Clavier. Will you please suggest how many Inventions a student should have studied before beginning the Preludes and Fugue. Also, I would be grateful for a list of which ones to assign.*

Before attempting to answer your question, let me put in a word about the *intrinsic* value of the Bach Inventions. Great artists return to the Inventions again and again, with ever-increasing pleasure and insight.

Of course, they are also the best possible preparation for the WTC, and "the more the better." If you plan to limit the number your student studies, I suggest you select them on the basis of variety. For instance, No. 1 in C major and No. 13 in A minor both have short subjects, developed by imitation with frequent use of inversion. No. 3 in D major, No. 4 in D minor, and No. 14 in B♭ major have longer subjects and the imitations often repeat only a portion of the theme. In No. 5 in E♭ major, No. 6 in E major, No. 9 in F minor, and No. 11 in G minor, there are long subjects with well-marked countersubjects and many fragmentary entrances of thematic material.

Be sure not to neglect the *Sinfonias* (Three-Part Inventions), especially those that are almost fugal in nature. They are excellent preparation for the fugues of the WTC. *(April 1977)*

Bach: The Well-Tempered Clavier. *The National Guild of Piano Teachers requires a student to perform from memory a Bach Prelude and Fugue from the* Well-Tempered Clavier *to earn a High School Music Diploma. Please list three or four that are easiest to perform and memorize.*

I can answer this question only in general terms by suggesting some possibilities for you to consider. So much depends on the individual student, on his technical skills and musical understanding, on which Bach works the student has previously studied and performed, and on the other standard repertoire he is currently studying. The Preludes and Fugues I generally teach first are from the *Well-Tempered*

Clavier Book I, No. 21 in B♭ major and No.2 in C minor. After those I often assign No. 6 in D minor, or No. 13 in F♯ major. It is tempting to select No. 10 in E minor because it is the only two-voice fugue, but resist the temptation — it is far from easy! *(July-August 1987)*

Bach: Keys of the Inventions. *My high school piano class would like to know why J.S. Bach wrote both the Two-Part and Three-Part Inventions in only 15 keys, while the Preludes and Fugues are in all 24 keys.*

The keys Bach used for the Inventions are C major and minor, D major and minor, E♭ major and minor, E major and minor, F major and minor, G major and minor, A major and minor, B♭ major and B minor.

The reason for the omission of the other keys is an interesting one. At the time the Inventions were composed, the method of tuning the piano by what is called "equal temperament" had not been introduced. By the older method, not all keys could be equally well tuned; those that were less satisfactory were the keys with many sharps and flats. So Bach chose to avoid all keys having more than four sharps or flats.

When equal temperament had been introduced, Bach became its great champion and the artistic result is the *Well-Tempered Clavier*, a double series of Preludes and Fugues in all 24 keys. *(February 1983)*

Bach: "Allemande" in A Major. *I have come across an Allemande in A major in several collections. Sometimes the composer is listed as Bach, sometimes as Telemann. Since this Allemande appears in your Piano Literature 5a-6a, can you tell me which composer is correct?*

Not absolutely, but the best Bach scholars today agree that the composer is Telemann. The story is this: a fragmentary Suite in A major, consisting of three movements (Allemande, Courante, and Gigue) appears in the manuscript for the Klavierbuchlein fur Wilhelm Friedernann Bach. The piece is copied in W.F. Bach's hand without any composer attribution. A concordant source (and one which contains the best musical readings) attributes the work to Telemann. The attribution to J.S. Bach appears in four less authoritative sources. Whereas the editors of the original complete Bach works (our source) indicated that "the work may be spurious, perhaps the work of Bach's colleague, George Philipp Telemann," the editors of the Neue Bach Ausgabe accept it as a work by Telemann, and I believe we can do no better than to follow their lead. *(July-August 1981)*

Bartok: "Hungarian Folk Melodies". *I have just ordered* Forty-Two Hugarian Folk Melodies *by Bartok, believing that they would give my intermediate students good experience in interesting rhythms. To my dismay, I find that not one of them is in compound meter. What music of Bartok's should I have ordered?*

As far as I know no Hungarian folk songs or dances occur in compound meter (apparently it is not characteristic of that particular national idiom), but you will find a few examples of compound meter in Bartok's *Slovakian Folk Melodies.* However, don't put aside the *Hungarian Folk Melodies* just because they don't include compound meter. They are all excellent studies in rhythm, full of interesting accentuations, sudden changes in meter (2/4 to 3/4 or 3/4 to 3/2 within a piece, for example), many tempo changes and extensive use of fermata, as well as dramatic changes in dynamic levels and touch. I don't consider this collection ideal for the average young intermediate student because the pieces are not easy. Perhaps as an introduction to Bartok, you should consider instead the two volumes entitled *For Children*, published by Boosey & Hawkes. *(September 1981)*

Bartok: "Mikrokosmos". *Where can I get help on teaching Bartok's* Mikrokosmos? *The parents of one of my beginners have requested that I use it as a basis for teaching their 7-year-old son.*

The six volumes of Bartok's *Mikrokosmos* (Boosey & Hawkes) are probably in stock at your local music store. Obtaining the music should be much less of a problem than using it as a basic study material for a young beginner.

The material in Volume I has been systematically arranged by Bartok for use with beginners — young or old. He believed that the pieces presented all problems encountered during the first stages of study. However, he was careful to point out that *Mikrokosmos* differed from a traditional "piano method" by the absence of any technical or theoretical description or instruction. The series begins, therefore, without any material for teaching reading, rhythm, or theory.

I think it would be very difficult and time-consuming to use these books without a basic instruction book, nor would I recommend using the Bartok pieces until all the basics they require had been taught. Perhaps you could show the parents the beginner's book you usually use and compare it to Volume I of *Mikrokosmos*, explaining the differences and difficulties.

After the student has had several months of lessons in a conventional method and has developed the reading, rhythm, and technical skills required for the first Bartok pieces, you could introduce Volume I as supplementary material. Despite its omissions, it has two real advantages: there is a systematic approach to various level one technical problems, and the music is by a master composer.

If you decide to use the material, I would recommend that you make a detailed study of the music and of the companion technical exercises in the Appendix of each volume. In addition, you will find the Preface and Notes sections helpful. When Bartok titles his pieces, it is usually to describe their pedagogical purpose: "Dotted Notes", "Repetition," "Syncopation," and "Parallel Motion."

I would also recommend Benjamin Suckoffs *Guide to the Mikrokosmos*, published by Music Services Corporation of America. Chapters 2, 3, 4, and the Annotations and Commentary sections are especially helpful.

Although other collections of Bartok's student pieces are not as systematically arranged, you may find that the material in *For Children* Vols. 1 and 2 and *First Term at the Piano* affords far more musical variety and pleasure than the purely pedagogical material of the *Mikrokosmos*. *(November 1980)*

Beethoven: "Country Dances." *I have tried to order the Beethoven "Country Dances" (arranged for 8-hands by Parlow) with no success. Are they no longer available?*

They were re-issued in sheet music by Summy-Birchard in April 1991.

Beethoven: Easiest Sonatas. *What do you consider to be the four or five easiest Beethoven sonatas?*

The only sonatas that can by any stretch of the imagination be called "easy" are Op. 49, Nos. 1 and 2. Both are two-movement sonatas, often called "sonatinas." It's interesting to note that the tide "Leichte Sonata" ("easy sonata") is Beethoven's own.

Aside from these two, it is difficult to say which are the least difficult, for the answer depends on what you are considering — technical difficulty or interpretive difficulty. From both standpoints, it is probably safe to suggest trying Op. 79, and Op. 2, No. 1. *(October 1969)*

Beethoven: Op. 49. *I have been criticized for listing Beethoven's Op. 49, Nos. 1 and 2 as "sonatas" instead of "sonatinas." Which is correct?*

Either term is correct, but I prefer "sonatas" because Beethoven included these works in his collection of 32 piano sonatas and gave them opus numbers. He also wrote at least seven sonatinas, none of which has an opus number. Six of the sonatinas are very well known and are available together as a set from many publishers. These include the Sonatinas in Eb major, F major, and D major, which Kinsky has catalogued as WoO 47, Nos. 1, 2, and 3 and Sonatina in G catalogued as WoO 51. The remaining two, the familiar G major and F major Sonatinas are the easiest of all. These are of doubtful authenticity and although they are included in all of the collections of Beethoven sonatinas, they have not been ascribed a number in the catalogue. In Volume 9 of the 1965 Supplement to Beethoven's Collected Works, published by Breitkopf and Härtel under the editorial direction of Willy Hess, a seventh sonatina is included, WoO 50 in F major.

Sonatas Op. 49 Nos. 1 and 2 are the easiest of the sonatas and have only two movements each, it is not really incorrect to call them sonatinas, and many recent editors, in compiling collections of sonatinas by various composers, have taken the liberty of including them. I know of no evidence, though, that Beethoven viewed them as sonatinas. *(May-June 1979)*

Brahms: Waltzes, Op. 39. *The Schirmer edition of the Brahms Waltzes, 39, for piano duet, does not give the arranger. Can you tell me who made the arrangement?*

The duet version of the waltzes is the original. Brahms originally wrote Opus 39 for 1 piano, 4-hands, and later made the solo version. *(February 1967)*

Brahms: 51 Exercises. *I recently read an article in which there was a reference to a technique book by Brahms. The dealer in our music store never heard of it, and I can't find any teacher who knows anything about such a book. I would appreciate knowing just what it is and where I can get it.*

Brahms wrote a collection of short etudes called *Fifty-One Exercises for the Piano*. It is Volume 1600 of the Schirmer Library and is readily available through G. Schirmer Company.

The collection of etudes (one page or less in length) does not have a Preface or Table of Contents, but a quick glance through the book shows there must have been a clear organizational plan in Brahms' mind.

For example, the first six exercises are numbered 1a-1f and all are based on one family of related problems. 1a and 1b are devoted to playing three against four; 1c and 1d to playing four against five; 1e and 1f to playing six against seven.

As another example, 2a and 2b are studies in legato thirds, alternating hands (2a ascends, 2b descends); 3 is an exercise in legato thirds, ascending and descending, hands together.

Because many exercises have two or more parts, there are actually 87 exercises in all. The studies are advanced technique, of the sort Brahms probably assigned to his artist students. *(December 1969)*

Chopin: Easier Pieces. *I have three high school girls who especially enjoyed studying the two Chopin Preludes and the Mazurka included in your Piano Literature Book 6. They are begging for more Chopin. I'd like to assign each of them one of the Chopin Etudes, but I need help in selecting the right ones. Please tell me which three Etudes are the easiest and how to go about assigning them.*

Don't! There are no easiest Etudes, only hard, harder, and hardest. I'd suggest making their next Chopin assignment either from among the less difficult of the Preludes, or from one of the volumes of easier or minor Chopin works.

In the Paderewski edition of Chopin's complete works, there are two volumes that I especially recommend for your purpose. The first is *Selected Easy Pieces, An Introduction to Chopin*. It contains seven preludes (A minor, E minor, B minor, A major, C major, E major, and Db major, all from Op. 28), six mazurkas selected from Op. 17, 24, 33, 67, and 68, three nocturnes, and five waltzes. The second collection to consider is *Minor Works* (Volume XVlll) which contains fourteen miscellaneous pieces (Bolero, Tarantelle, March Funebre (in two versions), Three Ecossaises, Two Nocturnes, Contradanse, Cantaile, Feuille D'Album, Largo, and Fuga). Most of the works in this collection are not very well known and are a rich source of less difficult material for the beginning Chopin student. Both volumes are published by the Chopin Institute in Warsaw and are available in this country through Hal Leonard.

Perhaps you will want to restudy the Etudes yourself. There are good study notes in back of the Chopin Institute Edition. In addition, I recommend an excellent book called *Mastering the Chopin Etudes* by Abbey Whiteside, published by Charles Scribner 's Sons. *(March 1977)*

Chopin: Easiest Nocturnes. *I have a student who is ready for Chopin's Nocturnes. Please tell me which Nocturne you consider the easiest.*

The two easiest Chopin Nocturnes are those in C minor and C# minor, to be found in the Chopin Institute Edition (Vol. XVlll, Minor Works), edited by Paderewski. While they are certainly not minor, they are considerably easier than any of the well-known Nocturnes and both are exquisitely beautiful and rewarding. *(November 1967)*

Clementi: Sonatinas. *I have questions about playing the Clementi Sonatinas, Op. 36. No two editions are alike, especially in the realization of the ornaments (appoggiaturas, turns, and trills). Is there an urtext edition available?*

The closest thing to an urtext is the fine new edition of Op. 36 prepared by Willard Palmer (Alfred Music, 1978). In his preface Palmer explains that the autograph has never been found but that the original edition was published circa 1803 by Clementi's own publishing company. Because this was Clementi's own edition, it may well have been more carefully edited than the manuscript.

In this edition all of Clementi's slurs, staccato marks, finger numbers, and ornaments appear in dark print, with editorial suggestions light print. The edition includes a table of ornaments compiled from Clementi's book, *Introduction to the Art of Playing on the Pianoforte.*

> *The appoggiatura is a grace note, written as a small note above a principal note; its length is borrowed from the principal note and in general is half its duration. The turn*

begins on the note above the principal note, and the lowest note is usually a half step below. Trills begin on the note above the principal note, but their performance is left to the taste and judgment of the performer, whether long, short, transient, or turned.

The entire edition is both scholarly and helpful, and I recommend it highly. *(November 1981)*

Clementi: Sonatas. *Is there a complete edition of the Clementi Sonatas currently available from any publisher? If not, which is the most nearly complete edition, which do you recommend as best, and which sonatas do you consider most worthwhile?*

Clementi wrote over 100 sonatas, 64 of which are for piano without accompaniment. (The others are duets or trios for piano with violin or flute, or for violin or flute with cello.) The only complete edition of the 64 piano sonatas is a three-volume publication by Breitkopf and Hartel, available in this country through Associated Music Publishers.

I believe most musicians would agree that his best sonatas include the Sonata in F minor, Op. 14, No.3; the Sonata in B minor, Op. 40, No. 2; and the three sonatas in Op. 50 (A major, D minor, and G mi- nor). Each of these has a clarity of form, conciseness of expression, and purity of style that mark them as works not of genius, but certainly of real musical worth and lasting value. *(February 1974)*

Debussy: "Dr. Gradus ad Parnassum". *I am going to play "Dr. Gradus ad Parnassum" by Debussy in a recital soon, and I would like to know who Dr. Gradus ad Parnassum is. My teacher suggested that I write to you to find out.*

"Dr. Gradus ad Parnassum" is the first piece in a suite by Debussy called the *Children's Corner.* All six pieces in the set are full of delight and fancy. Debussy gets his title for the first piece from a work by Clementi called "Gradus ad Parnassum," a series of one hundred pieces in progressive order of difficulty, written to increase the student's technical skill. Clementi took his title for this series of technical studies from Mt. Parnassus in Greece, a mountain sacred to the Muses and therefore supposedly a center of excellence in poetry and the arts. Freely translated then, "Gradus ad Parnassum" means "steps to artistic excellence."

Debussy's charming piece is really a parody on monotonous technical exercises at the piano. He himself says, "They are a kind of progressive, hygienic gymnastic exercise, to be played every morning fasting; beginning moderato and working gradually to animato."

I have heard the piece described as a student struggling at the piano with some monotonous finger exercises and, at points throughout the piece, pouting at the difficulties and enjoying the pleasure of the distractions that present themselves. I have also heard it described as a student beginning with finger exercises; as he becomes bored with the exercises, he decides to improvise and of course it is the improvisations that give the piece its charm. The fact that Debussy turns the title into a man's name is just another part of the joke. *(May-June 1972)*

Diabelli, Burgmüller, Hanon, and Czerny. *In all the years that I have subscribed to Clavier, I have never read any articles on, or seen any mention of, teaching materials which I consider basic, namely the Diabelli Duets, Op. 149, for elementary students; Burgmüller Etudes for intermediate students; Hanon Exercises, and Czerny Studies, Op. 740, for high school students.*

Please include in your column your opinion of this material or at least some explanation of why it has been omitted.

It's interesting that the material you mention has not been included in an article in Clavier during the years you have been a subscriber. I have not researched the accuracy of your statement, but if such standard and well-known teaching materials have been omitted, perhaps it is just because of their unquestioned position as staples in many teachers' pedagogical material. However, I cannot resist this invitation to evaluate them. As you will see, I have a few reservations about them.

Diabelli, "Melodious Exercises," Op. 149. These duets, primo for student and a much more elaborate secondo for teacher, are rather engaging musical fare in a straightforward 19th century style. While we use them, we do so very sparingly for several reasons. First, throughout the entire collection, both hands of the primo part are written in treble clef, so that the student's reading experience is quite limited. Second, a large portion of the primo parts are written in parallel motion with hands an octave apart, again a limited and limiting experience. By far the most important reason for using the material sparingly is the fact of its musical sameness and the resulting narrow demands on interpretive variation and nuance. This is nice music and students really enjoy the ease with which they can almost sight read the primo parts, but a little of it goes a long way.

Burgmüller, Twenty-five Studies, Op. 100. We frequently use the studies in Op. 100 for the student in Levels 3 and 4 who needs additional music. These studies vary greatly in difficulty. Played up to the tempo indications, we find Nos. 2, 8, 9, 11, 15, 16, 20, 22, and 23 good technical studies and rather effective musically.

Hanon, The Virtuoso Pianist in Sixty Exercises. If, and when, we assign the exercises by Hanon, we do not ask the student to buy the volume. Each Hanon study is based on repetition of one short pattern. This pattern can be learned easily by rote as a technical exercise and does not need to be written out in 32 or 64 measures. In my opinion the only person who should ever own a volume of Hanon is the teacher. In their written-out form, even the sections based on major and minor scales, arpeggios, trills, thirds, sixths, octaves, etc., seem not only to be a waste of precious paper, but actually prove to be a hindrance in developing a student who understands and thinks about what his hands are doing.

Czerny, The Art of Finger Dexterity, Op. 740. This volume has been of great value in developing facility, and has been used by many, many teachers for a long time. My concern, based on your question, is not the value of the work, but simply with which students you are using it.

In all the years I have taught, I can remember only three high school students whose technique was developed to the point that they could play these exercises up to tempo. Consider, for example, No. 1, which is made of non-stop sixteenth notes to be played at M.M. ♩ = 92, or No. 2, made of arpeggio crossings in sixteenth notes, to be played at M.M. ♩. = 60, or No. 6, made of broken chords in thirty-second notes, to be played at M.M. ♩ = 92.

The purpose of each study is made clear in the introduction. In every instance, it is designed for tonal control of a particular aspect of technique at a rapid tempo. Unless the student is ready to play the studies at the metronome mark indicated, I would certainly recommend using something less demanding. *(February 1976)*

Finney: "25 Inventions." *In the 1950s Summy published a set of* Inventions *by Ross Lee Finney, excerpts of which appear in your* Contemporary Piano Literature *books. Is this set still available and, if so, from what publisher? Also, could you tell me something about Finney and give me some ideas for presenting his use of tone rows to students?*

The 25 Inventions (without opus number) were composed in 1956 while Finney was working at the American Academy in Rome, and were published by Summy Publishing Company in 1957. Ten of the pieces from the collection were simultaneously published in our *Contemporary Piano Literature* books: "There and Back," "Berceuse," "Skipping," and "Reflections" in Book Four; "Vacation," "Mirrors," and "Song" in Book Five; and "Hopping," "Swinging," and "Night;" in Book Six. These excerpts are still available in our books, now obtained through Summy-Birchard, Inc., a division of Warner Brothers Music. The complete set of *25 Inventions* was republished by C.F. Peters in 1971 and is still available through them.

Finney is one of our leading contemporary American composers. Born on December 27, 1906 in Wells, Minnesota, Finney grew up in North Dakota. He remembers his childhood there as "normal and wholesome... the prairie, the fox tails blowing like waves in the wind, a hillside blue with crocuses, the wide sky, the mystery of the Cheyenne River winding its way through woodland, the skating for miles up river in early winter before snow fell, the wild ducks and geese overhead."

The memory of these typically American scenes has woven itself into his music.

He was brought up in a musical household; his brothers played violin and trumpet, and Ross studied cello. Even as a young child he began to compose. After graduating from Carleton College, Finney traveled to Europe, where he studied with Nadia Boulanger and later with Alban Berg and Roger Sessions. In 1929 he joined the faculty of Smith College, founded the Smith College Music Archives, and started the Valley Music Press, a series of publications devoted to contemporary American music.

Finney's setting of poems by Archibald MacLeish won the Connecticut Valley Prize in 1935. In 1937 he received a Pulitzer Scholarship, a Guggenheim Fellowship, and a Fulbright Traveling Fellowship. His works have been commissioned and performed by the Philadelphia Orchestra, the Baltimore Symphony, and the Erick Hawkins Dance Company, among others.

During the Second World War Finney served with distinction in the U.S. Office of Strategic Services and was awarded a Certificate of Merit and the Purple Heart. In 1948 Finney joined the faculty of the University of Michigan School of Music, where he organized and headed the composition department and served as composer-in-residence. He retired from the university in 1973 and now divides his time between Ann Arbor and New York.

Finney is a member of the Academy and Institute of Arts and Letters in New York City and the Academy of Arts and Sciences in Boston. He has taught many distinguished American composers, including Leslie Bassett, George Crumb, and Roger Reynolds.

His chamber works, orchestral works, piano pieces, and songs have been widely performed here and abroad. Although he has written many compositions for piano, including four sonatas, the *Inventions* remain his only works for student pianists. He is also the author of a wonderful introduction to the study of harmony, *The Game of Harmony* (Harcourt, Brace, 1942), written to amuse his 12-year-old son when he was in bed with the flu!

Composers Recording Incorporated has just issued a splendid compact disc of Finney's piano works performed by Martha Braden. It includes *Fantasy* (1939), *Sonata No.3 in E Major* (1942), *Sonata Quasi une Fantasia* (1961), and *Narrative in Retrospect* (1948).

To illustrate Finney's use of tone rows in his Inventions, let's look at two of the shorter pieces.

Puzzle

In line one of "Puzzle," the twelve-tone row is introduced in two halves, the first half presented by the right hand, the second half by the left hand.

In line two, each half of the row is used backwards: the right hand reverses its first-half notes (6, 5, 4, 3, 2, 1), and then the left hand reverses its second-half notes (12, 11, 10, 9, 8, 7).

The accompanying tones, circled above, are the outside points of the two halves of the row. In line one, tone seven accompanies measures 1-2, while tone six is sustained to accompany measures 7-8.

Skipping
From *25 Inventions*

In "Skipping" Finney assigns each hand its own row, but keeps the two rows, and therefore the hands, a major third apart throughout the piece. The rows are presented in line one, then used in reverse order in line two, so that the piece ends on the same tones with which it began. (*April 1989*)

Finney: "The Game of Harmony." *Help! Contrary to your April 1989 column, Harcourt, Brace says they do not publish* The Game of Harmony *by Ross Lee Finney.*

I wrote to Ross Lee Finney and learned that *The Game of Harmony* was indeed published by Harcourt, Brace in the 1930s but is now out of print. I'm sorry to have misled you.

Finney confirmed that his *Inventions* are still available through C.F. Peters. He also reminded me that although the pieces in our *Contemporary Piano Literature* books are similar to the *Inventions*, they are not the same pieces. In addition, he told me that Peters has issued a recording of his *Youth's Companion*, a collection that will enrich your repertoire of teaching pieces by Ross Lee Finney. *(October 1989)*

Finney: "32 Piano Games". *I've recently heard of a book called* Piano Games. *Could you tell me who wrote it and what it is for?*

I think you must be referring to *32 Piano Games* by Ross Lee Finney, published in 1969 by Peters (66256). According to the composer's Preface,

The object of this work is to introduce children to the entire sonority and articulation of the piano and to the types of notation that contemporary composers use. A child senses the fact that he is not permitted to use the sounds that he can produce most naturally at the piano and that the musical vocabulary open to him is limited. He finds it hard to sustain his original excitement for learning to play the piano. This volume assumes that the child has been taught conventional musical notation, can reach the two extremes of the piano keyboard, and that he can reach the pedal. In some of the pieces he is asked to be very free. His teacher should encourage him to improvise and if possible to find a notation for what he has improvised.

The collection is full of the richly imaginative sounds we have come to expect from the pen of Ross Lee Finney, and the excursion into a broader contemporary idiom is both exciting and rewarding for the piano student. In addition, the experiments with contemporary notation prove stimulating. *(October 1970)*

Finney: "Inventions". *There is an interesting article by Mr. Hinson, "The Solo Keyboard Works of Ross Lee Finney," in the June-July issue of the* American Music Teacher. *In it he highly recommends the collection called* Inventions *and regrets that they are no longer in*

print. Are these the same pieces that are included in your Contemporary Piano Literature, *Books 4, 5, and 6? And if so, does this mean that they will be removed from your series, too? I would hate to see this happen, because both young students and adults have found them very interesting.*

Yes, the piece in the *Contemporary Piano Literature* books are from the complete set of Finney inventions and will remain as part of our series. Mr. Hinson apparently did not realize that the *Inventions* are now available again, published by Peters.

I'm interested to learn of your students' response and I agree with Mr. Hinson that these pieces are among the finest contemporary music available to students. Not only are they rewarding from the standpoint of their beautiful and original sounds, but also from the standpoint of the fine introduction they make to tone-row construction. Mr. Finney invites us into his workshop with these pieces, for they are easy to analyze and to understand. The student who is not immediately taken with the sound often becomes interested in the 12-tone technique, and is won over to the new sounds through the experience of analyzing. *(October 1971)*

Gershwin: "Song Book". *At your study course in Princeton last summer we heard a high school student play selections from the Gershwin Song Book. I'd like to know who published it and who transcribed it for piano. I have some juniors and seniors in high school who want to play only popular songs, and I think these pieces might please them.*

The Gershwin Song Books in two volumes are published by Warner Brothers, and the transcriptions were made by Gershwin himself. However, before you assign these books, I would like to make two suggestions. First, remember that what was popular in one generation may not be popular in another. Second, get the books yourself and play the music through before deciding to whom to assign it. These pieces are subtle, sensitive, and rhythmically very difficult. The student you heard at Princeton had also studied and performed during that same year Scarlatti Sonatas, a Haydn Sonata, a Schubert Impromptu, the Gershwin Preludes, Copland's Four Piano Blues, and a group of pieces by Mompou.

In other words, you need to be certain your students will like the Gershwin songs, and that they will have the technical and rhythmic control and the musical sensitivity to play them. *(December 1981)*

Ginastera: "Rondo on Argentinian Folktunes". *I am interested in a set of variations on an Argentinian folksong by Ginastera, but have been unable to locate it either through my music store or publisher's catalogues. Could you come to my rescue?*

I'm not sure Ginastera has written a set of variations on a folksong. I wonder if you might be thinking of his *Rondo on Argentinian Folktunes* published by Boosey & Hawkes. I highly recommend this delightful, humorous, and brilliant concert piece;

it's sure to be a recital favorite. *(May-June 1987)*

Handel: Easier Pieces. *I have neglected to teach any music by Handel, and feel that I should be teaching his suites to my high school students who have already played several of Bach's two-part inventions. I don't know where to begin and would welcome your advice as to which suite is the easiest.*

I would not recommend introducing the music of Handel to a high school student by giving him a whole suite. If he has not previously studied any of the Handel keyboard music (and there is a veritable treasure-trove of it), I would assign first either some of the easier movements from the suites or, better still, some of the simpler miscellaneous pieces. I recommend a collection of Handel's easier works, such as the album called "G.F. Handel, Easier Pieces," published by Hinrichsen (No. 3) and available in this country through C.F. Peters Corporation. It includes some miscellaneous pieces and suite movements in their original form. They are heavily edited, but nonetheless provide a delightful introduction to Handel's music. The collection includes four transcriptions of non-keyboard music arranged for piano. Better skip these! *(March 1976)*

Haydn: Concertos. *I heard recently that Haydn composed concertos other than the D Major. Could you tell me what they are and who publishes them?*

We know that Haydn composed one "concertino" and at least four concertos, the most familiar of which is the D Major. Following are brief descriptions of the editions we prefer.

International publishes Haydn's *Concerto in G Major*. Its three movements — Allegro, Andante, Rondo (Presto) — contain many sections of equal or greater difficulty than comparable sections of the Major Concerto.

In 1955, Boosey & Hawkes brought out the first published edition of Haydn's *Piano Concerto in C*. This short work (about eleven minutes duration) contains three movements: Allegro (the cadenza, which is not original, may be omitted), Menuetto and Trio, and Finale (Allegro). It is a charming work, and all of it is a great deal easier than either the G Major or the D Major Concertos.

A *Concerto in F*, which we have not seen, is published by Schott.

In 1953, Peters issued for the first time a *Concertino* in C Major (Peters 4611). This easy and brief keyboard piece is published with accompanying parts for two violins and cello (or bass). Its three very short movements are: Allegro (4 pages), Menuetto and Trio (2 pages), and Allegro di molto (1 page). *(January-February 1966)*

Haydn: D Major Concerto (cadenza). *I have an outstanding eleven-year-old boy who is* *playing the first movement of the Haydn D Major Concerto. Which cadenza do you recommend that he play?*

I suggest Haydn's original cadenza, which can be found on page 18 of the Teichmüller edition (Peters 4353). This edition also includes a supplement that presents an alternate cadenza. *(May-June 1970)*

Heller. *Why isn't Stephen Heller's music popular today? I was brought up on a diet of Heller's music and have found it very valuable for students. Yet, in speaking of it at our piano teacher's forum, I found contemporaries who thought he was passé and younger teachers who didn't even know his name. Yet Baker's Biographical Dictionary of Music and Musicians describes his music as "distinguished for its elegance and refinement, varied and forceful rhythms, exquisite melody, bold and original thematic treatment." I'd like to know if you teach Heller's music.*

Yes, I teach some of Heller's music. His familiar "Avalanche" and "Curious Story" pop up occasionally in our repertoire classes, and we have a few students in the school who are currently studying his *Twenty-Five Melodious Studies*, Op. 45.

I agree with you that the literate piano teacher would certainly know something about Heller and have at least a nodding acquaintance with his piano music; there are the etudes, ballades, sonatinas, sonatas, waltzes, mazurkas, caprices, nocturnes, and variations to choose from. However, we also need to take into account the vast amount of fine piano teaching material written since his death in 1888, and choose the best from all periods. Probably this would not leave room for what you call a diet of Heller.

This changing perspective is demonstrated in Baker's dictionary to which you refer. In the 1940 edition from which you quote, Heller is accorded a full column out of the 1200 pages. In the 1979 revised edition, Heller rates only half a column in a book of 1955 pages. In Maurice Hinson's *Guide to Pianist's Repertoire* (1973), Hinson lists ten fine collections by Heller but precedes the list with this comment "Although old-fashioned by today's standards, Heller's works include plenty of fine pedagogical material readily available." *(March 1980)*

Hovhaness: Music for students. *Has Alan Hovhaness written any music suitable for young students?*

Yes, he has written some charming student pieces. The easiest is a collection called *Sketchbook for Mr. Purple Poverty*, Op. 309, in two volumes, published by Broude. Only Volume I has been released, but each of the two volumes is to contain 13 short, programmatic pieces. A composer's note on the title page of Volume I explains, "Mr. Purple Poverty is an idiotic, clownish poet who dreams himself in love with Lady Purple, a great and beautiful poetess who lived around a thousand years ago." In this spirit, titles include such imaginative offerings as "Purple's Empty Purse," "Purple Patches," "Purple's Empty Stomach," "Love Song to Lady Purple," etc. The pieces vary in length from 14 measures to two pages and are approximately Level 1 in difficulty. The music is major, minor, modal, pentatonic, and just plain Hovhannes. It runs the gamut from very simple to very sophisticated, and all of it is special in sound. Highly recommended as a supplement to the basic diet of contemporary repertoire for the sensitive young student and especially rewarding for older beginners.

Hovhannes has also composed two short works which appear in a single piece of sheet music as part of the series, *Piano Music for Students by Contemporary Composers*, published by Leeds and available through CPP/Belwin, 5800 N.W. 48th Ave., Miami, Florida. "Slumber Song" (Level 2) is a simple, expressive piece, two pages long. The one-page "Siris Dance" (Level 1) is a lively etude in eighth notes.

Twelve Armenian Folk Songs, published by Peters (No. 6432) is a collection of exquisite settings of Armenian mountain village tunes (Levels 3-4). And finally there is a three-page sheet called "Mystic Flute" (Level 4) published by Peters (No. 6470).

Hovhannes is also included in two collections of student works: "Lullaby" (Level 3) is part of *American Composers of Today*, published by Maris; and "Mountain Idylls" (Level 3), is part of the *Young Pianist's Anthology of Modern Music*, published by Associated and available through Hal Leonard. *(January 1981)*

Iturbi: "Pequena Darua Espanola". At a student recital recently I heard the piece "Pequena Danza Espanola," with the composer listed as Iturbi It is the identical piece I have often heard in the past whose composer is Navarro. Who did write this piece?

lturbi is the composer. When "Pequena Danza Espanola" was first published by G. Schirmer in 1934, lturbi used the pseudonym "Navarro", but for some time now it has been published under his own name. *(September 1968)*

Kabalevsky: Tempi for familiar pieces. *The teachers in our Piano Teachers Association cannot agree on the tempos of some of the Kabalevsky pieces included in your* Contemporary Piano Literature *books, especially "Dance on the Lawn," "Toccatina," and "A Little Joke" from Book 4, and the three movements of the Sonatina from Book 6. Will you please settle the matter for us?*

Easier said than done! The metronome marks for "Dance on the Lawn" and for the second movement of the Sonatina are the only parts of the problem we can settle with much certainty. For the other pieces, the wide range of metronome marks below will, I'm afraid, only tend to confirm that the disagreements among you are natural ones.

Dance on the Lawn	♩ = 138
Toccatina	♩ = 144 to ♩ = 126
A Little Joke	♩ = 144 to ♩ = 100
Sonatina	
First Movement	♩ = 138 to ♩ = 138
Second Movement	♩ = 72
Third Movement	♩ = 160 to ♩ = 200

The very rapid second metronome mark in each case is the tempo at which Kabalevsky himself plays these pieces on Monitor Records (MC 2039). The first metronome mark indicates the slowest tempo at which we believe this piece can be played effectively. Above all, the pieces must be clearly articulated and phrased and, though fast, must not sound breathless. The tempo at which each individual student can accomplish this clearly articulated performance is, of course, up to the judgment and standards of the teacher. *(April 1968)*

Kabalevsky: "Youth Concerto". *I have a very talented 14-year-old girl who would like to study a concerto. She has played the Haydn D Major and is not interested at present in studying a concerto by Mozart, Beethoven, Mendelssohn, etc. She is most interested in studying a contemporary concerto that is not too difficult. Could you suggest one?*

If you have not already considered *Piano Concerto No. 3, Op. 50* by Kabalevsky (often called the "Youth Concerto"), I'd suggest you examine it to see if it meets her needs. It is arranged for two pianos, 4-hands by the composer (M.C.A. Music). *(March 1969)*

LaMontaine: "Copycats." *Do you know any collections of canons for young students by composers other than those by Konrad Kunz?*

John LaMontaine has written a collection of 14 canons called *Copycats*, published by Fredonia Press, 3947 Fredonia Drive, Hollywood, California. The music is elementary level, written in large notes, and filled with child-like illustrations. The title, lyrics, and pictures are appealing and the music (all in 5-finger positions) is delightful. All of the pieces are in pure canon, 13 of them at the octave, one at the fifth.

LaMontaine has also prepared a recording of *Copycats*, in which he follows each canon with a delightful improvisation designed to guide student improvisation. The record is also available from Fredonia Press. *(July-August 1984)*

Menotti: "Poemetti". *I have a junior high school student who took part in his school's production of "Amahl and the Night Visitors." As a result, he wants to play something by Menotti. Has he composed any piano music easy enough for a student in Level 4?*

I know of only two piano compositions by Menotti. Long ago he composed a collection called Poemetti, published by Ricordi in 1937 and now available through Hal Leonard. This is a set of twelve one-page pieces, ideal for intermediate piano students. The music has great variety and charm, filled with colorful and idiomatic sounds, more romantic or impressionistic than contemporary in flavor.

The set of little poems includes: Giga, Ninna-Nanna (a lullaby), Bells at Dawn, The Spinner, The Bagpipers, The Brook, The Shepherd, Nocturne, The Stranger's Dance, Winter Wind, The Manger, and War Song. I have taught these pieces successfully for years and I recommend them to you and your student with great enthusiasm.

In 1953, Menotti composed a *Ricercare and Toccata* on a theme from "The Old Maid and the Thief," also published by Ricordi. This, too, is appealing melodic material but much too difficult for an intermediate student. *(February 1980)*

Mozart: "Viennese Sonatinas." *I have not had much success in teaching the "Viennese Sonatinas" of Mozart. Do you consider it absolutely essential for a student to master them?*

Actually, these pieces come from a collection of *Five Divertimenti* (K. 439B) for two clarinets and bassoon, which Mozart composed in Vienna in 1783. Various selected movements from these Divertimenti have undergone many arrangements and transcriptions, both for piano and for other instruments. Since early in the 20th Century, it has become customary to group 24 miscellaneous pieces from the set into an arbitrary sequence and key scheme (quite altered from the original) and to call them "Six Viennese Sonatinas."

A number of editors have made fairly satisfactory piano transcriptions of the music, but at best it is a transcription and does not lie under the hand the way real piano music does.

For students who find these pieces unrewarding, I suggest trying some of the charming original pieces from the "London Notebook." This music is far less sophisticated than the *Divertimenti* so it is easier students to comprehend, and, because it was written for piano, is far more playable, especially for younger students.

The "London Notebook" consists of 43 pieces which Mozart composed on a visit to London when he was eight years old. The pieces range in difficulty from late elementary to late intermediate level, and have all the naiveté and charm of Mozart's other childhood compositions. Fifteen of the pieces are available in a collection of Mozart and Beethoven dances, called "The Classic Dances," edited by David Goldberger and published by Consolidated Music Publishers. *(February 1968)*

Saint-Saens: "Carnival of the Animals." *Is there a piano arrangement of* The Carnival of the Animals *by Saint-Saens?*

There is a transcription of the complete work for 1 piano 4 hands by L. Barban and a transcription for 2 pianos 4 hands by R. Berkowitz. The complete work has not been transcribed for solo piano, but the following excerpts are available:

> Introduction and Royal March of the Lion
> Wild Jackass
> Turtles
> The Elephant
> Kangaroos
> The Aquarium
> The Cuckoo in the Woods
> The Birds
> The Fossils
> The Swan

All of the above are published by Durand and are available in this country through Theodore Presser. *(September 1968)*

Scott: "Zoo." *I am interested in teaching* Zoo *by Cyril Scott. Please tell me who publishes it, and also if the pieces in that collection are what you would consider Level 3.*

Zoo is published by Schott, catalogue number 2115. There are eight charming small pieces in the collection, colorfully characteristic of the animals they describe. Four of the pieces (Elephant, Bear, Giraffe and Rhinoceros) are definitely Level 3. Snake and Tortoise, though Level 3 in reading, are more difficult technically because of legato thirds and fourths. Squirrel and Monkey are harder, Levels 4-5. *(September 1968)*

Shostakovich: Preludes and Fugues. *How can I order the Prelude and Fugue by Shostakovich (G major, I think) which I heard performed at a summer study course in Princeton? I've been trying to procure it ever since then without any luck.*

So far as I know, none of the Preludes and Fugues is published separately. The set, *Twenty-Four Preludes and Fugues*, Op. 87, was composed by Shostakovich in 1951 and was published in this country by Leeds in 1955. There are two volumes and an excellent preface by Irwin Freundlich is to be found in Volume I. The set is available through CPP/Belwin.

The pieces are organized according to Bach's key scheme: C major, A minor, G major, etc. The first twelve comprise Volume I, and the last twelve make up Volume II. Eleven of the fugues are in three voices and eleven in four; one (E minor) is in two voices and one (F# major) is in five. The entire set is available on Concert Hall Long Playing Records, recorded by the composer. *(May-June 1968)*

Shostakovich: "Prelude and Fugue," Op. 87, No. 15. *Would you be kind enough to give me the tempos you recommend for the Shostakovich Prelude and Fugue, Op. 87, No. 15? Also, I would greatly appreciate your recommending an especially good book on Shostakovich.*

In his edition of the *24 Preludes and Fugues* by Shostakovich, Irwin Freundlich has added suggested metronome markings that I find very helpful. For Prelude No. 15 he suggests ♩. = 84 and for the Fugue ♩. = 188. These tempo markings conform very closely to the tempi chosen by the composer himself in his recording of the opus on Concert Hall Society Long Playing Records.

Four biographies have been written about Shostakovich: *Dmitri Shostakovich: The Man and his Work* by Ivan Martynov, translated by T. Guralsky and published by Greenwood Press, New York, 1947; *Dmitri Shostakovich: The Life and Background of a Soviet Composer* by Victor Seroff, published by Scholarly Press, New York, 1943; *Dmitri Shostakovich, Composer*, translated from the Russian by George Hanna and published by Lawrence and Wishart, London, 1959; and *Shostakovich* by Norman Kay, Oxford University Press, 1972. *(January 1974)*

Stravinsky: "Five Fingers." *I have a very good young student with sophisticated taste who enjoyed studying the* Five Fingers *by Igor Stravinsky. He would like to study more of Stravinsky's piano music, but I can't find anything else easy enough for him. Do you have any suggestions?*

Although Stravinsky's piano output was large he wrote very little for student pianists, and nothing else as easy as *Five Fingers*. However, two collections of his piano duets (both published by Omega Music) may be of interest. *Three Easy Pieces* contains "March," "Waltz," and "Polka"; the dedications (to Alfredo Casella, Erik Satie, and Diaghilev respectively) indicate the style of the pieces. *Five Easy Pieces* has an "Andante," "Espagnola," "Napolitana," "Balalaika," and "Gallop." The parts are not equal in difficulty: in *Three Easy Pieces* the secondo is the easier part, and in *Five Easy Pieces* it is the primo. It appears that Stravinsky intended for a young student to participate with a more advanced player. In this way a young musician can hear and perform music far more difficult than he could experience by himself. *(November 1978)*

Tcherepnin: "Ten Bagatelles," Op. 5. *I need advice on tempo markings for the* Ten Bagatelles, *Op. 5 by Tcherepnin. I have consulted several editions and the markings are quite different in each. Can you help?*

There are two very good recordings of the *Ten Bagatelles*, one by the composer himself and one by Margrit Weber, a fine artist whose close association with Tcherepnin makes her an authentic interpreter of his music. Tcherepnin's own performance is included in a record called *Tcherepnin Pieces for Piano* issued in France by l.M.E. Pathe Marconi (CVC 2124). The disc also includes *Sonata No. 1, Op. 22; Four Nostalgic Preludes,* Op. 23 and some miscellaneous pieces. Weber's record includes, in addition to the *Bagatelles*, Rachmaninoff's *Paganini-Rhapsody* and von Weber's *Concert Piece in F minor*. This recording is issued by Deutsche Grammaphon (138710).

The tempos at which the two artists play the various pieces are approximately the same for some of the *Bagatelles*, quite different for the others. A comparative listing may prove helpful. *(March 1969)*

	Tcherepnin	Weber
No. 1	96 ♩	92 ♩
No. 2	104 ♩	104 ♩
(meno mosso)	44 ♩.	56 ♩.
No. 3	108 ♩.	126 ♩.
No. 4	80 ♪	63 ♪
No. 5	66 ♩.	54 ♩.
No. 6	84 ♩	116 ♩
No. 7	152 ♩.	192 ♩.
No. 8	152 ♩	160 ♩.
No. 9	88 ♩	72 ♩
No. 10	168 ♩	152 ♩

Tcherepnin: "Ten Bagatelles," Op. 5. *Two of my students are playing the* Ten Bagatelles, *Op. 5 by Alexander Tcherepnin in a recital this spring. Could you send us some ideas for program notes? Also, is it true that there is an arrangement of the* Bagatelles *for piano and orchestra?*

Tcherepnin's *Bagatelles* rank among the most enduringly popular sets of piano pieces in 20th-century piano literature, and the story of their origin is charming. As a boy in Russia, Tcherepnin was in the habit of composing little piano pieces as birthday and Christmas presents for members of his family. Tcherepnin's father, Nikolay, affectionately called them "blochki" (little fleas) "because they contained melodic skips that were 'wide' and 'unpredictable'." Between the years 1912 and 1918, Alexander composed over a hundred of these short works. In 1922, at the suggestion of lsidor Philipp, with whom he studied in Paris, Tcherepnin compiled ten of the pieces into a set titled *Bagatelles* and first performed them that year in London at a recital that marked his Western debut. The set has appeared in many editions, including two American publications by Leeds in 1953 (available through CPP/Belwin) and by G. Schirmer in 1955 (available through Hal Leonard). The edition that Tcherepnin considered most authentic was the revised edition of 1964 published by Heugel in Paris.

Yes, there is a version for piano and orchestra, prepared by Tcherepnin himself in 1958-59, also published by Heugel. *(April 1987)*

Tcherepnin: "Bagatelles," Op. 5. *We have scheduled a performance of Tcherepnin's* Bagatelles *Opus 5 for Piano and Orchestra on our University Music Series, a series in which both faculty and students perform. To date, we have not been able to locate the orchestral score. If you have information on this we would greatly appreciate a reply.*

There are two orchestral versions of the Bagatelles. One is *Bagatelles for Piano and Orchestra*; the other is *Bagatelles for Piano and String Orchestra*. The scores and parts of both versions can be obtained through Theodore Presser Company, Presser Place, Bryn Mawr, Pennsylvania.

There is an excellent recording of this work by Margrit Weber, pianist with the Radio Symphony Orchestra of Berlin. It is available on Deutsche Grammaphon Gesellschaft. *(December 1972)*

Tcherepnin: "Chinese Bagatelles," Op. 51, No. 3. *I have taught the Tcherepnin Bagatelles, Op. 5 with great success to my high school and college students. Recently I heard of a second collection of bagatelles by Tcherepnin but have not been able to locate them. What is their Opus number, who publishes them, and are they of about the same difficulty as Op. 5?*

The only other set of bagatelles by Tcherepnin is the *Chinese Bagatelles*, Op. 51, No. 3, published in Paris by Heugel and available in America through Theodore Presser. The set contains 12 delightful pieces, nine of which are one page (or less) in length, and all less difficult than Op. 5. We use them for students of late intermediate/early advanced level and find them as satisfactory as any contemporary piano music available. I highly recommend them as an addition to your teaching repertoire, and as perfect preparation for the *Bagatelles*, Op. 5. *(January 1983)*

Tcherepnin: "Toccata." *Years ago, when I was in my teens and studying piano in Germany, I played a stunning piece by Alexander Tcherepnin called "Toccata." I have advanced students now who would enjoy and profit greatly from a study of this piece but I can't locate it. I have lost my own copy and not even a big city music store can obtain it for me. Do you know if it is still available and, if so, how to get it?*

Tcherepnin has composed two toccatas, Op. 1, No. 1 and Op. 20, No. 2. Op. 1, No. 1 is published by M.P. Belaieff and is available from C.F. Peters, sole agents for the Western Hemisphere for the entire Belaieff catalogue.

Op. 20, No.2 was originally copyrighted in 1925, but has been reissued under a 1974 copyright by N. Simrock, Hamburg-London (Elite Edition 3326), and is available in this country through Hal Leonard. Incidentally, it is dedicated to Rudolph Ganz.

In addition, you might like to look at his Canzona, Op. 28, which also was originally copyrighted in 1925 and has been reissued by N. Simrock (Elite Edition 3327). It, too, is available in this country through Hal Leonard. The Canzona is a very different kind of piece, and not as demanding technically as the Toccata. I recommend it highly for your advanced students. *(April 1975)*

Tcherepnin: "Technical Studies." *Years ago when I was studying in Germany, my teacher highly recommended a book of technical studies by Alexander Tcherepnin. I don't recall the exact title or publisher, and wonder if you know of the book, if it is still in print, and if you recommend it?*

The book is *Technical Studies for Pianoforte on the Five-Note Scale*, 53 by Alexander Tcherepnin, published by Edition Peters (No. It is still available and I highly recommend it for the development of advanced technique.

The famous French pedagogue, lsidor Philipp, who wrote the preface describes the collection with these words:

"There is nothing new under the sun, yet here is a novelty in the sphere of piano technique. Alexander Tcherepnin... has made a very valuable contribution to pedagogic piano literature by an original thesis on the so-called pentatonic scale.

"Double notes, octaves, arpeggios, stretches, chords, and scales are analyzed and prepared by special exercises which are quite invaluable for the pianist's greatest obstacle – the passing of the thumb.

"Any sound piano technique must depend on a thorough mastery of the thumb and it is used here in conjunction with the equal employment of all remaining fingers.

"We are convinced that this contribution by Alexander Tcherepnin will achieve the success it so thoroughly deserves."

I know of no other set of technical studies that emphasizes the passing of the fifth finger over the thumb to such an extent or in such way. For example, here is the first exercise: (July-August 1986)

Tchaikovsky: Complete Works. *I have been trying to get a list of Tchaikovsky's complete works for piano. I have inquired at various music stores and have looked through publisher's catalogues, but to no avail. Shouldn't there exist somewhere a list of major composers' works in complete form? I will appreciate any help you can give me on this.*

Grove's *Dictionary of Music and Musicians* contains a catalog of works for each of the major composers, as well as for many minor composers. I'm sure you will find a copy in the public library of any major city and in most college libraries.

In the case of Tchaikovsky (and many other composers), there is also a separately published catalog of complete works in which, of course, you will find the piano works listed by genre. In Tchaikovsky's case the catalog is called Systematisches Verzeichnis der Werke von Pjotr Iljitsch Tchaikowsky, published in 1973 by Hans Sikorski, Hamburg, Germany (Ed. Nr. 975). As its title indicates, it is a systematic catalog of the complete works, including stage works, vocal music, instrumental music (and this includes the piano catalogue), arrangements and even his literary works and editions. *(February 1974)*

Composer Articles

Dello Joio, Norman (1913-). *Sometime ago you wrote articles on Tcherepnin and Persichetti. I left them on my reading table and found students not only reading them, but discussing them together. Could you do more of this? If so, will you please begin with Norman Dello Joio? I have used his* Family Album *and* Five Images *with great success, ever since you first recommended them. We would like to know more about Dello Joio, what else he has composed for piano, what else he does besides composing, what he looks like, etc.*

I think Norman Dello Joio will be of great interest to all piano teachers and students, and I am happy to devote this month's column to providing some of the information you request.

I'll begin by answering your last question: "What else does he do besides composing?" Dello Joio is active in many phases of music in addition to his most important role as a leading American composer. For example, in 1964, the U.S. State Department sent him to Russia, Romania, and Bulgaria on a cultural exchange program. The following year, the U.S. Office of Education invited him to join the Research Advisory Council, and later he was the U.S. representative to the Festival of the Arts of this Century held in Hawaii. Mr. Dello Joio is also Chairman of the Policy Committee for the Contemporary Music Project, administered by the Music Educator's National Conference, under a grant from the Ford Foundation. Among its functions is the placing of young composers in school systems throughout the country to write for high school orchestras, bands, and choruses. It has also established six institutes in Comprehensive Musicianship for teachers, involving thirty colleges and universities across the country.

Dello Joio is also a teacher. For many years he was on the faculty of Sarah Lawrence College and later, Professor of Composition at the Mannes College of Music in New York City.

Dello Joio has written prolifically for the orchestra, chamber ensemble, chorus, voice, and piano, and has also written music for band, for organ, for ballet, and three operas. His most recent piano compositions include "Capriccio (on the interval of a second)," "Christmas Music," for piano duet, and "Lyric Pieces for the Young." All are published by E.B. Marks. Recently Dello Joio made choral arrangements of the seven carols he had previously arrange as "Christmas Music," making use of the duets as accompaniments, almost without change. The duet book was so well received by piano teachers that many will be glad to know of this new edition of the same material for chorus and piano duet. Each of the seven carols will be published separately.

In addition to the *Five Images* and the *Family Album* you mention (both published by E.B. Marks), Dello Joio has also composed the following music for piano:

Aria and Toccata for Two Pianos*	Carl Fischer
Night Song (published as part of *American Contemporary Composers of Today*)	E.B. Marks
Nocturne in E*	Carl Fischer
Nocturne in F#*	Carl Fischer
Prelude to a Young Dancer*	G. Schirmer
Prelude to a Young Musician*	G. Schirmer
Sonata No. 1*	Hargail Music Press
Sonata No. 2*	G. Schirmer
Sonata No. 3*	Carl Fischer
Suite* from the ballet *On Stage*	G. Schirmer
Suite for Piano*	G. Schirmer
Suite for the Young	E.B. Marks

*Performing rights non-exclusively licensed by BMI

Dello Joio is descended from three generations of leading Italian organists. His father, Casimir, came to America in the early 1900s and became the organist at Our Lady of Mount Carmel Church in New York. The composer was born in New York City on January 24, 1913. His early musical training was under his father's direction, and he showed remarkable aptitude and facility from the start. At the age of 14 he was appointed organist and choir director of the Star of the Sea Church on City Island!

Later he studied organ with his godfather, Pietro Yon, who for many years served as organist of St. Patrick's Cathedral in New York. After three years of composition in the Juilliard Graduate School, Dello Joio went to the Yale School of Music to study with Paul Hindemith.

Since that time his accomplishments as one of America's leading composers have brought him limitless rewards. In 1948, his *Variations, Chaconne and Finale* were introduced by Bruno Walter and the New York Philharmonic and received the New York Music Critics Circle Award as the outstanding new orchestral work of that season. He won the same award again in 1960 for his opera, The Triumph of St. Joan. A work for string orchestra, Meditations on Ecclesiastes brought him the Pulitzer Prize for Music in 1957, and his score for the NBC-TV News Special on the Louvre, Scenes from the Louvre, received the Lancaster Symphony Composers Award for 1967.

In an article in the Musical Quarterly (April, 1962), music critic Edward Downes wrote, "Among established composers of serious music in this country, Norman Dello Joio is outstanding for an outgoing directness of expression and a simplicity of manner, if not always of means, which have an intentionally broad appeal. A strong melodic vein, rhythmic vitality, a relatively restrained harmonic vocabulary, an infectious brio and freshness of invention, are among the earmarks of his style. Inseparable from this style is Dello Joio's conviction, resembling almost an ethical attitude, that his music should communicate with a broad contemporary public — not merely with an alert avant-garde, not with a few fellow composers, not with some hypothetical future public, small or large. The style in which this conviction is expressed sets Dello Joio somewhat apart from a majority of his peers." *(December 1971)*

Ferandez, Lorenzo (1897-1948). *I am planning to have my students give an all-Spanish program this fall and want to include some biographical information about the composers in the printed program. Could you tell me something about Lorenzo Fernandez?*

Oscar Lorenzo Fernandez was not Spanish but Brazilian. He was in Rio de Janiero on November 4, 1897, and died there on August 26, 1948. He was well known as composer, conductor, and pianist in his own country and other Latin American countries and for years served as professor at the Instituto Nacionale de Musica in Rio. His works are marked by a strongly national style, derived from Brazilian folksongs. *(December 1982)*

Grovlez, Maykapar, Dumesnil. *I would like to ask you whether there is any textbook or review concerning Gabriel Grovlez who composed "L'Almanach aux images" or "A Child's Garden"? I would also like to have information concerning Maykapar. I only know he is a Russian composer. Is there any textbook published by Maurice Dumesnil, who often wrote articles in* The Etude?

Gabriel Grovlez, a French conductor, writer, and composer, was born in Lille on April 4, 1879 and died in Paris on October 20, 1944. He was for some years conductor of the Paris Opera and also conducted at the Chicago Opera during two seasons. He composed operas, symphonic poems, string pieces, more than 50 songs, and many piano pieces, including the "A Child's Garden" to which you refer. He was also an editor of Rameau's works and the author of a book entitled *Introduction to Orchestration*, published in Paris in 1944.

Samuil Moysseyevitch Maykapar was a Russian pianist, composer, and teacher who was born in Taganrog on December 18, 1867 and died in Leningrad on May 8, 1938. For 20 years he was professor of piano at the St. Petersburg Conservatory. His compositions are limited almost exclusively to piano works, and he was most successful in miniature forms. Among other works he composed "Biriulki" (a suite of 26 pieces), "Twenty Four Miniatures," "The Marionette Theater" (an album of seven pieces), two sonatinas, and various piano studies and exercises. In addition he was author of two books, *The Musical Ear* (Moscow, 1900) and *The Years of Study and of Musical Activity* (Moscow, 1938); the latter is partly autobiographical.

Dumesnil's publications include *An Amazing Journey* (1932), *How to Play and Teach Debussy* (1933), and *Claude Debussy, Master of Dreams* (1940). As I am sure you know, Dumesnil was a student of Debussy and became a specialist in the performance and teaching of Debussy's piano music. *(February 1975)*

Hanon, Charles-Louis (1819-1900). *I have checked two Oxford editions and many other reference books, but can find no background information on the composer C.L. Hanon. Can you give me any information about him?*

Charles-Louis Hanon (1819-1900) was a French pianist and pedagogue, remembered primarily for his book of musical exercises, *The Virtuoso Pianist*. While not to be ranked as a great composer, he was undoubtedly, next to Czerny, the best-known composer of piano exercises in the 19th century, and his *Virtuoso Pianist* has been used by countless diligent piano students the world over.

Hanon also wrote a set of 50 piano pieces called *Elementary Method for Piano* and was the editor of a useful collection of *Excerpts from the Major Works of the Great Masters*. He composed some church music but no piano repertoire as such. *(November 1979)*

Kuhlau, Friedrich (1786-1832). *Will you please give a brief biography of Friedrich Kuhlau? He is not listed in any of my encyclopedias, and I can't afford to buy Baker's Dictionary of Music and Musicians.*

Kuhlau was born in Germany in 1786 and died in Denmark in 1832. To escape conscription into the army, he fled to Copenhagen where he became a flutist in the royal orchestra and a flute and piano teacher. He composed a series of operas, music for violin, flute, and many sonatas and sonatinas for piano students.

Concerning the unaffordability of Baker's, you might try the solution that a small group of teachers related to me in a recent letter. They have begun a communal reference library. They pooled their resources to buy reference books that they all needed but which none could individually afford.

Their library began with a single volume, *The Harvard Dictionary of Music*, and now includes Hinson's *Guide to the Pianist's Repertoire*, and Baker's *Biographical Dictionary of Music and Musicians*. The books are now kept at one teacher's home or studio for three months, then rotated to the others every three months. Books are available to members at all times. *(July/August 1984)*

LaMontaine, John (1920-). *Will you include in your column something about John LaMontaine? The* Child's Picture Book *has caught the fancy of many of my students. I have had students who played the whole collection on a recital, and I have also presented a recital in which the whole collection was performed, but with a different student playing each piece.*

My students have asked me to ask you the following questions. Is he a pianist? What, if any, awards has he won? (this looms very important in their young lives.) What else has he composed? What does he look like? I think what they really want to know is what is he like. I assume you know him since he has written for the Library.

Your request arrived just as Mr. LaMontaine's latest work, *Wilderness Journal*, was being premiered in Washington, D.C. A symphony for bass-baritone, organ, and orchestra, it was commissioned for the dedication of the Filene Organ at Kennedy Center.

Yes, I do know John LaMontaine personally, and for reasons both personal and professional it is a pleasure to answer your question. To do justice to LaMontaine, I will need to answer in greater length than usual, so will devote the entire column to this exceptional man who is one of America's most gifted composers.

You asked if he is a pianist. Indeed he is! If I tell you that he was the pianist and clavecinist for the NBC Symphony under Toscanini for four years you'll get an instant picture of the quality of his pianism. Your own ears will tell you still more. Because of your interest in his *Child's Picture Book*, I suggest that you hear his own recording of it on Dorian records, a recording that also includes his *Toccata* (a stunning piece for early advanced students), a piano sonata of his own, and the Chopin *Sonata in B-flat minor*.

Don't apologize for your students' questions on awards. I'm sure adult readers will be just as interested in them. In LaMontaine's case they are really too numerous to list here, but I will mention a few of most significant ones. He received the Pulitzer Prize in 1959 for his Concerto for Piano and Orchestra, Op. 9. In 1961 he wrote the first work ever commissioned in honor of a presidential inauguration, *From Sea to Shining Sea*, which was performed at the Inaugural Concert for President and Mrs. John F. Kennedy. He was the recipient of two Guggenheim Fellowships and commissions from both the Ford Foundation and the Koussevitsky Foundation, and now this latest commission for the dedication of the new organ at Kennedy Center.

LaMontaine was born and grew up in Oak Park, Illinois and had his early musical training with Chicago teachers, especially at the American Conservatory with Stella Roberts. He apparently knew from earliest boyhood that he would be a composer. He laughs with delight as he recounts his early forays to the public library to study books on composing and composers, and the earnestness with which, at age 10 or so, he explained to the librarian that he was a composer, too.

He attended Eastman School where he studied with Bernard Rogers and Howard Hanson, and he has also studied with Bernard Wagenaar and Nadia Boulanger.

Perhaps the most pleasant thing about Mr. LaMontaine is that his personal gifts are as rare and precious as his musical ones. The quality that leaps to mind whenever one thinks of him is his outpouring of joy at just being alive. He walks miles every day, with apparently boundless energy. He announces his arrival with a gay, whistled version of the Siegfried motiv. He rolls out of bed in the morning and often finds himself at the piano on his way to the kitchen for breakfast. He is a delightful host and a gourmet cook, a happy, well-rounded, well-read, well-disciplined creative spirit.

In the last ten years he has produced a great deal of music, and complete list of his piano works appears at the end of this column. But two major works of the last decade are perhaps most representative, both of the artist and of the man. The first of these may be familiar to you and your students already, for it has been nationally televised during several Christmas seasons. It is a trilogy of Christmas operas: "Novellis, Novellis" (1961), "The Shephardes Playe" (1967) and "Erode the Greate" (1970), all commissioned by and premiered at the National Cathedral in Washington, D.C. The spirit of this project is best described in the composer's own words:

> "The project of a trilogy of Christmas operas began almost inadvertently in May 1958, while I was searching for a suitable text for the Christmas carol that I traditionally compose each year for my friends... l chanced upon the remarkable book by Thomas Sharp, Dissertation on the Pageants or Dramatic Mysteries, Anciently performed at Coventry, by the Trading Companies of that City (1825). Specifically the words that ignited me and the entire project were:

> > *A ha! now ys cum the cyme*
> > *That old fathurs hath told*
> > *Thatt in the wynturs nyght soo cold*
> > *A chyld of meydyñ borne be he wold*
> > *In whom all profeciys schalbe fullfyld.*

I copied the words on the back of a receipt for groceries, and they became my carol for that year. They have haunted my life ever since.

> "Concerning the music itself, the only guiding principle has been that of appropriateness. I did not try to impose a technique or style upon the

material, but rather to find, as nearly as I could, its own true expression. It seemed to me that the people who first wrote and acted out medieval miracle plays were very close to creating for themselves the first true opera.

"Perhaps it was presumptuous to try to bring all these elements together to write the opera that they were so close to writing for themselves, but the challenge fed my imagination. My greatest help was to be guided constantly by their own aim, which was quite clearly the portrayal of plain people whose lives were transformed by a miracle."

In reviewing the middle of the three operas, "The Shephardes Playe," in the Washington Post, December 28, 1967, critic Paul Hume wrote, "One of the loveliest moments in the history of music in the theater occurred last night in... John LaMontaines's new Christmas pageant opera... there is a mood of natural honest beauty that marks the whole radiant piece... Far beyond the sum of the individual parts, John LaMontaine has created a work of special impact because of the power of its inner meaning. It is hard to think of a way of marking the Christmas season that might more vividly bring home its central message."

In his latest major work, *Wilderness Journal*, John LaMontaine has what Paul Hume has called, "the latest chapter in the enduring love affair between nature and music." It is a symphony for bass-baritone, organ, and orchestra, based on texts from the *Essays and Journals* of Henry David Thoreau. Again, the inception of the project is described in the composer's own words:

"It seemed to me that to celebrate a noble undertaking like the planning and building of Kennedy Center a work of large design and breadth of purpose was needed.

"I began by reading again *Walden* and the other published essays of Thoreau, and finally launched into the three million words of Thoreau's Journals — an absorbing task not yet completed. From these studies grew a huge shelf of texts that I felt suitable for setting to music. You cannot deal with Thoreau unless you deal with his sentences.

"My rediscovery of Eliot Porter's magnificent photographs in the Sierra Club book *In Wildness is the Preservation of the World* was the crystallizing factor. Could I find an imaginative realization of the aural aspect of Thoreau's words, as Porter had found a rich realization of their visual aspect?

"Using four of the texts chosen by Porter, I added eight others, drawn always to those that would provide vivid occasion for music and give some glimpse of the depth, breadth, humor, and sheer variety of Thoreau's thought. The twelve songs, together with the movements for organ, form a Symphony of fifteen movements.

"My chief joy in all this has been in search for musical means to convey the delight and sense of discovery that Thoreau found in nature. My chief reward has been in allying myself, as Eliot Porter did, with Thoreau's central idea that 'in wildness is the preservation of the World.'"

I hope that together LaMontaine and I have succeeded in giving some picture of the artist and the man.

LaMontaine's compositions include works for strings, orchestra, opera, and voice. Among his works for voice and orchestra are two exquisite song cycles, *Songs of the Rose of Sharon*, premiered by Leontyne Price and the National Symphony Orchestra and *Fragments from the Song of Songs*, premiered by Adele Addison and the New York Philharmonic. His piano works include the following:

Toccata for Piano, Op. 1 (Braude Brothers)
Sonata for Piano, Op. 3 (Carl Fischer)
A Child's Picture Book, Op. 7 (Braude Brothers)
Concerto for Piano and Orchestra, Op. 9 (Galaxy)
Twelve Relationships (set of canons), Op. 10 (Carl Fischer)
Fuguing Set for Piano, Op. 14 (Carl Fischer)
Six Dance Preludes for Piano, Op. 18 (Broude Brothers)
Sonata for Piano, Four Hands, Op. 25 (Theodore Presser)
Copycats (canons for young pianists), Op. 26 (Fredonia Press)
Birds of Paradise (piano and orchestra), Op. 34 (Carl Fischer)
Sparklers (Summy-Birchard)
(*February 1973*)

Mendelssohn, Fanny (1805-1847). *My music teacher's group is making a study of women composers, past and present. We have heard that Fanny Mendelssohn, Felix's sister, composed some published music, but we have not been able to locate it. Can you help us find it and tell us a little about Fanny and her music?*

You will find Fanny cross-referenced in *Baker's Biographical Dictionary of Music and Musicians* under Mendelssohn and also under Hensel, her married name. *Baker's* offers a brief paragraph about her, but you can learn a great deal more about her in any of the biographies about Felix. They had a particularly close personal relationship and each played an important part in the other's musical development. Fanny was born in 1805, four years before the birth of her famous brother. Of the four Mendelssohn children, only Fanny and Felix showed musical talent at an early age, so they received special musical instruction throughout their childhood and adolescence. Fanny studied piano with her mother, then with Ludwig Berger and Ignaz Moscheles, and theory with Carl Friedrich Zeiter. Zeiter wrote in a letter to

Goethe that Fanny "plays as well as any man."

After a long battle, Felix's parents allowed him to take up music as a profession, but they never even considered a career for Fanny. In 1829 she married Wilhelm Hensel, a painter at the royal court of Prussia. The couple had one son, Sebastian. Although her primary role was as wife and mother, Fanny played the piano at a professional level and composed songs and piano music all her life. She died suddenly in 1847, shortly before her 42nd birthday. Felix, desolated, died a few months later.

Fanny's first published compositions appeared in 1827, but under her brother's name. In his first collections of lieder, Op. 8 and 9, three songs in each volume are Fanny's. Felix was on tour at the time and gave Fanny sole responsibility of selecting from among his compositions and hers. When the choices were sent to him, he wrote of her songs, "... they are more beautiful than words can describe. I know no better music than this."

Shortly after her marriage, Fanny tried her hand at large-scale works — several cantatas, one overture, and a string quartet. Corrections by Felix appear throughout the manuscripts. After about 1835 she limited herself to songs and piano pieces which seem to have been her natural milieu. Shortly before her death, Bote and Bock (Berlin) published three volumes of her compositions. After her death, her family had several additional songs and piano pieces published and in 1850 Breitkopf and Hartel (Leipzig) issued a memorial edition of her works in several volumes.

We are fortunate that in 1986 G. Henle released a new edition of 11 of her previously unpublished piano pieces, with a preface and critical comments by Rudolf Elvern and fingering by Hans-Martin Theopold. The music is a delightful addition to Romantic piano repertoire in the style of Felix Mendelssohn. It is at an early advanced level of difficulty, lyric, and bravura by turn, rather reminiscent of Felix's "Song without Words." The first two pieces, both marked "Allegro moderato" and "Andante cantabile" are titled "Practice Pieces." The third and fourth are unmarked and untitled. The fifth is a lush "Noturno" and the sixth an expressive "Departure from Rome." The seventh and eighth are untitled, respectively marked "Allegro molto" and "Andante cantabile." The ninth, marked "Andante espressivo," bears the Romantic title, "O Dream of Youth, O Golden Star." The tenth and eleventh are untitled, respectively marked "Allegretto" and "Allegro vivace." This rich, effective, accessible recital music deserves to be widely known and used. (*May-June 1984*)

Persichetti, Vincent (1915-). *I have taught* Parades *and the* Little Book *by Vincent Persichetti with great success, ever since you introduced them in a summer study course several years ago. Could you provide me with a complete, graded list of his piano compositions? Also, any information about Mr. Persichetti himself would be of great interest to me and to my students.*

Vincent Persichetti is one of America's most interesting, prolific, and versatile composers. His major works, in almost every medium, are highly regarded and widely performed, both here and abroad. Over eighty of his compositions have been published and many are also available on records.

Persichetti was born in Philadelphia on June 6, 1915, and still makes his home there today. He began music lessons at an early age, and by the time he was eleven was already appearing as piano soloist with local orchestras. At the age of 15 he was appointed organist of St. Mark's Reformed Church in Philadelphia.

He is a graduate of Combs College, the Curtis Institute, and the Philadelphia Conservatory of Music, and has studied piano with Olga Samaroff, composing with Paul Nordoff and Roy Harris, and conducting with Fritz Reiner.

In addition to composing, conducting, and frequent appearances as piano soloist (or, with his wife, as duo-pianist), Persichetti has had a significant career as a teacher. For 20 years he was head of the composition department of the Philadelphia Conservatory. In 1947 he joined the faculty of the Juilliard School of Music in New York where he is presently head of the composition department. In the classroom he is a brilliant and exuberant teacher, whose ability to illustrate, at the keyboard and from memory, rapid-fire examples from the entire literature of music, is legendary.

Two full-time careers would be sufficient for most men, but Persichetti's seemingly limitless energies have ranged even farther. Since 1952 he has been director of publications at the Elkan-Vogel Company in Philadelphia and frequently serves as music critic for leading journals. In addition he is the author of three books: *William Schuman*, G. Schirmer, New York, 1954; *Twentieth-Century Harmony, Creative Aspects and Practice*, W.W. Norton, New York, 1961; and Essays on *Twentieth-Century Choral Music*, University of Oklahoma Press, 1963.

As a composer, Persichetti has written extensively for orchestra, chamber ensemble, voice, piano, miscellaneous solo instruments, band, and chorus. Not only is his contribution to the literature of modern music great, but he has made a significant mastery of all the techniques and idioms of twentieth-century music. By joining no particular "camp," he has avoided the narrowness and stylistic limitations of many of his contemporaries. His output is eclectic in the best sense, and his individual achievement is a synthesis, not only of twentieth-century styles, but of our entire musical heritage. His piano works are among his finest, suited to the instrument as only a virtuoso pianist (who is also a virtuoso composer) could make them. *(May-June 1984)*

Tcherepnin, Alexander (1899-1977). There have been a number of questions recently about Alexander Tcherepnin, whose many accessible pieces have endeared him to thousands of piano teachers and students.

Teachers write to ask where he is now living and what he is doing, to ask if he has written new piano pieces for children, or sometimes to request a complete list of his piano compositions.

Children ask for his address so that they can write him directly, asking for his picture, autograph, or even his advice on the interpretation of his pieces which they are studying.

This constant testimony to the popularity of his music is heart-warming, and proves again the universal appeal of greatness, even when it has been distilled into miniature for elementary and intermediate piano students.

There is hardly room here to answer adequately the questions about Mr. Tcherepnin which we receive. But it is an opportune time to try, for only last year Tcherepnin's place in twentieth-century music was recognized by his native Russia in a dramatic way. He received an official invitation from the Union of Soviet Composers to Russia, where he appeared performing his own piano music with orchestra and in solo recital. The only other Russian emigre composer to be so honored by his country is Stravinsky.

Earlier this season I received a letter from Mr. Tcherepnin about this tour, which he has granted permission to reprint here. Nothing will give the reader a better insight into Alexander Tcherepnin, the man, than these excerpts.

> "Perhaps the most important event in my life (both sentimentally and artistically) was a concert tour in the Soviet Union to which I was invited by the Union of Composers of the U.S.S.R., to which my wife was also officially invited, and which took place last May. The reception was touching, warm, spontaneous, and generous. I performed my compositions in recitals and with orchestras in Moscow, in Thilisi, and in my home town, Leningrad.

> "It was the first time in 49 years that I was in the country of my origin. Not only did I feel as if I had never left Leningrad, where in the center of the city nothing has changed, and I felt familiar with every corner, but I also visited my old home where I lived with my dear parents from the age of 7 to

the age of 19 (where, incidentally, the "Bagatelles," "Sonatine Romantique," "Episodes," "First Piano Sonata," etc. were composed), visited my room where I had my piano, my desk, and the icon in the corner, to which I used to pray to become a composer, finding it not changed since the time I left, and amazed that the new inhabitant, a young girl, also has an icon in the same right corner of the room in which, according to the Russian tradition, the icon to which one prays is to be placed.

"I met with Russian composers of all generations, became aware of the tremendous progress in education, both general and musical, and at the end of my stay in Moscow, on the eve of my departure, attended a concert of my compositions performed by Soviet artists in my honor. Somehow I felt like Simeon, ready to say, 'Lord, now lettest thou thy servant depart in peace, according to thy word,' but on the other hand this contact with the country of my origin gave me a new stimulus to live, to create, and to work.

"The idea to serve people by their art, to unite people by means of music, that animates my Russian colleagues, was and is always my idea. The only difference is that this attitude in my case is not limited to one country, but to the whole humanity, and that Iam trying to serve people by my music and activities, wherever I am, and especially in the U.S.A., of which I am proud to be a citizen. "The profession of a musician — composer, performer, pedagogue — in my mind is not just a profession, but rather a mission, similar to that of a priest. I felt it from the very beginning of my life, and feel it as strongly now. Music unites people. It "fixes" a particle of time. Thirteen-and-a-half minutes of Bach's *Passacaglia*, for instance, has fixed thirteen-and-a-half minutes of Bach's life, of Bach's time; it fixes also thirteen-and-a-half minutes of our time, that we live again at each hearing. Music is the only art that allows us to return back in time, to revive the past. The music which fixes the present is the music that will live in the future, if the composer was able to present in a work of art that which he has absorbed from the community in which he lives. The importance that mu sic has taken in the last three or four decades (since the invention of radio and records) in our culture, makes the composer, performer, pedagogue of today more responsible than ever. Music has to bring to people a positive message. Rather than new "words," new "thoughts" are needed in music. One has to speak the musical language that can be understood by music-eager people. One should not flatter the bad taste of people, but also should not indulge in bolstering one's own ego by producing musical puzzles. In this I believe, and this is how I try to compose."

The reader now knows from the composer's own pen a great deal about Alexander Tcherepnin, the man and the musician. Perhaps a few more facts, both biographical and musical, will help to enlarge this picture.

Tcherpnin's colorful childhood in Russia, in a home dominated by music, art, and religion, is charmingly described (from his own letters to us) in the biographies that Adelle DeLeeuw prepared for our *Contemporary Piano Literature* series.

His early career, too, is well documented, from the time in 1921 when he made Paris the springboard for extensive concertizing throughout Europe, the United States, and the Far East. His prodigious stream of compositions during this period would be amazing for a man who sat at home and did nothing but compose. But even when Tcherepnin's life was lived almost entirely out of suitcases and in concert halls, he composed without any let-up in quantity or quality; operas, ballets, works for orchestra, chamber music of all sorts, songs for chorus and for solo voice, and an enormous output for his own instrument, the piano.

After years of touring he decided to settle and work among us. He not only concertized and conducted all over this country, but for 15 years taught composition at DePaul University in Chicago. In 1958 he became a United Stated citizen, which means that his delightful children's pieces may be used for compositions and festivals requiring works by American composers.

Since his retirement from DePaul in 1964, Tcherepnin's pace has only increased. He and his wife divide their time between New York and Paris, where an apartment in each city, charmingly decorated with artistic and personal memorabilia, awaits their coming half the year. Springing to life on their arrival, the rooms are suddenly filled with music, laughter, animated conversation, the comings and goings of musical greats or just plain friends. But a home for Tcherepnin is still a springboard, and whether it is New York or Paris, he is always up and away, for a solo recital, an appearance with an orchestra (as pianist or conductor), or a lecture.

During an afternoon spent with Mr. and Mrs. Tcherepnin in their New York apartment recently, I learned of his most recent activities. In addition to the memorable journey to his homeland, Tcherepnin recently performed his *Piano Concerto No. 5* and his *Triple Concerto* in Paris, recorded some of his piano music for the BBC in London and lectured at the Summer School in Dartington (England) where he also performed his Piano Quintet with the Delme Quartet. In Munich he conducted his *Suite, Op. 87* with the Bavarian Radio Symphony Orchestra and performed the *Piano Concerto No. 5* with Rafael Kubelik. He lectured at the Austrian Music Society and recorded some of his piano music for the Austrian Radio in Vienna. In New York, an entire program of the American String Quartet was devoted to Tcherepnin's works, with the composer at the piano. Alexander

Tcherepnin is working on *Symphony No. 5*, commissioned by the Koussevitsky Foundation, and on the score for a BBC production of Tolstoy's Ivan the Fool, to be produced in London with Peter Ustinov as narrator.

Unfortunately, Tcherepnin's only recent piano music for children, a book of duets for teacher and student called *Exploring*, is not presently available. However, a *First Suite in C* and *Second Suite in C*, both very easy, are available in this country through Presser.

His most recent piano compositions include *Second Piano Sonata*, commissioned by the Berlin Festival in 1961, *Piano Concerto No. 5*, commissioned in 1963 by the Berlin Festival, and *Piano Concerto No. 6*, just published but not performed; all are available in this country through Boosey & Hawkes. Of particular interest to teachers is the fact that the popular set of *Bagatelles, Op. 5* is now available through Presser with a delightful orchestral accompaniment. The orchestral version has been recorded by Margrit Weber and the Berlin Radio Symphony Orchestra (Deutsche Grammophon 18710).

Tcherepnin was particularly excited about a new booklet (in French), just received that day from Boosey & Hawkes in Paris, describes the lives and works of the Tcherepnin "dynasty." Tcherepnin's father Nikolai was a student of Rimsky-Korsakov and became a famous Russian composer and conductor. For many years the elder Tcherepnin served as conductor of the famous Diaghileff Ballet in Paris, and illustrations of the original ballet sets now decorate his son's New York apartment.

Famous fathers of famous sons are not uncommon in the music world. But how often does such a sustained creative effort extend to a third generation? Mr. and Mrs. Tcherepnin have three sons: Peter, Serge, and Ivan. Taught piano by their mother (Lee Hsien Ming was one of China's finest women pianists when she met and married Alexander Tcherepnin) and composition by their father, Serge and Ivan are already published composers, making their own mark. Peter? A stock broker!

On January 15, the Tcherepnins left New York for three months in Europe, where Alexander continues his seemingly tireless round of public appearances. Looking back on his first youthful public performances, Tcherepnin once said, "I felt natural and happy on stage, and never experienced any stage fright. On the contrary, I was always longing to be on the stage, was delighted to perform on any occasion; and I continue to feel exactly the same now."

From the beginning, it seems, Alexander Tcherepnin was destined to be what he became – a brilliant concert pianist, a distinguished composer, and a great human being. On January 21, somewhere in England, he celebrated his 69th birthday. As he enters his 70th year, he is still in full possession of his artistic and creative powers, still boyishly eager and excited every time he ascends the concert stage, still experimenting and growing as a composer, still a warm, buoyant, humble, and devoutly religious servant of music and of mankind.

Isn't it wonderful that a composer of this dimension should have spent the time and engaged in the exacting discipline to fashion per· feet little gems for young piano students, so that at the beginning of their artistic experience they could encounter, in miniature, one of the great artistic expressions of our time? [Tcherepnin died in 1977.] *(March 1968)*

Zabrack, Harold (1929-1995) *I have recently discovered* Preludes for Piano *by Harold Zabrack and am enjoying teaching them to a gifted high school student. I have not been able to learn anything about Zabrack and do not find him listed in Baker's Biographical Dictionary of Music and Musicians. Is he primarily a composer? Has he written other music for piano?*

I seldom receive a question as easy to answer as this one, for Harold Zabrack is one of my colleagues at Westminster Choir College. Yes, he is primarily a composer (when composing), but is also primarily a pianist (when giving concerts) and primarily a teacher (when teaching). He is continually active in all three areas, bringing to each enormous talent, unbelievable energy, and ebullient enthusiasm.

You will find Harold Zabrack in the latest (sixth) edition of *Baker's Biographical Dictionary of Music and Musicians.* He was born in St. Louis and educated at the Chicago Musical College where he studied with Rudolf Ganz. Later he studied composition with Nadia Boulanger at Fontainebleau and in 1957-59 held a Fulbright Fellowship for study in Europe. He toured Germany for the U.S. State Department and was a Diploma winner at the International Piano Competition in Munich. Zabrack has performed widely both here and abroad. His First Piano Concerto was commissioned by the St. Louis Symphony, and he appeared as soloist with the Milwaukee Symphony Orchestra in the world premiere of his Symphonic Variations for Piano and Orchestra. On several occasions he has been in residence as a composer at the MacDowell Colony, and has received awards from ASCAP every year since 1975.

Harold Zabrack presently divides his time between his studio in Baltimore and his position as professor of music at Westminster Choir College.

His published piano compositions include a collection of eight difficult piano solos, including Dialogue, Elegy for the Left Hand, Etude, Introspection, Landscape, Prelude, Quasi Improvisation, Toccata; three virtuosic etudes, one in thirds and two in octaves; six delightful Preludes in a conservative contemporary style, ideal for early advanced high school students; Piano Sonata No. 1, a demanding bravura work in four movements: Allegro con brio; Adagio espressivo; Interlude; Finale; Piano Sonata No. 2, an equally demanding, equally brilliant work in three movements: Allegro moderato; Andante espressivo; Allegro con brio; Piano Variations, a charming and simple theme with 11 moderately difficult variations that advanced high school students can handle; and Scherzo: Hommage a Prokofiev, a popular and engaging work, reminiscent of Prokofiev, that early advanced high school students can play effectively. There is also a four-hand version of this piece. *(January 1986)*

Special Purpose Pieces

Ensemble standards. *I have just finished a semester's tour of music schools and made a surprising discovery: overall, students' solo performances exceeded my expectations, but their ensemble playing was far below what I had anticipated. This was true for students of all ages, from preparatory department students to college piano majors. Even the best soloists were a disappointment when they collaborated in music for four hands. Would you give the gist of a series of illustrated lectures you gave on ensemble music a number of years ago?*

As teachers we need to recognize that a beautiful performance of an ensemble piece requires the same thought and effort as a solo performance, times two. It requires another step as well: putting together two students' minds, ears, hands, and musicianship in the performance of a single work. This extra step, which I call togetherness, is an additional challenge that in no way replaces any other step.

I think the problem of poor ensemble performance may begin, consciously or unconsciously, in the minds of students who think, "If I don't get off to a good start, my partner will carry the piece," or, "My partner will cover up any mistakes I make," or, "I can rely on my partner to provide the inspiration."

Such attitudes inevitably produce poor ensemble performances. What's more, if these attitudes prevail, one of the fundamental values of ensemble playing is lost — the awareness that if one student misses, both miss. Each student needs to feel completely responsible not only for his part and the whole score but also to his partner.

The difference between teaching ensemble music and teaching solo repertoire is twofold. There are two students performing one piece, and each part needs the same thought and care that a solo requires. In addition, everyone has to remember that neither performer is a soloist; both have to work together to create a musical whole.

This blending of prima and secondo requires teachers and students to develop a new level of listening skills. From a pedagogical point of view, this is one of the significant benefits both of playing and of teaching duets. Ensemble performance is demanding business. Fortunately, it is so rewarding that students will do anything to be able to play more duets.

Learning to listen and play together should begin early in the first year of study, in solos that the beginner can play with teacher accompaniment. Even at the start, students should become thoroughly familiar with both their own part and the sound of the teacher's accompaniment. Play the accompaniment for them without the solo part, calling their attention to its color, harmony, and overall style. If the accompaniment's rhythm patterns differ from those of the solo, point them out, making the student aware of how the teacher's part against the longer note values that the student is sustaining in his part.

Put the duet together only when each student has achieved a beautiful performance with the teacher playing the other part. This is a must until students have played many duets over a period of several years. The students' first practice together should be a big moment, after details of tempo, dynamics, and phrasing have been carefully worked out.

Each student should learn both parts, so that he knows his partner's part as well as he knows his own. In rehearsals have them exchange parts until each is completely secure with both primo and secondo. Of course this does not apply to duets in which the parts are of equal difficulty.

Pairs of young students, both at elementary and intermediate levels, should play many duets together prior to playing together in public. An ability to perform well with a partner is not something students are born with or that happens for a one-time occasion.

Listen to the duets from a distance, whether in a small studio or a large one. In a recital hall always listen from the back of the room. Balance between melody and accompaniment is a sensitive matter, especially if the accompaniment is written above the melody, or if the melody is in an inner voice.

Things that are most apt to go wrong in student performances are twice as apt to go wrong in ensemble playing. Students often infect each other; a student who is inclined to rush, for example, may push a normally steady partner into a faster and faster tempo. A student who tends to over-ritard endings may cause a partner to get slower and slower as the end approaches. Dynamic contrasts are particularly vulnerable in ensemble performance and need to be jealously guarded so that piano doesn't become mezzoforte or mezzoforte become fortissimo.

Generally speaking, ensemble music needs less pedal than solo music. Even if pedal is carefully indicated, the teacher should question whether or not it is right for these two students at this stage in their development, and change it if necessary.

Too much pedal or careless pedaling is doubly destructive in a duet. (*September 1985*)

Problems with ensemble music on recitals. *For years I have included ensemble music in all my recitals. It provides a welcome change from a large number of solos, and the parents like it; but I'm about to give it up. Students are too busy to get together for adequate practice, and I can't stand to hear ensemble music played in public as if the performers were two soloists vying for attention. If you have any ideas on how I can include ensemble music in my programs under these conditions I'd be surprised, but I would give your suggestions my serious consideration. Otherwise, from now on, my recitals will be solo programs.*

I must admit that I am disturbed by what seems to be your reason for teaching duets. While duets do help to make an interesting program, that surely is not the reason for teaching ensemble music, just a side benefit.

I hope that I can persuade you to continue using ensemble music as a big part of your teaching repertoire by telling you a bit about the ensemble work we do here at the New School.

We begin duets, student with teacher, from the very first lesson, to enlarge the student's musical experience from the beginning. And we continue this experience until he has learned what ensemble playing entails — being as aware of the teacher's part as he is of his own part and knowing that the two parts together make the whole piece. It is not only easy but exceedingly beneficial to develop a student who is acutely aware of phrasing, dynamic levels, imitation, bass line, and division of the pulse in music that is far more complicated than he himself is yet ready to play alone. Of course I am referring in this case to the teacher's accompaniment. In this way, the student grows up knowing that to play duets he needs to know (at least in his ear) bot h the primo and secondo parts. After months of this kind of experience he's ready to play duets with a student at his own level, eager to learn both the prime and secondo parts, and conditioned to listening to the whole piece, not just to his part.

Even at this point we play the duets with each of the two students involved while they are learning them, so that the first time they play together they are free both technically and musically to enjoy listening to each other, to be acutely aware of the whole piece, not just their own part.

Ensemble playing is one of the rich musical experiences that can so easily be included in group teaching or repertoire classes. If your students do not have group lessons or repertoire classes, you might consider scheduling students who might play together on the same day, one right after the other, then use the last few minutes of one lesson and the first few minutes of the next for their ensemble work. At any price, I would provide more and more ensemble experiences for their own musical growth and I would do this even if you never included ensemble music in a recital. *(November 1972)*

Practicing ensemble music. *I have a real problem in getting students together to practice duets. I like to have my students play duets, especially for recitals, but they don't seem to have time to learn their parts and then practice together. How do you get them to spend the necessary time?*

I'll answer your question by asking two other questions.

Is it possible that the duets you have assigned are too difficult? I question the grading of much ensemble music. Too often the grading seems to be based on the difficulty of the single parts, ignoring the real difficulty, the ensemble itself. I recommend assigning ensemble music in which the single parts are at a much easier level than the rest of the assignment. In this way, learning the parts is a cinch, and putting them together a possibility.

Is each student wholly confident of his own part (and his own part in relation to the other part) before he plays it with his partner? Rehearsal time will be greatly reduced if you postpone having the students practice together until each has learned *both* parts (his partner's as well as his own) and until each has a secure feeling for the ensemble through having played it with *you* many times. *(November 1967)*

Duet collections. *I'm looking for more good ensemble music. I have used everything you recommended in the past, and with great success. Do you have any good new duet collections to recommend? I can't seem to get enough of them.*

Our own supplementary material includes a series of three duet books by Jon George: *Two at One Piano, Books 1, 2, 3,* published by Summy-Birchard. The music is exceptionally engaging, and the parts are of equal difficulty, so that the duets can be played by two students at the same level. Our students study this as a part of their core curriculum and it wins, hands down, as the favorite part of their repertoire. In addition, three good collections have come to my attention:

Three for Two by Madeline Dring, (Hal Leonard), is just what the name implies: three duets for two pianists. The titles are "Country Dance," "The Quiet Pool," and "Hobby Horse." The music is colorful and imaginative. These duets can be handled nicely by a level 1 student and his teacher, or two level 2 students.

Round and Round by Jack Beeson, Oxford University Press, is a set of seven clever rounds and canons for level 3 students. The music is interesting and students will respond to the game of analysis as well as to the fun of performance.

Jamaican Folk Songs arranged by Barbara Kirby-Mason, Oxford University Press, is a set of exciting duet arrangements of 8 folk songs from Jamaica. Except for No.3, "Water Come to My Eye," which is more difficult, these are just right for teacher and level 1 student or two level 2 students. *(January 1972)*

Music for piano and violin. *I am trying to include more ensemble playing in my teaching, using music for piano and violin. The students have responded enthusiastically to all this music and are asking for more. Do you have suggestions for piano-and-violin music for students at the early intermediate level? I will appreciate knowing of any good music for piano with violin or another instrument.*

I can recommend highly a new collection by Hansi Alt published by Oxford University Press. Called "Red Clouds," it includes twelve folksongs from Austria, Switzerland, and the Tyrol. The folksongs are arranged for violin (or recorder or flute) and piano with an optional part for cello. The pieces are short (one or two pages in length). I consider this a fine addition to the teaching repertoire for any teacher who appreciates the value of chamber music for his intermediate students. *(October 1971)*

Which player should pedal? *What great composers of the 19th century, aside from Schubert, Schumann, Brahms, and Grieg, wrote original music for piano duet? In playing this music, which player should use the pedal – prima or secondo?*

The list is very long, but the greatest 19th century composers of piano duets would undoubtedly include, in addition to those you mention, Beethoven, von Weber, Mendelssohn, Bruckner, and Bizet. Great composers born in the 19th century, whose duets were written early in the 20th century include Dvorak, Faure, Arensky, Debussy, Satie, Reger, Rachmaninoff, Ravel, Stravinsky, Casella, and Poulenc. Pedaling depends largely on harmonic changes, and because harmonic motion is often seen most clearly in the bass, it is usually best to have the secondo player pedal. However, this is by no means a hard-and-fast rule; each duet requires an individual decision, based on the nature of the music itself. *(September 1980)*

Mozart duet sonatas. *I have been searching for months for some easy duet sonatas by Mozart; I played them with my teacher when I was in junior high and remember them with great pleasure. Apparently I used my teacher's music or have lost my own copy.*

The only duet sonatas I have been able to find are those in D major, K. 381 and Bb major, K. 358 – definitely not the ones I played, and far too difficult and mature for the students I have in mind. Do you know the easier ones and who publishes them?

Mozart wrote no duet sonatas that can be considered easy. Probably the duets you played at that age were the *Leichte Sonatinen* published by Peters (No. 4456).

Sonatina No. 1 is in F major and contains four movements: *Allegro spiritoso, Andante, Menuetto and Trio*, and *Contredanse en Rondo*.

Sonatina No. 2 is in B major and also contains four movements: *Allegro, Andante grazioso, Menuetto and Trio*, and *Allegro*.

The Sonatinas are delightful music, just right for the student not yet ready for the more mature duet sonatas. *(November 1975)*

Duets by Diabelli. *Please send me the list of 4-hand music by Diabelli that was referred to in the Summer Study Course in Chicago.*

The following music by Diabelli for one piano, four hands is published by Peters:

> Sonatinas in Five Notes, Op. 163 (Peters 2440b)
> Melodious Exercises, Op. 149 (Peters 2442)
> Sonatas, Op. 32, 33, 37 (Peters 2443a)
> Sonatas, Op. 38, 73 (Peters 2443b)
> Two Sonatas Mignonnes – Rondeau Militaire (Peters 2441)
> Sonatinen, Op. 24, 54, 58, 60 (Peters 2440a)

This is charming music, of intermediate or early advanced level. *(November 1967)*

Use of popular music. *I would like your opinion concerning the use of popular music as occasional supplementary material for young students with an interest in "playing something I know." I have heard strong opinions for both sides of this issue, but your opinion would settle this question me and several other piano teachers I know.*

You put a heavy burden of responsibility on one person's opinion! In reality, I can't settle the question for you or for anyone else — it is a decision each teacher must make independently. However, I can tell you what we do and don't do here at the New School, for you to consider in reaching your own conclusion.

Every program of study is made up of the most well-rounded musical diet possible for that particular student, taking into account his level of advancement, his own preferences and tastes, his family background and interests, and his developmental needs as we see them.

Part of this diet for most students is contemporary music — some of it art music, some of it in a lighter and more popular vein. Most youngsters have a desire, indeed a need, to play some of the really good lighter pieces in jazz, blues, folk, or rock idioms. When I say "really good" I mean pieces that are well-composed, that lie within the student's rhythmic and technical limitations at his level, and that do not violate our concept of good pedagogy.

Most of these pieces, however, do not meet the specific interest you mention of "playing something I know." Many of our students play popular music they hear on radio or TV, and some of them play it exceedingly well. They may pick up the music at the music store and work it out on their own, or they may just pick it up by ear.

Last June one of our biggest recital hits was a lengthy and skillful improvisation on the "Exodus" theme, done by a 12-year-old whose teacher has been encouraging improvisation of all sorts in order to hold his interest in piano study while coaxing him gently into a serious study of the classics. One of our most ardent Bach enthusiasts, too, often stays after an evening Repertoire Class to improvise on popular songs, to his own satisfaction and our delight. *(May-June 1975)*

Teenagers who want to study nothing but jazz. *Every once in a while I have had a teenager who wants to study nothing but jazz. Right now I have two high school boys who I know will drop if I try to give them any serious music. What do you do in such a case? Shall I teach what they want just to keep them at the piano? They are good kids who have studied with me for several years. I can't bear to lose them, or have them stop lessons just because I don't want to teach the only thing they want to learn.*

This is a question only you can answer. I'm sure every teacher has a similar experience from time to time, and I don't believe there is a hard-and-fast rule to follow. You have to solve each case on its own merits. However, maybe it will help to share the story of two specific examples from our own recent experience.

Jack is a senior in high school. His parents want him to know and love the classics, and to spend this last year getting farther in serious music before he goes off to college. Jack says he's had enough serious music, and wants to spend his last year concentrating on jazz. He hopes that during college he can have the fun (and maybe the extra income!) of playing in a combo, and knows that his jazz skills aren't good enough for that yet.

Fortunately, we have on our staff a young man who is a fine pianist and skillful teacher, who also had the experience of playing his way through college in a jazz combo. So we made a bargain with Jack. He could study with this teacher, and we would make jazz the major part of his assignment, providing he would also prepare one piece from the great piano literature to play for each repertoire class. He agreed. So, both he and his parents are happy, and we believe that we are helping to prepare him for college in two meaningful ways.

Tom is a freshman in high school and has studied with us from his first lesson. Last spring, with great embarrassment and disappointment, his mother came to tell me that he had decided to change teachers, and why. Tom wanted "a fling" with a jazz teacher in the area, and he wanted it so badly that she and his father felt they couldn't fight it. She thanked me for all we had done for Tom, and hoped that we would understand his decision. I told her we certainly did understand, and thanked her for coming in person to explain. I also asked her to keep us informed about Tom's progress and to tell him that I hoped he would come to play for us sometime in the fall.

In September she called again and asked if she and Tom could for an appointment to discuss his summer experiences. Tom did all the talking, describing his summer study, first in a two-week jazz workshop and then at a music camp where he met many other youngsters his age who were totally involved with serious music. The opportunity to compare the two worlds in a short, concentrated time had made him realize that he really belonged in the world of serious music. He asked if we would take him back as a student, and I said we would be delighted. After the conference, his mother told me that our understanding of his first decision and our not trying to persuade him to change his mind had as much to do with his second decision as the summer experiences he had described. Moral: the way to lose a student is to try to hang on to him.

These two stories have happy endings, but not all do. I have occasionally lost a good student whose interest in real jazz improvisation was so intense that I could do nothing but recommend a teacher whose specialty that is; it isn't mine, and there's no point in pretending that you can teach it if you aren't good at it. Another warning: if a student is genuinely interested in serious jazz, I think it's wrong to give him the placebo of books with "jazz" in the title if they aren't real jazz and don't fill his needs in a meaningful way. *(November 1976)*

Carols for early intermediate students. *I have looked over at least ten Christmas Carol books and can't find what I want for my early intermediate students. The arrangements all seem so trite and unmusical. Is there any book you especially recommend for third and fourth year students?*

A book that was published many years ago (in 1935) is as good as any I know and far better than most. It is *The Diller-Paige Carol Book*, published by G. Schirmer. It consists of 34 Christmas tunes, both religious and secular. Carols from ten countries are represented, and in most cases the complete text is included. The arrangements are tasteful and pianistic, but harder than they appear. *(October 1971)*

Christmas duets. *During the holiday season, I give my students a holiday vacation in that there are no assignments. Instead, we spend the lesson time sight-reading and playing Christmas music. I would like to find a good book of duets for late elementary and early intermediate students which I could play with the student at the lesson.*

I believe that *Carols for Two*, 15 carols arranged for piano duet by Thomas Johnson, will satisfy your need. The tunes in this collection include: Away in the Manger;

Silent Night; The Holly and the Ivy; While Shepherds Watched; The Coventry Carol; See Amid the Winter's Snow; I Saw Three Ships; Once in Royal David's City; Good Christian Men Rejoice; We Three Kings of Orient Are; Come All Ye Faithful; The First Noel; Good King Wenceslas; Hark the Herald Angels Sing; God Rest You Merry Gentlemen. The carols themselves are kept in their simple song form without elaboration· the accompaniments (more difficult than the prima parts) are tasteful and interesting without being too difficult. The collection is Hinrichsen Edition No. 881, available through C. F. Peters Corporation. *(October 1969)*

Carols for high school students. *My advanced high school students are giving a recital in December. I would like to include something on the program that represents the Christmas season, but have not been able to find any arrangements of carols that seem worthwhile. Can you recommend any really musical settings for students at this level?*

There is a distinguished new collection that fills the bill exactly. Called simply, Christmas Music, it is a volume of piano duets by Norman Dello Joio, published by Marks Music Corporation. The set includes transcriptions of four traditional carols (O, Come All Ye Faithful; God Rest Ye Merry Gentlemen; Silent Night; and Hark! The Herald Angels Sing) as well as three original Christmas duets by the composer.

The original Christmas pieces are exceptionally beautiful music in mild contemporary idiom. The transcriptions are dignified and tasteful yet wonderfully fresh and often quite unexpected. The pieces are of early advanced level and offer a real challenge to high school students, both technically and interpretively. Highly recommended. *(November 1968)*

Christmas recital. *Can you suggest some arrangements of Christmas carols that could be used in an interesting all-Christmas program? I would like to include all of my students from elementary through early advanced.*

Congratulations on planning ahead, but your question poses one problem for me: Christmas carols were meant to be sung! A whole program of piano arrangements of carols not only seems inappropriate but might also be somewhat dull. So my suggestion would be to include performances of piano transcriptions of carols, interspersed with student accompaniments of carols sung by the audience. Following is some music to consider for such a program.

Possibly begin with your elementary students playing familiar carols in simple, tasteful arrangements. If you don't already know it, take a look at *First Book of Christmas Songs and Carols for Piano* by Rachael Beatty Kahl (Carl Fischer, 1976). It includes 22 traditional carols. The arrangements are exceedingly easy, very good for the beginning student. I'd suggest using the piano parts without singing both because these arrangements are a little low in range for children's voices and because beginning students are not the most secure accompanists. For variety, some of the carols could be done as solos, some as duets.

A second part of the program could be performances by late intermediate students of the very beautiful *Appalachian Christmas Carols* (after John Jacob Niles) arranged for one piano, four hands by Vincent Persichetti (Eikan-Vogel, 1975). This collection consists of seven lesser-known carols that have been exceptionally well transcribed.

Next you might use a group of standard carols, sung by the audience. In a Christmas mood by this time, they will enjoy singing along, and the experience of accompanying a "chorus" will be invaluable for your young students.

An excellent collection of standard carols is the *Diller-Page Carol Book* (G. Schirmer, 1935). The first half of the collection includes 10 familiar carols, while the second part introduces 20 lesser-known carols from 10 foreign countries. Doubtless the audience would enjoy learning some new carols, along with singing old favorites.

As a last group on the program, consider having the more advanced students play *Christmas Music*, transcribed by Norman Dello Joio (Marks Music Corp., 1968). This collection includes three original Christmas pieces by Dello Joio ("A Christmas Carol," "Bright Star the Light of the World," and "The Holy Infant's Lullaby") and settings by Dello Joio of "God Rest Ye Merry Gentlemen," "Hark! the Herald Angels Sing," "O Come All Ye Faithful," and "Silent Night."

If you carry through with your plan for an all-Christmas recital, I'd appreciate receiving a copy of the program. *(September 1977)*

Appalachian Christmas Carols. *Forty years ago I came across a wonderful collection of Christmas carols, arranged by Vincent Persichetti. I think it was published by G. Schirmer. Recently I wanted to teach them again, but find they are not listed in the Schirmer catalogue. Do you know if they are still available?*

The set entitled "Appalachian Christmas Carols" was reissued in 1975 by Elkan-Vogel, Inc., a division of Theodore Presser Company. The collection contains 7 carols from the Appalachian mountains arranged for one piano, four hands. The subtitle, "after John Jacob Niles," probably identifies the source of the carols and certainly gives a sense of their evocative quality.

The music is of late intermediate to early advanced level. The carols themselves are hauntingly beautiful, and the arrangements by Persichetti are full and colorful without in any way clouding the simple and natural quality of this mountain music.

Included are "Down in Yon Forest," "The Cherry Tree," "The Seven Joys of Mary," "Jesus, Jesus, Rest Your Head," "Jesus Born in Beth'ny," "Lulie Lullay" and "Jesus Christ is Born."

We have frequently programmed some or all of the carols on Christmas recitals where they stand out for their beauty and authenticity. This set is highly recommended. *(December 1988)*

Music for one hand. *Occasionally a pupil will sprain or break one arm, and rather than stop lessons during his convalescence, I continue the lessons and concentrate on working with his "good" arm alone, until the other arm is healed again. We do scales, arpeggios, chords, exercises, sightreading, ear training, and pieces for one hand.*

Is there a listing of piano pieces, and their approximate grade levels, written for the right hand alone or the left hand alone?

To date, most of the one-hand music I've come across is either banal or contrived. These pieces are composed for an exceptional teaching situation rather than a meaningful musical experience.

A delightful exception is the C minor Solfeggietto by C.P.E. Bach. It is available in a left-hand version that can be refingered for right hand alone.

I agree that it is wise not to stop lessons during the student's convalescence. Much ground is lost if lessons are discontinued for such a long time. But, more important, this can be a great teaching period, a golden opportunity which we should not miss.

I usually use the student's regular repertoire, playing the part for the injured hand while he plays with his "good" hand. This can be great fun and good ensemble experience. It never fails to result in more careful work and more attentive listening. If the broken or injured arm is the "clever" one, the opportunity is twice blessed, as it presents the chance to really concentrate on the less skilled side. I suggest the student practice less during his convalescence (if he chooses) but expect more careful work, greater attention to detail, and more rapid progress for the one hand.

Often, we start new material and have the one hand completely learned before the injured hand is ready to take up its part. In addition, through playing the piece as a duet with the teacher, the student can acquire a total concept of the music before he is ready to try it with both hands. *(March 1971)*

Every year I seem to have at least one student who is handicapped for a month or more with a broken finger, wrist, or arm. Sometimes the student discontinues lessons for that period, but often I try to make interesting assignments for the hand that was not injured. Is there music written for left hand alone and for right hand alone for students of early grades? If so, I will order it at once, to be prepared for this annual problem.

This year, the Boston Music Company has published *Elementary Piano for One Hand* by Joseph Riccardi and August Vella. This book, which claims to be a course of study, was written for handicapped individuals who have the use of only one hand and arm. I cannot recommend it as a course of study because it progresses much too fast, it offers a real solution for teachers such as you and is suitable for students at various stages of development. For example, the first three exercises are just around Middle C and the C below: melody with no accompaniment. By No. 5 there is melody and accompaniment in one hand, and two-thirds of the way through the book the melody and accompaniment within one hand is very complicated and demanding.

This book has a few drawbacks: all fingering is for the left hand so that in the case of a left-hand injury, right-hand fingerings would have to be substituted by the teacher. The second problem is that the left-hand finger numbers are written both above the treble staff and below the bass staff. The numbers above the treble staff give an unusual and awkward appearance, and there is a temptation to misread them for the right hand. A third difficulty occurs in connection with using slurs over parallel octaves. The slur helps the student sense the phrasing and play as smoothly as possible, but the word "connect," appearing between notes that cannot be connected, is misleading.

I agree with your sensible suggestion that all teachers should keep a copy of one-handed music on hand, so that when students suffer sprained or broken fingers, wrists, or arms, there is no delay in locating music for them to play. *(March 1982)*

Other Repertoire Issues

Early 20th century materials. *Can you tell me something about piano teaching materials available in the early part of this century? I myself started lessons with the John Thompson course, but I am interested in what preceded it.*

Four names stand out in the history of American piano courses: W.S.B. Mathews, John M. Williams, Angela Diller, and Louise Robyn. Some materials by all four are still available in print.

In the early years of the 20th century W.S.B. Mathews compiled the *Standard Graded Course of Studies for the Pianoforte in Ten Grades* published then and now by Theodore Presser Company. Presser could not help me find the original edition, published before 1920. The current edition, first released in 1931, is a great improvement over the original as I remember it, which presented many lessons on the treble staff alone, then many lessons on the bass staff alone before the grand staff was introduced. The current edition begins with the grand staff, and the Grade I book includes over 100 pieces, varying in length from two to six scores and in difficulty from a first piece all on Middle C to material which most of us would consider at least Grade II.

Even though the ten grades differ greatly from our present standards and knowledge of pedagogy, Mathews' undertaking in preparing this first comprehensive course was a giant step in the right direction.

John M. Williams (1884-1974) lived through a period of enormous development and was able to see the ideas he first introduced in his piano method carried far beyond his original concepts by later writers of piano courses.

His books, published by the Boston Music Company, are used in Canada, Great Britain, and Australia, and they sell in Spanish translation in Cuba and South America. The first pedagogue to lecture widely to piano teachers, he traveled extensively to major cities in the Untied States and the British Isles. He was also the first to give piano lessons over the radio, developing a course of 26 15-minute lessons called "Piano Playing for Adult Beginners."

His 35-book course included a preparatory level and five subsequent grades. In addition he edited, annotated, and fingered over 200 pieces of sheet music for students in the five grades.

As a beginning teacher I heard Williams lecture on his first and second grade books and found him to be a literate, personable, and intelligent salesman of his methods and materials.

Angela Diller (1877-1968) was our first great woman pedagogue. Her writings were not a course of study in the same sense as those of Mathews and Williams, nor did she become the household word that Williams was in his day, but the impact she made on piano teachers, students, and on the art of piano teaching will be felt for generations. Although she did not write a course of study or develop a unique pedagogical concept, she collected and edited educational piano materials of the highest musical and pedagogical quality, in which she paid meticulous attention to nuance and phrasing. Her collections were often prepared in collaboration with colleagues: Elizabeth Quaile (her partner in founding the Diller-Quaile School), K. Stearns Page and Harold Bauer. Her *First Theory Book appeared* in 1921, her landmark Keyboard Harmony Course between 1936-49, and a book about her life in music, *The Splendor of Music*, in 1957.

Unfortunately many of her publications are no longer in print, but a list of those currently available can be procured through her publisher, G. Schirmer.

Like Diller, Louise Robyn's educational piano materials were slight in output (compared with Mathews and Williams) and did not constitute a real course of study. She is remembered instead as a pioneer in the development of a systematic and comprehensive course in piano pedagogy which she taught for many years at the American Conservatory of Music in Chicago. The students who studied with her there, and the teachers who attended her summer normal courses, received invaluable insights into teaching-learning principles as they apply to piano study. As an early advocate of pre-school musical training, her "Robyn System" was oriented to young children. Because she studied early childhood education and taught young children, she shared her ideas in an intelligent and thoroughly modern way. Teachers attending her courses saw live teaching demonstrations of her principles using children enrolled m the Children's Department of the American Conservatory.

Robyn's books for young students, published by Oliver Ditson, include *Keyboard Town* (piano instruction in story form for young beginners), *Technic Tales*, Books 1 and 2, *Chord Crafters*, and the *Robyn Rote Cards*. In collaboration with Howard Hanks she prepared a series of keyboard harmony books, *Robyn-Hanks Harmony* Books 1, 2, and 3.

Again, not everything Robyn prepared is still available, but materials currently in print may be procured through Theodore Presser. (October 1982)

Elementary music with a fresh sound. *There has been a great emphasis in study courses on choosing elementary piano music with a new, fresh sound. I agree, but I find that some students really love some of those old pieces that may not be so fresh in sound but are rewarding in other ways. They are big without being too difficult, or they have pretty melodies that parents like, too, or they have chords. Am I terribly old-fashioned?*

You don't sound old-fashioned at all to me. Apparently we agree about the importance of choosing music with a new, fresh sound; but let's modify that to read some music. All students, regardless of their level, need some music with new, fresh sounds: music that stretches their ears and minds as they explore the various styles and idioms of their own day.

Most students also need some music that is big without being too difficult, that has pretty melodies, and that gives experience in full rich chords. No intelligent teacher would recommend a diet of con: temporary sounds to the exclusion of all other types and styles. That would make as little sense musically as a diet of anchovies and ripe olives would make nutritionally. Indigestion is apt to develop in either case!

The best way to insure the development of a healthy, well-rounded musician is to follow the basic principle used by nutritionists: plan a well-balanced diet. Such a diet for piano students should include such staples as the keyboard works by master composers from Baroque, Classic, Romantic, and Contemporary periods for the main course; a bit of the freshest modern idioms for relish; some jazz or other popular styles for dessert.

Of course the early elementary student is not ready for even the easiest works by master composers, yet he, too, must have a well- balanced diet. This can be accomplished only if his very first study material is designed to provide early experiences in a variety of classic, romantic, and contemporary sounds, not a bland diet of I, IV, and V chords.

When he is ready to play the master composers from all periods, he still needs occasionally that fresh, new music for added spice, that not-too-difficult, big-sounding piece, and that piece with lovely melody or with full, rich chords. *(December 1969)*

The black hole in intermediate repertoire. *I've been hearing recently about the black hole in piano teaching. I assume it's a play on the term black hole as it applies to outer space, but even teachers who use it don't seem sure of its meaning.*

I believe the term was first applied to piano teaching (specifically to an area of piano literature) at the National Conference on Piano Pedagogy at the University of Illinois, Urbana-Champaign in October, 1980. Professor Rita Fuszek of California State University at Fullerton read a paper entitled "The Black Hole" in which she said: "The lack of knowledge of intermediate repertoire for the future piano pedagogue creates a 'black hole' in music that is not easily remedied. The lack of experience in the (future teacher's) own training as well as the inability to easily learn or sight-play repertoire of this development, perpetuates the void." The expression "black hole" caught on with the 250 teachers who attended the conference, and dotted the sessions from then on.

The expression is useful in pointing out a lack of preparation of college piano majors in the intermediate repertoire they will almost certainly be teaching in the future. Even more, it points to a hole in the early training of a large percent of piano majors when they enter college.

I have already emphasized in this column the need for piano students to grow up with the music of the great composers, studying their smaller works year by year, in preparation for understanding major works later on. Yet, I still interview many college freshmen whose first piece of Bach was an Invention, whose first piece of Grieg the A minor Concerto, and whose first piece of Bartok was Op. 14. For such students, the first year of college piano study has to be filling in holes, so that their future study of major works can be more meaningful.

If enough of us emphasize the enormity of this black hole, perhaps it will alert pre-college teachers to omissions in their teaching which at present the college undergraduate or graduate teacher has to fill. *(October 1981)*

Collections of Bach, Mozart and Beethoven. *I have a group of six outstanding students, ages 10 to 12, who are just about to finish the First Grade John Thompson Book, and will soon begin the Second Grade Book. They are impatient to begin playing what they think of as real music, especially Bach, Mozart, and Beethoven. I'm considering giving a Bach book to two of the students, a Mozart book to two others, and a Beethoven book to the last two. Which collection of each of these composers do you recommend for students at this grade?*

I take issue with your plan of giving each student a collection of pieces by one composer. Bach, Mozart, and Beethoven composed very little music which can be considered easy in any way. Even collections under such titles as "My First Bach Book" or "Easiest Keyboard Music of Mozart and Beethoven" (to name but two) include music at many levels of difficulty, some of which your students would not be able to play well for several years. This can be frustrating for students and discouraging for parents.

Further, I believe that when students begin to study music by the great keyboard composers, they should experience as full and well-rounded a diet as possible. There are available many fine, tastefully chosen and carefully graded collections of the easiest original piano music of such composers as Bach, Haydn, Mozart, Beethoven, Schubert, Schumann, et al. Such a book, containing only music that the late elementary student can reasonably expect to master, is a far better introduction to the great composers than any single-composer collection I know. *(October 1975)*

Intermediate repertoire by contemporary composers. *I have several students who have completed the "Contemporary Piano Literature " series of the Frances Clark Library and need more contemporary music. They are especially interested in compositions by Kabalevsky, Tcherepnin, Bartok, and Prokofieff. Will you please send a list of other music by those four composers?*

The following list is by no means comprehensive, but does provide a starting place for more experience with the composers you name.

Kabalevsky
    Sonatina, Op. 13, No. 2   Leeds
    Four Little Pieces, Op. 14   Leeds
        A Brisk Game

The Drummer
In the Gymnasium
Soldier's March
Five Sets of Variations, Op. 51   Leeds
Five Happy Variations on a Russian Folksong
Merry Dance Variations on a Russian Folksong
Gray Day Variations on a Slovakian Folksong
Seven Good-Humored Variations on an Ukrainian Folksong
Variations Op. 40   Leeds
Tcherepnin
Chinese Bagatelles, Op. 51, No. 3
Mercury
Bagatelles, Op. 5   Leeds
Expressions, Op. 81   Leeds
Songs Without Words (No. 6015)   Peters
Bartok
Mikrokosmos   Boosey and Hawkes
Ten Easy Piano Pieces   Boosey and Hawkes
Three Rondos   Boosey and Hawkes
Nine Little Piano Pieces   Boosey and Hawkes
Vol. I, II, III
Prokofieff
Visions Fugitives   Marks
Music for Children, Op. 65   Leeds
(November 1967)

Music for small hands. *Each year I seem to have some advanced students whose hands are too small to play octaves comfortably, and who can't play big chords at all. At present I have a high school senior and two college students, all of whom are excellent students and fine musicians, but who are handicapped in this respect. Will you please suggest music for them?*

The two-voiced pieces of Bach do not demand large stretches nor do they use big chords. In fact, a large part of Baroque keyboard music fits comfortably into these limitations.

Following are a few of the many Scarlatti sonatas that can be played by small hands. Our listing is taken from the Kirkpatrick edition (G. Schirmer) with the Longo numbers in brackets.

Volume I	Volume II
K. 1 [378]	No. 33 [359]
K. 3 [397]	No. 34 [454]
K. 4 [416]	No. 40 [470]

K. 11 [10]   No. 46   [8]
K. 18 [215]   No. 48 [82]
K. 19 [457]   No. 49 [206]
K. 23 [238]   No. 59 [497]
K. 27 [27]
K. 29 [103]

A great many of the sonatas of Haydn and Mozart, too, are possible for small hands.

From the Romantic period, consider the following works of Chopin, especially suitable for small hands:

Mazurkas   *Waltzes*
Op. 6, Nos. 1 and 2   Op. 69, Nos. 1 and 2
Op. 7, Nos. 1 and 2   Op. 70, No. 2
Op. 17, No. 1
Op. 30 No. 2
Op. 67, Nos. 2 and 4   *Posthumous Polonaises*
                                              G minor
Nocturnes   B♭ major
Op. 32, No. 1

And, of course, music for small hands is not limited to 17th, 18th, and 19th century repertoire. Modern piano literature is replete with music suitable for small hands. A comprehensive list would take pages, but as examples consider Toch's *Etudes*, Ibert's *Histoires*, of Tcherepnin's *Bagatelles*, and a great many works by Bartok, Rachmaninoff, Kabalevsky, Kodaly, and others.

Repertoire for high school students. *I have a high school student who is playing several Beethoven sonatas, Chopin waltzes, and Czerny, Op. 740. Please suggest some pieces for her to work on next.*

For any high school student who can play Beethoven sonatas and Chopin waltzes and is able to play Czerny, Op. 740 (up to tempo), the world of great keyboard literature is wide open. I would need to know the individual student to recommend specific pieces, but I can make general recommendations. She should be studying music from every period: Bach Inventions, Sinfonia, Preludes and Fugues, or suites; Haydn or Mozart variations and sonatas; works by Mendelssohn, Schubert, Schumann and Brahms; Debussy or Ravel; and much music of the 20th century. At this time I surely would not assign more Beethoven or Chopin; instead, widen her musical horizons. *(May/June 1982)*

A variety of Preludes. Our piano teachers' organization is preparing a series of six recitals to be given by advanced high school and college students in our area. The series will feature preludes. To date we have selected preludes by Bach, Chopin, Debussy, Gershwin, and Kabalevsky. For variety and interest we want to include more composers and would appreciate your suggestions.

I suggest you consider the following additional sets of preludes:

> Casadesus, *Twenty-Four Preludes, Op. 5* (Eschig)
> Ginastera, *Twelve American Preludes, Op. 12* (Carl Fischer)
> Griffes, *Three Preludes* (Peters)
> Mendelssohn, *Three Preludes, Op. 104b* (Ricordi)
> *Muczynski, Six Preludes, Op. 6* (Schirmer)
> Rachmaninoff, *Ten Preludes, Op. 23; Thirteen Preludes, Op. 32* (Boosey and Hawkes)
> Resphigi, *Three Preludes on Gregorian Melodies* (Universal)
> Shostakovich, *Twenty-Four Preludes, Op. 34* (MCA)
> Tcherepnin, *Eight Preludes* (Heugel); *Twelve Preludes, Op. 83* (E. G. Marks); *Four Nostalgic Preludes* (Heugel)

(April 1986)

Grading music. *I find choosing music for my intermediate students very difficult because of the different grading systems used by composers, publishers, and reviewers. Can't you do something about getting reviewers together to set up some common basis for grading? The way it is now, a grade or level on the cover of a piece or in an ad for a piece is practically meaningless.*

Anyone who grades music, especially music beyond the elementary level, will agree, I'm sure, that grading is a very personal matter. Right here within our school, where there exists a real community of thought and purpose, there are as many ideas on grading as there are teachers on the faculty!

The teacher is the only one who can really determine how difficult a given piece will be for a given student at that particular time, and whether or not the choice is appropriate.

Music can be easy or difficult because of notation, because of technic, or because of intrinsic musical significance. Each of these areas must be considered in relation to each student. No two students are exactly the same place in their performance ability, nor are the performance standards of any two teachers exactly the same.

All in all, I fear I can only confirm the great difficulty that exists in the area of grading, and the fact that conformity is a perpetual impossibility. There are no blacks or whites, just varying shades of grey. I recommend being grateful that a reviewer has introduced you to a new piece of music and given you, in some broad and general way, his idea of its difficulty. How it suits your purposes then must be determined entirely by you as you teach it. *(April 1976)*

Consistent grading policy. *I am confused and concerned about the grading systems used. Can't there be some consistency between composers, publishers, and teachers? I have on my piano right now a piece of music that is marked grade 3, but it is too difficult for my grade 5 students. How do you interpret grading?*

The grading systems in use by composers and publishers are certainly a difficult problem, and I'm sure most teachers have felt the same frustration you express.

In general, composers and publishers know less than teachers about what makes music difficult for students; but there is even great divergence of opinion between teachers as to what is difficult and why. This is true partly, I think, because their performance standards differ so widely.

We usually grade our music at the earliest level at which our students can play the piece with understanding and enjoyment in what seems to them to be a reasonable amount of time. It might be possible that some students could play a piece at grade 3, others not until grade 4 or even 5. Should a publisher call it grade 3 or grade 5? There is a basis for either decision.

I think the only sensible solution to the problem is for teachers to view printed grade levels as approximations only — loose guidelines to be followed only in the most general way. The real test, of course, is how a piece works for you with your students. Unfortunately there is no certain way to discover this except by teaching it. In general, my own experience has been that music is more difficult than the publisher's grading would seem to indicate. *(December 1969)*

Terminology of editions. *Would you please include in your column some general information on editions? I'm not sure I understand such terms as autograph editions, urtext editions, first editions, etc.*

I believe I can best answer this question by reprinting excerpts from an article by David Kraehenbuehl that appeared in The New School's 1963-64 *Reference Book for Piano Teachers.*

Autograph Editions

The initial state of any masterwork is the composer's manuscript the autograph. Since composers and their students taught from these manuscripts, many markings appear in autographs that are not found in early published editions. It is difficult to determine what markings are those of the composer, those of a student working with the composer, and those of the many musicians who might have played or taught from the manuscript after the composer's death. The study and comparison of autographs can be illuminating. Facsimile reprints are quite valuable to scholars; for the studio teacher they are seldom more than interesting curios. There are, however, some modern autograph editions that are carefully done and very useful. These are engraved versions of the composer's manuscript to which nothing has been added editorially. Equivocal signs, unclear passages, notational mannerisms peculiar to the time or the composer are all cleared up by the scholars supervising the edition. The result is a modern edition that provides the student direct and vivid contact with the composer's manuscript.

First Editions

The earliest published version of a composer's work is the first edition. Although great importance is attached to first editions, they are often poor representations of the composer's work. The authenticity of a first edition depends on a number of conditions: What was the quality of the manuscript from which it was prepared? Was it published during the composer's life? If so, did the composer proofread the edition? Was it a careful or casual proofreading? Unless there is a positive answer to all these questions, the authenticity of a first edition is uncertain.

Critical Editions

A critical edition is an attempt to reconstruct from all available resources — autographs, editions of the past, earlier critical editions, letters and essays by the composer and his contemporaries- an exact engraved representation of the composer's work. Ordinarily, a critical edition includes only what the composer marked or, in the best judgment of the editors, intended to mark in the score. Whenever there are alternative interpretations of sources, the editors provide all the possibilities with careful notes supporting their decisions.

For the purposes of the studio teacher, critical editions have limitations. They are relatively expensive; they provide no interpretive assistance; the student, and often the teacher, is more hindered than helped by the detailed alternative readings. Such editions do provide a valuable reference for the careful teacher who wishes to choose the best of the many practical editions available to him.

"Urtext" Editions

A note of warning is in order regarding "urtext" editions. The German word "urtext" means nothing more than "taken from the sources." Most "urtext" editions are reprints, without alteration, of some previous edition. To call them "urtext" is not a falsehood; it is misleading. The merits of an "urtext" edition depend entirely on the quality of the edition reprinted. Some "urtext" editions are reprints of first editions; many of the better ones are reprints of the scholarly editions produced in the 19th century. Still others are unacknowledged reprintings of practical editions from the 19th and 20th centuries. If the critical or practical editions reprinted are of high quality, the modern "urtext" edition is very useful. If the sources are not of high quality, the modern "urtext" is not an assurance of authenticity.

Personal Editions

Personal editions are of limited value for teaching. They are an attempt by a master performer to indicate in a score the details of his personal interpretation of the masters. A famous example is the edition of the Beethoven sonatas prepared by Artur Schnabel. To indicate on paper all the subtleties of his interpretation, he emended many of Beethoven's markings, added many indications (some of which are not explained for the reader), and made it impossible to reconstruct the original score. In general, such specialized editions are too strong for students.

Practical Editions

Of greatest usefulness to the studio teacher are the modern practical editions of the standard repertoire. A practical edition continues where a critical edition leaves off. The critical edition serves as the basis for an edition prepared by a pianist and pedagogue who is acquainted with both the music and the needs of student performers. It is his function to add to the score those indications that will help the less experienced performer to interpret the work effectively. The usual editorial additions include pedaling, fingering, phrasing, and more detailed dynamic markings. Outmoded signs are replaced by modern equivalents. The engraving techniques and prefatorial notes should make it clear which are the composer's indications, which the editor's. Editions that do not make this clear should be avoided or, at least, verified through comparison with a good critical edition.

For further help we recommend the pamphlet, *Editions and Musicians* by Walter Emery, published by Novello. (September 1968)

New edition of Anna Magdalena Bach Notebook. *I understand there is a new edition of the Notebook for Anna Magdalena Bach but I have not been able to find the publisher. Could you tell me more about it and whether or not you recommend it for students?*

I believe you must be referring to the 1983 edition from G. Henle Verlag, prepared from original sources by Ernst-Günter Heinemann. This is the most useful critical edition of the *Notebook* I have seen. The engraving is beautiful, the pages are clean and clear, and the only addition to the music itself is sparse (and generally sensible) fingering. From the teacher's standpoint, it is a boon to have the *Notebook* available in full size with a single clean page or two for each piece. An informative foreword and abundant critical notes appear in German, French, and English.

For his notes on the composers and on the discrepancies between manuscript and early editions, Heinemann has made a careful examination of all available sources. The editorial commentary is meticulous.

As to composers, we learn, for example, that the familiar Minuets in G Major and G Minor (quoted below) are from the pen of Christian Petzold.

The Marches in D Major and G Major (quoted below) are in the hand of C.P.E. Bach and were probably composed by him.

The F Major Bourree, G Major Minuet, C Minor Minuet, and D Major Musette are among the many works for which the composer is unknown.

One insight from Heinemann's reexamination of the manuscript is worth quoting here. In the imitative G Major Minuet (quoted below), measure 24 has a right-hand eighth-note (D) on the second beat, printed without either sharp or natural sign. This leads Heinemann to conclude that the unknown composer probably intended

D♮. If are working with editions containing D# you may wish to consider changing them.

This edition of the *Notebook* is a must for every teacher's library. I do not recommend it for students because the difficulty ranges from the early intermediate pieces quoted above to music of the most profound complexity and difficulty. My preference for students is a collection of carefully graded and edited literature that includes the easiest selections from the *Notebook*, together with music of comparable difficulty from other master composers of the past and present. (*February 1986*)

Editions of Bach. *What editions do you recommend for Bach Inventions, Preludes and Fugues, Suites, Partitas, and so on?*

For many of the most commonly used sets of Bach pieces, the Peters editions are excellent. The editions recommended here are critical editions to which nothing has been added except fingerings. Almost all provide a helpful preface that includes Bach's own table of ornaments taken from his instruction for his son, Wilhelm Friedemann. The Peters volumes we recommend particularly are: the *Two- and Three-Part Inventions* (4201) with a detailed companion volume on their interpretation (420 1b); the *French Suites* (Peters 4594); the *English Suites* (Peters 4580 and 4580b); the *Partitas* (Peters 4463a and 4463b); the *Well-Tempered Clavier* (Peters 1a and 1b); the *Seven Toccatas* (Peters 4665); and the *Italian Concerto and French Overture* in one volume (Peters 4464). It is important to order Peters editions by number because, in its long history, this company has produced several editions of almost every important keyboard work. The quality varies markedly.

We recommend the Kalmus edition (a reprint of the old Steingraber edition edited by Bischoff) for the *Little Preludes and Fugues* (all markings except the ornaments are editorial additions); the *Notebook for Wilhelm Friedemann Bach* and the *Notebook for Anna Magdalena Bach* (which contains most of the famous easy pieces); and various single pieces such as the *Fantasy in C Minor*, the *Chromatic Fantasy and Fugue*, and the *Capriccio in B-Flat Major*.

The *Goldberg Variations* are beautifully presented in a special edition (G. Schirmer), prepared by Ralph Kirkpatrick, which includes a carefully written preface and detailed indications (added always on a second complete score) for the resolution of ornaments, division of the lines between the hands, phrasing, rhythmic variants, and many other performance problems. This edition is the epitome of editorial intelligence. From it the student can discover exactly what Bach wrote and, further, exactly how a fine performer-scholar interprets Bach's indications. *(January/February 1966)*

Editions of Debussy. *Could you give some guidelines for teachers and advanced students on the new editions of Debussy that have come out since the expiration of the Durand copyright? I have found the lack of pedaling and fingering indications to be a problem, although I realize that Debussy wanted players to discover their own approach.*

To answer your question I have reviewed the Debussy editions in my own library, including Durand, Henle, Heinrichshofen, Peters, Schirmer, Dover, and Alfred.

For the most part the editorial approach in all these editions is restrained. Although many of Debussy's performance indications for articulation, dynamics, and tempo are quite specific, he felt that details of fingering and pedaling should be left to the judgment of the individual performer, and publishers have followed his lead.

I believe that the Alfred edition, edited by Maurice Hinson, has the most pedagogical value, unfortunately only Volume I of the Preludes, the *Children's Corner*, and a collection of selected works entitled *At the Piano with Debussy* have been released to date. Hinson offers helpful editorial suggestions for teachers and students. In Volume I of the Preludes he gives a brief formal analysis of each prelude, discussing mood, color, visual imagery, and harmonic structure. In addition, he places the title and its translation at the beginning of each piece, indicating a concern for the relationship between title and musical content. English translations of all the French performance instructions are printed at the back of the book.

Debussy included only one metronome marking (for "Bruyeres") in Volume I of the Preludes. Hinson has included this and has added metronome markings for the remaining preludes in the volume.

Debussy offered only 20 pedal indications in his entire piano oeuvre, and only 2 in Volume I of the Preludes. Hinson has added pedal and fingering suggestions throughout, attempting to indicate the appropriate use of all three pedals. The improvisatory nature of the preludes leaves much to the discretion of the performer, and Hinson maintains that the final decision should be left to the ear.

As for the Etudes, Suites, *Images*, and *Estampes*, the Henle urtext edition is perhaps the best of the unedited texts.

Just a reminder: the May/June 1988 issue of *Clavier* included two articles on

Debussy's piano music: "Stewart Gordon on the Debussy Etudes" by Dean Elder and "Getting Ready for Debussy" by Celia Grasty-Jones. *(May-June 1989)*

Editions of Haydn. *Bach, Handel, and Scarlatti have had their 300th birthdays, and Mozart has had his* Amadeus. *Meanwhile, I have grown defensive about Haydn and want to make a much more comprehensive study of his solo piano repertoire, both as a performer and as a teacher. Which edition of the sonatas do you recommend and what are the best sources for information on his teaching pieces?*

There are five well-known editions of the Haydn sonatas: Henle, Kalmus (Belwin-Mills/Columbia), Peters, Schirmer, and Universal. The two most recent and scholarly editions, Henle and Universal, win my approval hands down. My personal preference is the Vienna Urtext Edition. It contains the complete sonatas (62) in three volumes, edited by Christa Landon with fingerings by Oswald Jonas, published by Universal Editions, Vienna, 1966. The catalogue numbers for the three volumes are UE 1337, 1338, and 1339.

I like this edition best because it is complete, its chronology has been meticulously researched, and the editors have upheld scrupulous standards of contemporary musicology and editing. The best part of the edition, though, is its preface, a work of brilliant scholarship that is indispensible to any serious study of Haydn's music. Each of the three volumes has the same preface and contains sections on authenticity and chronology, choice of instrument and interpretation, appoggiaturas and ornaments, and editing principles. Only the section on authenticity and chronology is different for each volume because it deals with individual sonatas. At the end of each volume there is a complete thematic index of all 62 sonatas.

For a comprehensive guide to all of Haydn's solo piano literature, I recommend Haydn Solo Piano Literature, edited by Carolyn Maxwell and published in 1983 by Maxwell Music Evaluation Books. This little book is a treasure-trove of information on all of Haydn's solo piano music from the sonatas to the easiest teaching pieces. The table of contents will give you an idea of its scope: Foreword; I. Authentic pieces (a discussion of eight larger independent compositions, including the five sets of variations); II. Sonatas (with a table of numbering systems used in the five most readily available editions); III. Authentic transcriptions (other works, transcribed for piano by Haydn himself); IV. Transcriptions from other media (works for other media, transcribed for piano but not by Haydn himself); y. Works of doubtful or unknown origin (including all of the well- known teaching pieces); VI. Works for musical clock; Bibliography; and Index. The guide has many admirable features: completeness, scholarship, readability, and easy format. Best of all, every entry includes thematics and a list of available editions. *(July-August 1987)*

Editions of Mozart. *What edition of the Mozart sonatas do you recommend?*

There are three very fine editions of the Mozart Sonatas: the relatively recent Presser edition, prepared by Nathan Broder (includes a fine preface on the performance of Mozart's ornaments); the Henle edition, prepared by Lampe (another fine explanation of ornamentation plus generally satisfactory fingerings); and the Kalmus edition. The main advantage to the Kalmus edition is that sonatas can be purchased separately. Otherwise, I prefer the Presser or Henle editions. In my own library I have all three of these editions, plus the modern reprint of the 19th-century Breitkopf and Hartel edition, now available through Edwards Brothers, Ann Arbor, Michigan. All are extremely useful for teachers but I believe I most often assign the Henle edition for students. *(February 1971)*

Editions of Liszt. *I try to use only the preferred editions of major composers. I have often begun with poor editions and profited greatly by changing to the more authoritative ones, but of course this has been expensive. I am about to add to my repertoire some of the music by Franz Liszt and want to begin with the most authoritative edition of his piano works. What do you recommend and what are the reasons for your choice?*

Your question regarding recommended editions of music by Franz Liszt came at an opportune time. The *New Edition of the Complete Works* by Franz Liszt is in the process of being published. This monumental project will include ten series. Series One, works for piano solo, will include eighteen volumes. The original edition that appeared during Liszt's lifetime will serve as the most important source, since in many instances the music was edited by Liszt himself. In cases where doubt exists, the reserved autographs, including reliable copies of engraver proofs and corrections, will be consulted for comparison.

Volume I and Volume II of Series One are now in print, published by Barenreiter and Editio Musica, available in the United States through Belwin-Mills. These two volumes are edited by two Liszt authorities, Zoltan Gardonyi and Istyan Szelenyi. Volume I includes twelve of Liszt's best know miscellaneous pieces, each of which is available separately. Volume II includes "Trois Etudes de Concert," "Trois Caprices poetique," "Ab irato," "Zwei Konzertetuden," "Grandes Etudes de Paganini," including the familiar "La capanella." The editorial notes and preface in each volume will be a great help in your studies. *(November 1972)*

Editions of Scarlatti. *I am trying to decide whether to use the Friskin or the Kirkpatrick edition of the Scarlatti sonatas with high school students. Which do you recommend?*

Both editions are excellent. First, your choice depends on which of the sonatas you have chosen to teach. Of the several hundred sonatas Scarlatti wrote, the Friskin edition includes 24 in two volumes, the Kirkpatrick 60 in two volumes. Friskin has chosen excellent sonatas for students, and has carefully fingered and edited the music, indicating down to the articulation how he performs them himself.

Kirkpatrick has neither fingered the sonatas nor added articulation marks. As he states in his Preface to Volume I, "My own specific ideas regarding interpretation will illustrate themselves far better in my recorded performances than in any verbal explanation." The en- tire Preface is invaluable, with chapters on fingering, technical problems, ornamentation, phrasing, melodic inflection, harmonic inflection, tempo and rhythm, dynamics, and expressive character. Volume II concludes with a scholarly report on the sources and numbering of the sonatas, editorial policy, and notes on the text. The material, while indispensable for teachers, is probably too detailed and scholarly for most students.

My recommendation is to own both editions yourself and to assign the Friskin edition to most high school students. *(April 1987)*

I have three questions concerning the Scarlatti Sonatas. How many sonatas did he write? What is the explanation for the "L" numbers and the "K" numbers? How should I program the Sonatas in the Friskin edition which have no numbers?

The "L" numbers refer to the first so-called "complete" edition, prepared by Alessandro Longo, an edition that contains 545 sonatas. This edition includes, for example, 68 sonatas in the key of D major, 31 in D minor, and 70 in G major, the keys you refer to in your discussion of the Friskin edition. So it is clear that to list a Scarlatti sonata simply by key is not very helpful.

The "K" numbers which are given along with the Longo numbers in the Kirkpatrick edition are the catalogue numbers assigned to each sonata by Kirkpatrick himself, a wholly new cataloguing system covering a total of 555 sonatas. Kirkpatrick's edition is the only one arranged, as nearly as possible, m chronological order. This explains the discrepancy you have noted between his numbering system and that of the earlier Longo edition.

To program the Sonatas in the Friskin edition, you really have only two choices: list them by volume, number, and key as they appear in the Friskin volume you are using, or find a complete Longo edition in a good music library and look up the Longo number (a fascinating detective game in itself!).

In a former issue of *Clavier* I recommended the Kirkpatrick edition and made a strong case for studying the preface to Volume I which includes a treasure-trove of helpful suggestions for teaching and performing Scarlatti. *(October 1972)*

Teaching suggestions for Scarlatti. *Could you direct me to some help in teaching the Scarlatti sonatas? I live too far from a major music center to avail myself of lessons from a master teacher.*

There is no better study source on the Scarlatti sonatas than the preface to a collection of *60 Sonatas*, edited by Ralph Kirkpatrick from the manuscripts and earliest printed sources, published in two volumes by G. Schirmer (Nos. 1774 and 1775).

The preface (Vol. 1) begins with information on Scarlatti's life and explanations of this particular edition. The "meat" of the preface is contained in the invaluable suggestions for performance that follow. Mr. Kirkpatrick states that the purpose of these suggestions is to provide a glimpse into his own working habits, and to aid the player in formulating general principles and methods of practicing and of sharpening the ear, which not only form the basis of his own interpretations but are so fundamental that they might serve equally well as the basis for interpretations radically different from his own.

He uses the question-answer method to discuss fingering, technical problems, ornamentation, phrasing, melodic inflection, harmonic inflection, tempo and rhythm, dynamics, and expressive character.

A study of this preface, along with Mr. Kirkpatrick's own recordings of the sonatas (Columbia), provides invaluable insight into the Scarlatti sonatas and how to teach them. To supplement this study, you might also read Kirkpatrick's book, *Domenico Scarlatti*, published by Princeton University Press. *(November 1966)*

Lea Pocket Scores. *What are the Lea Pocket Scores and where are they available?*

The Lea Pocket Scores are reproductions in miniature of scholarly editions of a great variety of music, including orchestral, chamber, choral and keyboard works. They have been a godsend to college music students because of their high quality and very low cost.

For example, the complete keyboard works of Bach, Handel, Rameau, Haydn, Mozart, Beethoven, Schubert, Chopin, Schumann, and Brahms are available in scholarly study scores, as is a reprint of the complete keyboard works of Bach in the famous Gesellschaft Edition. They are available through CPP/Belwin.

Of course these pocket scores are too small for studio use, but they do provide the teacher with a complete home reference library, against which to check and correct teaching editions. *(February 1968)*

Ornamentation. *Could you refer me to some book or literature that gives help in regard to ornaments in general? I am forever running into baffling problems with turns, trills and the like, and would like to know how to cope with them with more understanding.*

For ornaments in Scarlatti, read the excellent preface to Volume I of Ralph Kirkpatrick's edition of the Scarlatti Sonatas, published by G. Schirmer.

For ornaments in Bach and his contemporaries, see the book, *Bach's Ornaments* by Walter Emery, published by Novello.

For ornaments in classic composers, you will find C.P.E. Bach's *Essay on the True Art of Keyboard Playing* extremely helpful. It is published by Norton.

For ornaments in romantic and modern composers there is, unfortunately, no definitive work. Trills and turns remain much the same as in the classic era, except that they tend to start, much more frequently, on the principal note, rather than the note above or below. *(May/June 1967)*

Could you recommend a good all-purpose manual on the art of ornamentation and the proper articulation of ornaments in the different periods of music history?

Many fine, scholarly tomes on ornamentation, beginning with C.P.E. Bach's *The True Art of Playing Keyboard Instruments*, are available, but almost every comprehensive work on the subject limits itself to a single period in music history. The exception may be found in Howard Ferguson's Keyboard Interpretation (Oxford University Press, 1975). Chapter 8 of this volume is devoted to the art of ornamentation, treated by country and period.

This is the most compact historical survey of ornamentation I know, and I recommend the book to you in its entirety, but especially for this section. *(April 1982)*

Chopin Ornamentation. *How can I know for sure to play correctly the ornaments in Chopin's music? Where can I get this information?*

One of the simplest explanations can be found at the back of any of the volumes of Chopin's Complete Works in the Polish Institute Edition, edited under the direction of Paderewski and available in this country through E.B. Marks (now a part of Belwin). A discussion of Chopin's ornaments is included in the two pages under the heading, "The Character of the Present Edition." This section occurs at the end of each of the volumes except Volume 18, "Selected Easy Pieces." *(November 1975)*

Would you tell me how to play the trills in Chopin's Nocturne in F Minor, Op. 55, No. 1? I have listened to the record many times, but cannot grasp the detail as it happens so fast.

All the trills in the Chopin Nocturne are on Bb, but, with the exception of the first one, they are preceded by a small gruppetto which begins on A.

The first trill (measure 6) begins on Bb and trills between C and Bb, like this:

All of the trills after that begin with a gruppetto on A, proceed to Bb, and then trill between C and Bb, finishing with the varied after-turn which is written out in small notes by Chopin. For example, measure 14:

As you can see, the entire ornament must take place within the time of the last half of the measure. *(May/June 1967)*

Meaning of Hob. *I recently bought a new edition of the Haydn Sonatas and found that each sonata has a Hob. number. What does Hob. stand for?*

Hob. is to Haydn what K. is to Mozart or L. to Scarlatti. It stands for the catalogue of Haydn's complete works, compiled by Anthon y van Hoboken and published by Schott. The instrumental portion of the Hoboken catalogue, including the keyboard works, was released in 1957; and since that time most publications refer to Haydn work s by their Hob. numbers. *(January 1979)*

Music notation. *Where can I get help with the fundamentals of writing music? I'm not referring to composing, but to notating what I compose. I need help both for myself and for my more advanced students who are now composing music that they don't know how to notate properly. We all need advice in such practical details as stems, flags, beams, rests, slurs, ties, etc.*

The best advice I can give is to refer you to the two resources I myself use.

First, there is an excellent and very complete book called *Music Notation* by Gardner Read, published by Allyn and Bacon, Inc., Boston. Read is a teacher of composition and instrumentation and in this book has distilled the experience and wisdom gleaned over many years of correcting student manuscripts. In the course of these years he grew increasingly aware of the widespread lack of knowledge concerning correct notational procedures, and his book is an attempt to present a working tool for anyone interested in making music notation clear, accurate, and effective.

Part I of the book is a brief historical survey of the evolution of music notation. In Part II, each single element of notation (staves, systems, clefs, notes, rests, expression markings, etc.) is presented, first in traditional practice and then in modern usage. Sometimes he also suggests reforms in accepted practice. Part III deals with notation for voices and individual instruments. Part IV contains precise directions for writing music manuscript, reading proof, and preparing full and condensed scores.

I do not know of a comparable book and recommend it as the best written word on how to notate music as clearly and accurately as possible.

Prior to the publication of the Gardner Read book, I often sought the advice of a professional music editor. This was time-consuming and expensive, but it is magic to watch a confused page take on simplicity and clarity under the hands of the best editors. Now that this book is available, I recommend it as a daily source of help and inspiration. *(February 1983)*

About five years ago you answered a question in your column from a teacher who wanted to learn more about the proper way to notate music manuscript. You referred her to a text called Music Notation *by Gardner Read which I believe was published in the 60s. Has this book been revised and is there a more recent textbook which you recommend?*

Gardner Read's book was first published in 1969 and has since appeared in a second edition entitled, *Music Notation (A Manual of Modern Practice)*. It is a Crescendo Book, published by Taplinger. When it first appeared it stood alone as the standard reference work on music notation. Soon after, another landmark work appeared: *Music Notation in the Twentieth Century* by Kurt Stone, published by W.W. Norton. Stone was editor of many of the major music publishers in the United States and has become one of the world's leading authorities on contemporary music notation and its problems. As head of the Index of New Musical Notation, he collected and categorized the myriad new devices appearing in published music during the 20th century. Working with professional performers and conductors he evaluated the effectiveness of each device in its practical application.

In 1974 under his leadership the International Conference on New Music Notation met to discuss these devices. Eighty musicians from 18 countries were able to reach a consensus as to the devices and practices in contemporary music notation, and the results of that conference are incorporated into this book.

Both books treat traditional notation in the most comprehensive way, and both have extensive musical examples and detailed indices. Together the two volumes present far more information than any but the most serious professional composer or performer could possibly need to know. *(December 1988)*

Chapter Eight

Books and Reference Works

Grove's. *I will be a beginning piano teacher when I graduate from college in June, 1972. My piano teacher at college has suggested that I begin now to build a library of reference books for the piano teacher, and thinks I need to budget about $50 per year so that eventually I will own all the books I need. He suggested that I start by purchasing Grove's Dictionary of Music and Musicians. I understand it is very expensive, and wonder if you would recommend it for my first purchase.*

Certainly Grove's is a fine set of books to own, and you will undoubtedly want to have it in your library some day; but I would not recommend it for your first purchase. It is published in nine volumes by St. Martin's Press, and would consume your total budget for many years.

It seems to me it would be more practical to start with a one-volume dictionary such as the Harvard Dictionary of Music by Willi Apel, published by the Harvard University Press and perhaps, the second year, an additional dictionary of musicians, such as *Baker's Biographical Dictionary of Musicians*, published by G. Schirmer.

To these basic books I would then recommend that you add two additional reference works:

1) a compendium of piano repertoire, such as *The Teacher's Guidebook to Piano Literature* by Kern and Titus, published by Edwards Brothers, or *The Literature of the Piano* by Ernest Hutcheson, published by Knopf, or *Music for the Piano – A Handbook of Concert and Teaching Materials from 1580 to 1952* by Friskin and Freundlich, published by Dover.

2) a one-volume history of keyboard music, such as *A Short History of Keyboard Music* by F.E. Kirby, published by The Free Press.

If you can budget $50 for your first year, you would probably have enough left over to purchase *The Art of Piano Playing* by George Kochevitzky, published by Summy-Birchard. This book is the best synthesis I have found of workable ideas about developing piano technique.

To sum up, then, the Grove's dictionary will always be available to you in any college or municipal library, where you can consult it occasionally while you build a basic library of books you will use daily or weekly in your own studio. As soon as possible, turn your attention to some of the many excellent books on teaching and learning — you may find them even more helpful than books limited to your own special field! *(April 1972)*

Baker's. *What do you consider the best biographical dictionary of musicians? I can't afford Grove's and wonder what you consider next best.*

The best reference work available in English is *Baker's Biographical Dictionary of Musicians*. The sixth edition, edited by Nicholas Slonimsky and in preparation for over two decades, has just been released. The price is steep, but the work is the most valuable one-volume biographical dictionary I know. It contains approximately 12,000 en- tries, spanning the history of music from the Middle Ages right up to today. There are over 1000 new entries in this sixth edition. *(September 1979)*

Compendia. *I am particularly interested in a book which I have been told is out of print. The title is* Music for the Piano, A Handbook of Concert and Teaching Material from 1580 to 1952 *by James Friskin and Irwin Freundlich. Is a comparable text available?*

Music for the Piano by Friskin and Freundlich is now available in paperback, published by Dover. It still includes only music published up to 1952.

Following is information on three somewhat similar texts.

Guide to the Pianist's Repertoire by Maurice Hinson, edited by Irwin Freundlich, was published in 1973 by the Indiana University Press, Bloomington, Indiana. This is a much larger volume than the Friskin-Freundlich edition. It includes over 700 pages of solo piano works (publishers given) by individual composers, graded as to difficulty; anthologies and collections listed by country; an alphabetical list of composers under national designation; and an appendix of historical recital programs. It is an outstanding reference work for performers and teachers. In 1979 a supplementary volume by Mr. Hinson was released by Indiana University Press entitled Guide to the Pianist's Repertoire Supplement. It updates the 1973 publication and includes a great quantity of new or formerly unavailable music.

The Teacher's Guidebook to Piano Literature by Alice M. Kern and Helen M. Titus is published by Edwards Brothers, Ann Arbor, Michigan. It first appeared in 1954, went through five printings, and was revised in 1964. This is a comprehensive listing of recommended literature for students. There are four sections, each covering a different grade level (lower elementary, upper elementary, intermediate, and lower advanced) and within each section the music is listed by period (16th,

17th and 18th centuries, 19th century, 20th century). Within each section the material is arranged alphabetically by composer, and for each recommended composition, a variety of publishers or collections is included.

An older book, *The Literature of the Piano* written by Ernest Hutcheson in 1949 and revised by Rudolph Ganz in 1964 is published by Knopf, New York. This is a valuable textbook, providing discussion analysis of traditional piano literature; however, it omits earlier music and modern repertoire. *(May/June 1977)*

Maxwell Music Evaluation File. *I have heard about a music evaluation service for piano teachers. Can you tell me more about it?*

The Maxwell Music Evaluation File began as a compilation of favorite teaching pieces from many Colorado teachers. Gradually, sources for the file- expanded to include syllabi from 12 state music teacher associations, the M.T.N.A. "Course of Study," reviews of new music from Cla11ier and other music magazines, books, recital programs, and workshop lists.

Each title was cataloged according to information such as level, period, style, and technical difficulty. The cards were then taken to conventions, independent teachers, and university pedagogy classes where music professionals were asked to sign the cards if they used and approved of the music. Cards receiving at least five recommendations were included in the file.

In 1984, the Maxwell Music Evaluation File began to be issued yearly in notebook rather than file card format. To date, these annual notebooks, called "Update and Catch Up" have appeared in 1984, 1985, 1986-87. *(November 1988)*

Liszt. *Our piano teacher's group is having a series of programs this year on the teaching methods of some of the famous teachers of the past, especially their technical approaches. I volunteered to do the session on Liszt for the January meeting and have already looked up some source material, but I'm wondering if there isn't something more recent that I may not be aware of. Can you suggest any new books of special value?*

There is a brand new publication, just released this summer, that should prove both helpful and entertaining. It is called *The Liszt Studies* (Essential Selections from the Original 12-Volume Set of Technical Studies for the Piano including the first English edition of the legendary *Liszt Pedagogue* — a lesson-diary of the master as teacher, as kept by Mme. Auguste Boissier, 1831-32). The selections, editions, and English translation are by Elyse Mach, and the volume is published by Associated Music Publishers, New York ($5.00).

In the preface to this interesting collection, Dr. Mach explains:

"In 1869, Franz Liszt began to set down a series of formal exercises designed to improve the finger technique of advanced students. He completed the twelve volumes of Technical Studies in 1879. Although he had hoped to have these studies in readiness for publication in 1880, it was not until 1886, after Liszt's death, that these exercises were published by Alexander Winterberger through the Schubert Company in Leipzig, Germany. The exercises selected for this book have been compiled from these twelve volumes. The basis of selection is the unusual and unique fingerings which were intended to lead the advanced student of piano to the epitome of technical proficiency.

"Besides the twelve volumes of Technical Studies there was, apparently, a method book that accompanied them. Composer Camille Saint-Saens indicated that Liszt wrote a 'method' which was entrusted to others and mysteriously disappeared... Saint-Saens regarded the loss as irreparable, because Liszt's written method would have transmitted his most valuable teaching to generations of pianists.

"Some indication of Liszt's approach to the practice of exercises, however, survives in the testimony of his students – in particular the lesson-diary *Liszt Pedagogue*, by Madame Auguste Boissier... Madame Boissier, whose daughter Valerie was a private pupil of Liszt during 1831 and 1832, attended her daughter's lessons and took notes... The diary itself is divided into lesson segments, starting with Lesson Seven (there is no record of the first six) and progressing through Lesson Twenty-Eight. Madame Boissier has at-tempted to record not only what occurred throughout the lessons, but her intellectual and emotional reactions to various situations as well."

The lesson-diary has fascinating passages. Despite its flowery language, languorous repetitiveness, and romantic idolization of the young Liszt, there are a number of real insights into Liszt's character in various roles — technician, pianist, teacher, improviser, composer, and salon idol. The diary is almost embarrassingly romantic in style, but as we read it we must remember that it was written when the romantic period was at its zenith, by a woman composer who was also the concerned and conscientious mother of a precocious young pianist.

In evaluating the insights which Madame Boissier has provided, it is important to keep in mind that we see Liszt the pedagogue through the eyes of a devoted and anxious mother; might his lost "method" not have presented his teaching methods in quite a different light? Also, that through her eyes we see a very young Liszt (he was 21 and 22 years old when these lessons took place). What master teacher would wish recorded for all time the teaching methods and insights he espoused at 21 or 22?

Isn't it likely that Liszt outgrew his passion for Bertini, Kalkbrenner, Moscheles, Kessler, Czerny, Hummel, et al? Can we believe that in maturity Liszt would have linked Weber and Beethoven as composers before whom he felt "profound humility, maintaining that he was as yet unworthy of executing their works, though he sets the piano on fire whenever he plays them?" Can we believe that in later years he would still have found Haydn "old-fashioned, too rhythmical, and overripe?" Or did Madame Boissier misunderstand or misinterpret what the very young Liszt was thinking and feeling? Despite these seeming detractions of the diary, it is wonderful reading, light, entertaining, often amusing. And the technical exercises that follow afford fascinating hints as to how the prodigious 19th century technicians developed their flying steel fingers. Madame Boissier assures us that Liszt did his own technical practice at least three hours each day, while reading a book to avoid boredom!

But, in fairness to the master Liszt became, do keep in mind the contrast between the diary and the studies themselves. The studies were prepared for publication, by the fully-mature technical master, toward the end of his life; they must be considered the distillation of his lifetime inquiry into the development of absolute technical control. The diary, on the other hand, was prepared by someone else with no thought of publication, probably without Liszt's knowledge, certainly without his sanction; and it represents his work with one young student when he himself was but a youth. *(November 1973)*

Clara Schumann. *Our piano teachers organization is studying great women in music and I've been assigned a paper on Clara Schumann. I have John Burk's* Clara Schumann: A Romantic Biography, *but wondered if you know of a more recent publication.*

Yes! First, though, you should be aware that the most comprehensive material on Clara Schumann is in the volumes edited by Berthold Litzmann and published in English as *Clara Schumann: An Artist's Life, Based on Material Found in Diaries and Letters*, translated by Grace E. Hadow, and published in two volumes by MacMillan (London, 1913).

John Burk's volume was published in 1940. Since then there has been a surge of renewed interest in Clara, as shown by the serious research into her life and work, resulting in new translations of the letters and diaries, many scholarly periodical articles, and several doctoral dissertations. Two biographies have come out since 1980: John Chisells' *Clara Schumann: A Dedicated Spirit*, published by Hamish Hamilton (London, 1983), and *Clara Schumann: The Artist and the Woman* by Nancy Reich, published by Cornell University Press (1985). I believe the latter is the finest biography of Clara Schumann to date; this study forces us to take an entirely new look at one of history's great women artists.

To prepare her book, Reich not only studied all the old sources, she was also able to gain access to new, recently published or still unpublished primary sources. In her preface she writes:

"Though much has been written about Clara Schumann, she is still, more than 165 years after her birth, known to us only through the eyes and minds of her own era. She is viewed even today as her nineteenth-century contemporaries saw her — as saint or 'priestess,' as a dedicated wife, mother, and musician. In seeking a modern approach to this great artist, I have examined new sources and reexamined the old. This study has deepened my regard for the artist and woman; it has also convinced me she is worthy of the truth. Such a quest calls for the tools of musicological scholarship, the insights of psychology, and sensitivity to the history of women and their place in nineteenth-century musical history."

Reich used only the original German publications of all the best-known sources, providing her own meticulous translations for them. In addition, she had access to a remarkable collection in the archives of Robert-Schumann-Haus in Zwickau of Schumann documents that are being prepared according to contemporary scholarly procedures. The book is in two parts. Part I is organized chronologically, but the focus is less on Clara's life history than on the key issues of her life: her childhood and education; the strong bond with her father; the development of her brilliant early concert career; her romance with and eventual marriage to Robert Schumann; her struggles during his illness, suicide attempt, and hospitalization; and her astonishing ability to juggle the responsibilities of her large family and demanding career .

In Part II, under the heading *Themes from the Life of Clara Schumann*, Reich deals mainly with the 40 years of Clara's life after Robert's death. She discusses Clara's friendships (especially that with Johannes Brahms), her work as composer, editor, and teacher, and her unparalleled concert career. Reich's accomplishment in this volume is formidable. Her scholarship is profound, her search for the truth unstinting, and her willingness to submit old myths to careful scrutiny unrelenting. In addition, she shows sensitivity, compassion, and insight into a remarkable and complex personality. Studying the book greatly enhanced my appreciation and respect, if not my affection, for Clara Schumann as woman and artist. I recommend it to you as one of the best new musical biographies of 1985. (*February 1987*)

Alexander Tcherepnin. *At the college where I am enrolled, all piano majors have an hour private lesson each week and an additional one-hour piano class each week. For next term our class assignment is to write a paper on a contemporary piano composer who is living today. We are free to use the composer of our choice, so long as no two students choose the* *same composer. I chose Alexander Tcherepnin because I was brought up on his compositions in your Contemporary Piano Literature series and I have also studied some of his major works since I've been in college. Will you please tell me where I can get more information both on his life and on his compositions?*

If you check the back issues of *Clavier*, you will find an article I wrote about Tcherepnin, entitled "A Visit with Alexander Tcherepnin" in the March, 1968 issue.

My Tcherepnin file includes at least fifteen magazine articles on the composer and his work that have appeared in music magazines within the last decade. Since an important part of writing term papers is learning to do the research that goes into them, I'll leave you on your own to find these articles. If you haven't yet learned to use the various library resources and indices, ask your college librarian to teach you this important research tool.

There is a book-length pamphlet on Tcherepnin in French called *Alexandre Tcherepnine* by Willy Reich published in Paris by La Revue Musicale. If you read French it would prove very helpful. If it is not in your college library, perhaps the librarian could borrow it from a larger university or from your state library. *(April 1972)*

The New Grove Biographies. *I've just begun teaching and want to build up a library of good reference materials as quickly and inexpensively as possible. Can you recommend brief but comprehensive biographies of the great keyboard composers, preferably in paperback?*

I am happy to recommend a new series called The New Grove biographies, which are reprints in book form of articles that appeared in The New Grove Dictionary of Music and Musicians, published in London in 1980. Biographies of the Bach family, Handel, Haydn, Mozart, and Schubert are available at this time; these paperback editions range in price from $7.95, to $9.95 per volume.

Written in the mid-70s, the texts for these new books were completed at the end of that decade. For these reprints, the original author, or his representative, re-read, corrected, and modified the text. Because the texts originated as dictionary articles, their character is quite different from that of material conceived for publication as a book. They include a great deal of factual information in a format that offers quick and easy reference, treating the composers' lives and works in an encyclopedic rather than a narrative style. They contain proper source acknowledgements, comprehensive works lists, and extended bibliographies.

In short, the series contains definitive information in compact form and at reasonable prices. However, you will not find information such as thematics, analyses of the works, interpretive help, or critical evaluation; and keyboard students may find it frustrating to have to sift through all the works in every genre to find reference to keyboard compositions. Another lack is personal detail about the composer 's life or any attempt to interpret the music in terms of the composer 's mental, emotional, and psychological nature and development.

The new series is a gold mine of useful information, though devoid of the kind of analysis and interpretation that the best critical biographies offer. *(December 1987)*

About pianists. *I have accumulated quite a library of books on great composers. Now I'm interested in acquiring some books on great pianists. Will you please suggest three or four of the best? Also, is there a book that would be especially good as a gift to a student going off to college to major in piano?*

Of the many fine books available, I'll suggest three, the first of which would be particularly appropriate as a gift for a graduating piano student:

- *The Great Pianists from Mozart to the Present* by Harold Schonberg (Simon and Schuster, paperback). This is an historical and analytical compendium by a man who for many years was head music critic of the New York Times. The book is concerned primarily with piano playing and begins with Mozart and Clementi. The leading pianists from then till the present are discussed, not biographically, but as "keyboard specialists who had something unique to offer, and whose playing made a mark not only on their own generation but in many cases helped shape the playing and the keyboard philosophy of the generation that followed." A must for every serious pianist and piano teacher.
- *Great Pianists Speak for Themselves* by Elyse Mach (Dodd, Mead, paperback). Reviewed in the October 1980 issue, this new book is not about great pianists, but by them. Thirteen of the most important contemporary artists (Arrau, Ashkenazy, Brendel, Browning, de Larrocha, Dichter, Firkusny, Gould, Horowitz, Janis, Kraus, Turek, Watts) discuss, in their own words, the development of their art, per- forming careers, and ideas and viewpoints. The material for the book was drawn from personal interviews, and the artists speak informally and candidly with insights that are as revealing as they are entertaining.
- *Alfred Brendel, Musical Thoughts and Afterthoughts* (Princeton University Press, paperback). This slim, provocative volume is one in a series of "Princeton Essays on the Arts" which aims to provide an outlet for scholarly papers in the various disciplines of the creative arts. The major sections include essays on the piano music of Beethoven, Schubert, Liszt, Busoni and Brendel's teacher, Edwin Fischer. The book is scholarly and profound, invaluable for the most serious pianists and artist-teachers. *(April 1982)*

Sidney Harrison. *One of the things I always look for in your column is recommended books* on music and teaching. *You have not recommended anything new for some time. Do you have any goodies up your sleeves?*

Unfortunately, good books on music education don't come along on a monthly schedule. I wish they did! However, I am delighted to recommend a book that is not new, but new to me and about which I am very enthusiastic. It is called *The Young Person's Guide to Playing the Piano* by Sidney Harrison, published by Faber and Faber in London. Harrison writes in a commonsense manner, with a delightful sense of humor, and seems to draw his remarks from years of wonderful experience teaching young people.

Despite its title, and the fact that junior high and high school students will thoroughly enjoy it, I see it as a book for teachers of young people, or one that teachers and young people might use and enjoy together.

There are 22 chapters, ranging in subject matter from "A Piano is a Piano" (a short, amusing and intensely instructive discussion of how the piano works) to "Heavy Pianists, Light Pianists, and Jazz Pianists" (a funny, but very serious discussion of the differences between concert artists, salon musicians, and jazz pianists). There are good discussions of how to look at music, phrasing and pedaling, technique and relaxation, how to practice, accompanying, receiving applause, bowing, and much, much more.

It is extremely readable and entertaining, yet deeply insightful. I recommend it highly for your serious students and even more highly for you. *(January 1984)*

Abby Whiteside. *Some time ago you recommended a book that has meant the world to me,* Indispensables of Piano Playing *by Abby Whiteside. Could you tell your readers something about the author and list other books she has written?*

Abby Whiteside was born in 1881 in Vermillion, South Dakota and died in New York City in 1956. She was a student of Rudolph Ganz, taught for a number of years at the University of Oregon, and then in New York. I know her, as you do, only through her writings and through her extraordinary reputation as a great human being and a great teacher.

Her greatness as a teacher is perhaps best exemplified by her willingness to come face to face with the fact that there is no Great Divide separating the gifted from the ungifted unless it be the teacher himself. As a result she forsook the tools she had been using to spend the rest of her life discovering means by which everyone could play the piano beautifully and with enjoyment. Her contributions in this field are inestimable.

Last year a new Abby Whiteside book was released, *Mastering the Chopin Etudes and*

Other Essays, published by Charles Scribner's Sons, New York. This book is edited by Joseph Prostakoff and Sophia Rosoff and includes all the available manuscripts written by Miss Whiteside. We are indeed fortunate to have these essays on the Etudes brought to light, because it was in the mastery of them that she found ways to present the essence of her principles. *(April 1970)*

Howard Ferguson. *I recently heard of a book on interpretation by Ferguson. I would like to know more about this book and its author, and also how to gee a copy. None of our local music scores or book stores has it in stock or has heard of it. Is it available?*

The book you refer to must be *Keyboard Interpretation* by Howard Ferguson, published by Oxford University Press, and available in paper back edition. Ferguson is a well-known musicologist, born in Belfast, Ireland, in 1904 and educated at Westminster School and the Royal College of Music. He has composed piano, chamber, choral, and orchestral works and has appeared widely as a chamber pianist. He is perhaps best known in this country for his editions of early keyboard music, and anyone interested in this literature will find a rich treasure-trove of early music in his anthologies Early English Keyboard Music (42 pieces in two volumes), Early German Keyboard Music (30 pieces in two volumes), Early Italian Keyboard Music (35 pieces in two volumes), Style and Interpretation (71 pieces in six volumes), all published by Oxford University Press.

Keyboard Interpretation is a compilation and augmentation of the information about keyboard instruments, their literature, and its interpretation that first appeared in the introduction s to the various anthologies listed above. Both students and teachers will find it a clear, detailed, and practical guide to authentic performance of early music. *(November 1975)*

George Kochevitsky. *Our piano teachers group now includes two older Russian-born piano teachers whose training in Russia was in the classic 19th century European tradition. Heavy debate has arisen over the number of hours even a young student must practice to develop any technique whatsoever. They disagree with all the rest of us who do not require hours and hours of daily scales, arpeggios, Czerny, and Hanon. I have heard a book mentioned at your study courses that debunks this extreme emphasis on fingertraining. Will you please send me the name of the book, the publisher and enough about it to help us decide if it would be a good book for our discussions? I believe the author was Russian; if that is true it might help persuade our two dissenters!*

I believe the book to which you are referring is *The Art of Piano Playing* by George Kochevitsky (Summy-Birchard). Kochevitsky, born in Russia in 1902, graduated from the Leningrad State Conservatory in 1930 and later did post-graduate work at the Moscow State Conservatory with emphasis on what he calls the theory and history of "pianism and piano pedagogy." He came to the United States in 1949 and is now living and teaching in New York City.

As far as I know *The Art of Piano Playing* (subtitled, "a scientific approach") is his only published book; however, he has published articles in American magazines.

The Art of Piano Playing begins with an historical survey of theories of piano technique, including direct quotes from such technical specialists as Clementi, Hummel, Kulak, Czerny, and Hanon, each of whose technique Mr. Kochevitsky claims is based on fingers alone. The author also considers what he calls the progressive ideas in 19th century teaching where there is emphasis on the participation of the arm. Following this comes a chapter which deals with growing awareness of the role of the mind.

This leads directly to his theories on how technique is developed, and it is this chapter that warrants real study, for Kochevitsky believes that the central nervous system is the source of all pianistic movement and the seat of learning for all musical performance.

I most definitely recommend a serious study of *The Art of Piano Playing* by all piano teachers. I use the word "study" advisedly because parts of the book make real demands on the reader. When you come face to face with the concept that the roots of technique lie in the central nervous system, with muscular conditions and the out- ward appearance of the playing apparatus only secondary, you are entering a very different world of thinking from that which is prevalent in much teaching today.

Subjects discussed in the last half of the book include: Theory of Movement, Tone Production, Relaxation and Tension, Adjustment to the Keyboard, Finger Dexterity, Spatial Orientation, Regulation of Energy, Mental Dexterity, Grouping and Regrouping, Mental Practicing, and Stage Fright.

Even though the emphasis in this book on concepts of neurology and muscle physiology makes it appear as purely a book on the skill aspects of performance Mr. Kochevitsky concludes the book With these words:

"While striving to give as much scientific foundation as possible to our technical work, I still hope that there will always be a place in piano playing for inspiration of a high order, and that wealth of imagination will be the decisive factor in great performance." *(December 1972)*

Otto Ortmann. *In his book,* The Physiological Mechanics of Piano Technique, *Otto Ortmann explains that through laboratory experiments he found that the quality of piano tone cannot be changed by the way in which the piano is played. If this is true, why do we think that one pianist plays with a "hard" touch, another with a "beautiful" touch, on the* *same piano? Is it because one person's playing is more artistic than another's?*

Ortmann's book, published originally in 1929 and now available only in paperback from E.P. Dutton & Co., Inc., includes the findings of years of rigorous scientific analysis and experimentation in the field of piano technique. It is an oversimplification to say Ortmann concluded that the "quality of piano tone cannot be changed by the way in which the piano is played." It is more accurate to say that he proved beyond any scientific doubt that the single piano key can influence tone in one way only — dynamically; that the only tonal control a pianist has over a single key is loudness, which is directly proportional to velocity of key descent. In terms of loudness, it does not matter how the key is activated — curved finger, flat finger, high finger, close finger, or even by machine. A pianist cannot control the timbre (i.e., the overtone structure) of piano tone in the sense that a string or wind player controls this aspect of sound.

However, piano playing, as Ortmann was keenly aware, involves far more than control of single keys. More than we often realize, beautiful tone is a matter of proper dynamics or voicing within the harmony. There are also infinite degrees of dynamic inflection from pitch to pitch within a single line, as well as the degree of legato or non-legato, exactness and inflection of rhythm, and pedaling.

These are some of the many factors that make up the elusive quality of piano touch that we refer to subjectively as hard or beautiful, banging or singing. Ortmann would have been the first to admit that it is these elusive qualities that contribute to artistry and beautiful tone. *(October 1980)*

Helen Lanfer. *In a recent column you recommended* The Music Within Us* *by Helen Lanfer, published by Hebrew Arts Music Publications. I have tried to order the book, but neither my music store nor my bookstore can find it. Can you give me the publisher's address and the cost?*

Many teachers have written with this same question. The book is available in paperback through Tara Publications, The Hebrew Arts School, 129 W. 67th Street, New York, New York. *(March 1981)*

*For a review of this book, see Chapter Six

Books on general education. *I have planned my teaching schedule this year to allow time for a reading and study program. I would like some suggestions on books dealing with general education, but especially books that would help me as a piano teacher. I have already read Gilbert Highet's* The Art of Teaching *and enjoyed it, but I am interested in finding books to study, not just to read for pleasure.*

Bravo! Here are a few books on education which will take real study, and which I believe you will find significant as you apply them to your own teaching.

The Process of Communication by Berlo (Holt, Rinehart) is an excellent and readable survey of the whole problem of interpersonal communication, with practical suggestions for improving our techniques.

Experience and Education by John Dewey (MacMillan). Contrary to the popular belief that John Dewey was a perpetrator of "isms," progressivism in particular, his own writings reveal an educator who was basically a traditionalist, yet one who added to the educational framework a more alive and meaningful concept of learning. His contribution to education is a positive one, with far-reaching implications. It is important to understand what he meant, by reading not only this book but everything he wrote.

The Child from Five to Ten by Gesell and Ilg (Harper) is a detailed description of the average child, year by year, formulated as a composite of observations on hundreds of children at the Institute of Human Relations at Yale University. Generally regarded as a most accurate and reasonable description of the nature of children.

The Teacher and the Taught by Ronald Gross (Delta, paperback). The subtitle of this book is "Education in Theory and Practice from Plato to James B. Conant." The book includes essays about educators, covering two thousand years of teaching and learning in 305 pages! However, reading it will entice you to read the books by and about the 19 important educational leaders touched on in these essays.

The Analysis of Behavior by Holland and Skinner (McGraw-Hill) is a highly technical book, in a special question-answer format, which helps the reader to self-teach the vocabulary and basic principles of fundamental learning theory as they are currently understood by psychologists.

Talks to Teachers on Psychology by William James (Dover) is a collection of talks on psychology, first given at the request of the Harvard Corporation to the teachers of Cambridge. Every teacher should read and reread this book. The chapter on "The Laws of Habit" alone is worth twice the price of the book.

Learning How to Learn by Rambusch (Helicon) is a book on the Montessori techniques of child education, especially valuable for its clear description of the child's learning process.

There's Music in Children by Sheehy (Holt) is a book full of common sense about children, written by a woman whose lifetime of experience in bringing children and music together enables her to present the most profound observations in the simplest language. A must for every teacher who works with young children, and for every parent interested in recognizing and helping to develop the natural love for music that exists in every child.

The Aims of Education by Alfred North Whitehead (Mentor Books, paperback). Probably no one has had a more pervasive influence on education in our universities than the late Professor Whitehead of Harvard. Every student of education will find this book a persuasive protest against dead knowledge and inert ideas, and a strong appeal for alive teachers with living ideas, to deal with students and the process of their self-development.

What Do I Do Monday? by John Holt (Dutton) This is one of the best recent books I know on problems in general education. Holt is the well-known author of *How Children Learn* and *How Children Fail* which I have previously recommended. *(December 1966)*

Jerome Brunner. *Thank you for the fine list of books on education, I have read them with interest. Since you suggested that this was only a beginning, may I ask for a few more recommendations in the general field of teaching and learning?*

I enthusiastically recommend three books by Jerome Brunner, Professor of Psychology at Harvard, all three published in 1966 by Harvard University Press.

Toward a Theory of Instruction. This book is a compilation of eight essays, parts of which were given as lectures, written by Professor Brunner over a period of five years. The essays are the result of years of research and exploration into the nature of intellectual growth and its relation to methods of teaching children. The concrete illustrations make it an invaluable book for any teacher of young students, regardless of the subject matter being taught. *The Process of Education.* In this book Professor Brunner states his views of the conclusions reached at a conference on new educational methods at Woods Hole, Mass., in 1959. *On Knowing (Essays for the Left Hand).* A brilliant inquiry into the part that intuition, feeling and spontaneity play in determining how we know what we know, and how we can communicate what we know to others, that is, how to teach. *(September 1967)*

Children teach each other. *I recently attended a workshop for piano teachers, based on video teaching tapes made at the New School for Music Study. The whole theory that students learn more from each other than they ever learn from a teacher is quite new to me, but very exciting. Your tapes seem to confirm that you have applied this learning principle to the teaching of music at the piano. Are there any books written specifically on this subject, not as it applies to music teaching particularly, but to education in general?*

The only book I am acquainted with that bears directly on this subject is one called *Children Teach Children*, subtitled "Learning by Teaching." It is by Alan Gartner, Mary Kohler, and Frank Riessman, and is published by Harper and Row. It is a report of the processes used in some "youth-teaching-youth" projects and the experiences and insights gained. The book begins with a foreword by Ralph W. Tyler, in which the first sentence reads, "Children and youth learn far more when performing the teaching role than when acting as students in the classroom." Here at the New School for Music Study we have seen this happen- with children, with teenagers, and with the young adults who enroll in our post-graduate pedagogy program. At every age it seems to be true that the active role of teaching is a better way to learn than the relative passivity of just being the student. *(October 1975)*

Piaget and Montessori. *I have become interested in teaching children from pre -school through sub-teens. You mentioned some books by Piaget and Montessori on the young child. Will you please recommend which books I should read first, and also tell me if Piaget and Montessori are still alive?*

Jean Piaget, who died in 1980, was one of this century's most distinguished students of learning in early childhood. Most of his books have been translated into English. Perhaps you should begin with the first book available in English, *The Language and Thought of the Child*, Basic Books, Inc., New York (1926).

Maria Montessori, the famous Italian doctor who developed a learning theory, methodology, and materials, died in 1952 at the age of 81. Her methods are internationally recognized and used, and there are authentic Montessori schools in many parts of the world, as well as a good many off-shoots which are not recognized by the parent organization. One of the speakers on our European tour lecture series this past summer was Miss Elizabeth Stephenson, director of the Montessori Training School in Washington, D.C. Miss Stephenson recommended reading first, not a book by Montessori herself, but a book about her, *Maria Montessori, Her Life and Work* by E.M. Standing, available in a paperback edition published by Mentor-Omega. *(November 1969)*

Periodicals. *Sometime ago I heard recommended a little magazine devoted entirely to education. I don't know its name or how to get it, but remember seeing a copy. It was about 8 inches long by four inches wide, if that's any help. Do you know of such a magazine?*

I think you must be referring to the *Bulletin*, issued by the Council of Basic Education, 725 15th Street, N.W., Washington, D.C. 20005. Regular membership includes the *Bulletin*, issued every month except July and August, and *Occasional Papers* as they are issued. Perhaps more helpful, are the following fine sources of information on general education:

About Education, 219 Broad Street, Philadelphia. Penn.
Colloquy, United Church Press, 391 Steel Way, Lancaster, Penn.
Psychology Today, P.O. Box 60407, Terminal Annex, Los Angeles. Calif.
This Magazine Is About Schools, Box 876, Terminal A. Toronto, Ontario, Canada. *(September 1971)*

Chapter Nine

The Business of Teaching

Starting a studio. *After I graduate from the state university with a master's degree in piano performance, I plan to set up my own studio as a private teacher. I will be teaching in a town of about 40,000 and can have my studio in my parents' home. I am eager to work with young people and to prove that I can be a good teacher, but first I must have students. I would appreciate any suggestions you might have on how I can get started on my career.*

I am delighted you are entering our profession as a private piano teacher in your own studio. We need more teachers in that category in every part of the country. Here are some practical and professional ways to make yourself and your plans known in your community.

- In late summer give a recital, open to the public and free of charge. Advertise it widely, sending notices to newspapers and to radio and TV stations in your area. Include some brief, interesting facts about yourself and a photo. Be sure to select your program with your audience in mind. This will probably mean including repertoire that is not too heavy, too long, or too severely modern.

- Just before Labor Day, send a news release to the local papers announcing the opening of your studio. Feature your background, experience, and education and the types of instruction you are offering. Be sure to include your address and phone number. If possible, hand-deliver the article to the news editor, taking time to introduce yourself and explain the opening of your studio.

- At the same time, insert a small, attractive newspaper ad. Use large type and plenty of white space. The ad should announce the opening of your studio, its location, the dates of your teaching season, the types of instruction you are offering, and the fact that you are now scheduling interviews for new students. Make your address and phone number prominent. Do not include fees. Plan to run this ad for several weeks, and ask about the best location in the paper for your type of ad.

- As soon as your ad runs, it is important to have your telephone covered during business and evening hours. Arrange with someone else to take messages for you when you are not there, or invest in an answering machine. Return all calls as soon as possible; your phone contact with prospective students and their parents is one of the most important aspects of a successful start. Ask about the student's age, grade in school, musical experience, other interests and activities, and the parents' expectations concerning lessons. Make notes so that this information will not need to be repeated at the interview. Have a schedule of available interview times at hand.

- The interview itself is the single most important part of opening a new studio. This is where you sell yourself and your work, both to the student and to the parents. I'd allow at least 30 minutes per student, spending 15 or 20 minutes with the student and the balance of the time with the parent. An interview form on which you can record your impressions of and recommendations for the student is most helpful, and you'll need a printed sheet that includes your calendar, fees, and studio policies to give to the parent. You need to meet and evaluate each child to decide study plan, length of lesson, and materials.

- Get to know the music dealers in your area. Let them know your plans, and ask for their advice and help.

- Join the music organizations in your city and state. Get acquainted with your colleagues and try to play on a program early in the year. Many organizations refer students to teachers whose studios are not full.

- Because your studio will be in your home town, you probably already know a number of potential students. You could write their parents a letter outlining your plans and asking for their cooperation.

- Accept every invitation to play in public, regardless of the condition of the piano, the size of the audience, or if there is a fee. The important thing is to be known in the community.

- Remember that your best advertising is word-of-mouth. A few happy students and their parents will be more effective than newspaper ads. Once you have some students and can prove your success as a teacher, you'll soon have more students than you can handle. (May/June 1980)

How to decrease enrollment. *While many of the letters you receive question how to obtain more students, my letter asks the opposite: how may I decrease my enrollment? My problem lies in my commitments to my ever-growing family and my work at church. How may I fairly reduce my present enrollment from 24 to 12 students? Shall I patiently wait until students decide to quit? Or shall I keep the children a) who have studied with me the longest, b) who have attended most regularly, c) who exhibit the most talent and interest? Are such criteria unfair? I feel I am facing the impossible.*

Your desire to be fair is commendable, and it seems to lead you directly to a) the students who have studied with you the longest. That is the only objective criterion you have. It is matter-of-fact, provable, and explainable. Because they have studied with you the longest, this group probably includes a high percentage of students who attend most regularly and exhibit the most talent and interest.

So you end up being fair and getting the cream of the crop — a happy solution!

There is one other possible approach: announce at the end of the current season that you will be able to take only half your students next year, and that you will accept the first 12 students who enroll. This may not result in the students you want, but it puts the entire burden on the parents and relieves you of any risk of being unfair. *(May/June 1988)*

Interviewing beginners. *I understand you interview all new students, even beginners. Would you explain why you think this is necessary, and what you do at a beginner interview?*

We interview all our beginners to determine if they are ready for piano study and to learn as much about them as possible in advance of the first lesson.

Parents of young children often want them to begin piano study when the children first show interest in the piano, or when the parents themselves think the time has come. Our job is to make an objective evaluation of the child's physical, mental, and emotional readiness for a discipline as demanding as music study at the piano. Beyond determining readiness, however, the interview provides in- sight into the child's physical size and coordination, mental and emotional development and maturity, ability to concentrate, personality, and response to a new learning situation.

In addition, any teacher who works with beginners in groups knows that a careful interview is essential in determining whether or not a particular child is suited to group study and which of several groups he or she might fit into most comfortably.

Teachers who offer pre-piano programs may find interviews less important. The pre-piano program itself not only prepares the young student for formal lessons later on, but also serves as an ideal way of evaluating the child in all areas mentioned above.

At a beginner interview at the New School for Music Study we meet the student and parents and spend a few minutes getting acquainted. Then the parents watch a videotape of our study program while we work with the student. The interview typically takes about 30 minutes and has the format of a relaxed first lesson. It includes these activities:

Exploring the keyboard, black key groups and white keys, the direction and sound of up and down.
Testing the student's rhythmic responses, moving to music, tracing phrases, and clapping back short rhythm patterns.
Testing the student's ear, tracing the direction of upward and downward passages as you play them, identifying the difference between high and low pitches, and singing back short phrases.
Showing the student how to sit in a good position at the piano and what a good

piano hand looks like; experimenting with playing legato between two fingers in the same hand.

Following the interview, we meet with the parents, report to them on the student's readiness for lessons, answer questions, explain study plans, calendar, and fees, and discuss lesson schedules.

We always send registration materials home, asking the parents and child to make a decision together. The interview should feel open-ended, with time for discussion and evaluation at home before a decision is made. *(March 1986)*

Interviewing transfer students. *My question is in reference to interviewing transfer students before their first lesson. I do not have time in my busy schedule for an interview prior to the first lesson, so I use some of the first lesson for getting acquainted and find it works very well. What advantages do you see in interviewing students before they have their first lesson with you?*

There are two definite advantages to interviewing students before committing either side to the arrangement. The first concerns the mutual understanding that is necessary before we accept new students or before they accept us as their new teacher. This understanding includes everything from practical business matters (fees, schedule, policies, and so on) to our educational and musical goals, what we expect of our students, the parents' role, and what they can expect of us.

An interview that precedes registering for lessons allows the teacher to evaluate the student, and gives parents and student an opportunity to reconsider their commitment. An interview almost always ends with a meeting of minds and with an enthusiastic feeling about getting started. At the same time, it makes it easier for parents and student to change their minds if they are looking for a different type of piano study experience.

The second advantage concerns selecting repertoire for a new student. When we interview we hear students play repertoire they have been studying, so that we can begin to determine where they are musically, technically, and intellectually. After the interview we need lead time for planning — what the first assignment should include, what new repertoire is appropriate, and what emphases we should give priority. Such decisions can't be made on the spur of the moment.

For these two reasons we consider it essential to interview transfer students before accepting them or giving the first lesson. *(January 1985)*

Parents. *I need help in answering the many questions I get from parents of both present and prospective students. Teacher friends have recommended the booklet you wrote called* Parents Are Important People, *but I've been told it is no longer in print. Is there any way possible for me to get a copy?*

Because of many similar requests, here are some excerpts from *Parents Are Important People*.

Parents play a vital role in their child's musical growth, both because they initiate the lessons and choose the teacher and because only they can create and maintain the atmosphere of interest and encouragement at home so necessary to real pleasure and progress in music study. Their questions deserve careful, thoughtful answers. This is the way we might answer some of the most frequent questions.

My child has no special musical talent. Should I give him piano lessons anyway?

By all means. Thirty years of piano teaching have convinced me of two things:

There is music in every child.

Every child can learn to play the piano well and can thoroughly enjoy the experience.

Naturally, not all children have the same amount of musical talent, any more than all children are equally adept at reading, spelling, or arithmetic. But every child does have some musical ability, and this deserves to be developed.

The teacher is interested in discovering whatever talent a child does have, and then, no matter how much or how little, helping him develop it. (The interesting thing about learning is that it's something like compound interest — the more an ability is developed, the more there is to develop!)

The boy or girl who already has a highly developed sense of pitch or secure rhythmic coordination, for example, begins with a head start. But the teacher will not be at all alarmed if your child begins piano study without these advantages. It merely means that these are yet to be developed. This is the teacher's job.

My second statement, that every child can learn to play the piano well and thoroughly enjoy the experience depends on three ifs:

if the parents are actively interested,
if the student has a good teacher,
if the teacher uses good teaching materials .
How can I be sure of finding the best teacher?

You have to go shopping — not for price, but for product. First, find out who the most popular teachers in your area are, then ask the parents of their students such questions as these:

Does your child enjoy going to his lesson?

Does he come home happy and enthusiastic, eager to tell you what he learned that day and to play his new pieces for you?

Does he make constant progress?

Is he becoming an excellent sight-reader?

Does he enjoy playing for other people?

If feasible, attend recitals of the teachers you are considering — not a recital of four or five star performers, but one which includes all of this teacher's students, and particularly those who have been studying only a year or two. Even if you have had no musical training you will be able to judge for yourself whether they play with real enjoyment; with freedom, security, and confidence; beautifully, with obvious understanding of the music.

What is my part in my child's music study?

The greatest help you can give your child is active, constructive, daily interest. Being interested takes no special training or skill. It can consist of just asking, "What did you learn at your lesson today?" It can mean listening to him play one or two of his pieces, or checking to make sure he has covered his whole assignment, or even helping him during an entire practice period.

This daily and continuing interest of yours is the most expensive part of music study, far more expensive than the cost of lessons or the music you buy, but the rewards to you are limitless. What could be more satisfying than watching your child learn to enjoy listening to music, acquire a new mental discipline and physical skill, and gain poise and self-confidence through performing for others?

Are there other ways in which I can help?

Lots of them. Here are a few suggestions:

Some Dos

1. Do try to see that your child never misses a lesson except for illness or real emergency. He needs the inspiration of the teacher and the impetus of

a new assignment regularly every week to maintain his interest and rate of progress.

2. Do see that your child arrives at his lesson five minutes early, allowing him time to remove his wraps, get out his music, and catch his breath before the teacher is ready for him.

3. Do check regularly to make sure that your child has taken all of his music and study materials to his lesson (and brought them all home again!) Arriving at the lesson without one's music is a little like arriving at the tennis court without a racket.

4. Do buy new books or sheet music as soon as they are assigned. Children leave the studio eager to see their new music, anxious to get to work on it. The teacher wants to capitalize on this eagerness.

5. Do keep an open mind if the teacher you have chosen for your child teaches differently from the way you were taught, or uses different teaching material with a different look. Try to find out why he teaches the way he does, why he uses this material, why it looks so "different." Chances are, when you understand, you'll be delighted with the changes that have taken place in piano teaching since you were a child. If you have chosen your teacher carefully, you must expect that his methods and his teaching materials will be up to date.

6. Do encourage your child to play for you, your family, and friends. Since practicing is a lonely activity, the more you can do to make it socially rewarding the better. Every opportunity to play for others will increase your child's self-confidence, poise, and enjoyment of music study.

7. Do keep your piano tuned. Music is "sound," and it is the ear more than anything else that is being developed. An untuned piano can undo much of the good that was done at the lesson.

8. Do keep in close touch with the teacher. Feel free to ask questions and make suggestions. Teachers need your constant interest and help, too. They are better able to plan your child's work and gauge his progress if they have accurate reports from you about his practice habits and attitudes at home.

Some Don'ts

1. Don't give your child piano lessons if he is already taking ballet, riding, and swimming lessons. Either drop a few of the extracurricular activities to make room for piano study, or wait to begin lessons at a less busy time.

2. Don't "try out" music lessons with the lady next door with the idea that if they "take," you'll switch to a real teacher. Always choose the best teacher for the beginner.

3. Don't expect your child to maintain a consistently high level of interest in his music study every day of every week throughout the year. Months of high interest are apt to be followed by short periods of lower interest. You

should expect this. Progress is an interesting paradox; sometimes when it's happening fastest, it shows the least.

4. Don't express displeasure when your child "doodles" at the piano. Just make a clear distinction between doodling and practicing. Doodling is important, a necessity to the child, but it should never be confused with, or allowed to take the place of, real practice.

5. Don't allow your child to skip a lesson because he hasn't practiced. The student who hasn't practiced is most in need of his next lesson.

When should my child practice?

Every day. Learning to play the piano involves developing new mental disciplines and acquiring new physical skills. A short, regular practice session every day is worth far more than a longer period every other day or an irregular schedule.

How long should his practice period be?

Long enough to cover the assignment, short enough to stay within the student's attention and interest span. For this reason two short periods are often better than one long one, especially for young children.

Don't insist on your child's remaining at the piano for a specific length of time. From the outset your emphasis should not be on how long he practices but on how much he accomplishes. Ideally, the clock should enter into practice only as a starting point. When he has completed the outline for his daily practice, he is through for that day.

The thing to remember is this: practicing is not a matter of time spent, but a matter of mind spent.

Can I help my child practice even if I don't know anything about music?

Yes. Parents who don't play the piano or read music often feel unable to help their children, but they can. Here are a few suggestions:

1. Immediately after the lesson ask your child to tell you what he learned that day, to show you his new assignment, perhaps to play one of his new pieces for you, and especially to tell you what his teacher had to say about his lesson.

2. At the first practice period following the lesson spend a few minutes with your child talking over his new assignment and helping him practice one or two of his new pieces (even those of you who don't play the piano can be a great help to your child in making sure that he understands every step of the instructions in his assignment).

3. Each succeeding day of the week check to make sure that he has covered the entire assignment, and perhaps ask him to play one or more of his pieces to show you how they have improved.

Parent's guide to music lessons. *I am writing a paper which deals with parents' understanding and cooperation with their children's music lessons. I have found several pamphlets on the subject, as well as a number of magazine articles. I am eager to locate a book which I believe was written by a faculty member of a New York music school, but I don't know the title of the book or the name of the author.*

The only book I know that fits your description is *A Parent's Guide to Music Lessons* by Vera G. Wills and Ande Manners, published by Harper and Row. Wills is an assistant to the chairman of the pedagogy department at Mannes College of Music in New York City. Benny Goodman wrote the introduction, and in it he says, "*A Parent's Guide to Music Lessons* provides the parent with his own insight into what musicianship is and how it is developed in the child. The book provides practical advice about how the child can be interested in music, what instrument is right for a particular child, and how one goes about buying instruments. In short, the book is more than a discussion of the techniques of music lessons; it is an essential statement about the delicate state of musical awareness in the child and how that awareness can be guided into musicianship."

Every teacher and parent should own a copy of this excellent book. *(January 1983)*

Contact with parents. *How can I keep parents better informed about their children's progress?*

One of the most valuable ways to stimulate the parents' interest and ensure their cooperation is to talk with them frequently in person or by phone. This discussion can't be done on the run between lessons. A specified time needs to be set aside for an unhurried conversation. During the meeting or phone call it is very helpful to have on hand copies of the student's recent assignments in order to explain in detail the student's current work and his progress.

An even more effective point of contact is to invite parents to visit private lessons. With most students it works better not to have the parent at every lesson, but they should certainly be invited at frequent intervals, and should feel free to initiate visits with your approval in advance. I usually end such a lesson a bit early so that there is time for discussion of the lesson and the student's progress.

At the New School we schedule a special meeting for parents of new students each fall. It is divided into two sections, one for parents of new beginners and one for parents of students transferring to us. These meetings give us an opportunity to explain our educational philosophy, methods, and materials, and to discuss with them their role in helping with piano study. Most important, the meetings give us an opportunity to become better acquainted with the parents and to answer their questions.

For continuing contact with the parents of all our students, we schedule periodic visits to classes. These "open" classes are conducted as much like the regular class as possible, so that parents have a chance to see a variety of activities, to hear their own and other students play, and to see their child interacting with students and teacher. At the end of these classes the students are dismissed, and the parents invited to remain for discussion and questions.

Parents are indispensable for student progress at the piano. If we take the time to help them understand what we are doing and why, their cooperation will be limitless. Keep in mind that the parents need to be motivated, too. *(February 1978)*

Contact with parents. *When I interview all of my new students, I meet their parents and explain my fees and studio policies. After that I seem to lose touch with the parents. How can I maintain this important contact after the lessons have begun?*

I believe you can successfully establish a pattern of parent contact during the entire first year of study; once you establish it, you can maintain it with little effort on either side. Here are some of the ways we try to build real rapport with parents from the beginning.

Two or three weeks after school begins in the fall, we have a meeting for the parents of all our new beginners. We schedule it on a weekday evening in the hope of attracting both parents, and we make it an important occasion for which they will reserve time. We tell them about it at the interview, send home a reminder notice a week ahead, and make a follow-up phone call a day or two in advance.

At the meeting we explain how we teach and why, go through the students' first book (which will be different from the material with which most of them began), and play some of the music the students will be studying in the first weeks of the term. We follow this music with some pieces the students will study later in the year to show the scope of growth and progress we expect.

We ask for the parents' cooperation in many ways — making sure the student shows up regularly and on time for lessons, brings all materials to each lesson, practices regularly each day, follows the weekly assignment carefully, and so on. We ask them to check on the student's posture and hand position from time to time and to be sure the bench is the correct height. We explain the importance of regular piano tuning and maintenance. We ask them to keep in touch with us and to call us if they have questions or if there is even a hint of trouble about the assignment at home. We also urge parents to visit a private lesson occasionally, and often we invite them to step into the studio at the end of the lesson to hear how well a piece is going.

Around Thanksgiving we invite parents to attend what we call open classes. These are the students' regular weekly or bi-weekly classes, conducted as much like a normal class as possible, so that parents see all of the activities we use to develop concepts and skills and so that they understand more about our approach to reading, rhythm, technique, and theory. Each student plays one or more pieces, and the teacher and other class members work to improve the performance, just as we would at a regular class. These open classes are real eye-openers for the parents, who invariably express amazement at how much the children have learned, understand, and can perform in such a short period of time.

During the winter months we often invite the parents to informal programs. Performers range from the youngest beginners to the most advanced high school students, so that every musical experience gives both parents and students variety and the excitement of seeing what lies ahead.

I like to think of the relationship between parents, student, and teacher as a triangle: each side is required to complete the design, with no side more or less important than any other. Once parents catch on to the significance of their role, they are willing and eager to fulfill it. *(October 1986)*

Parents aren't serious about piano study. *Would you take a beginning student whose parents say frankly that they are not serious about piano study, that they don't want their child to become a concert pianist — no scales, no struggling to learn big pieces, just learning to play the piano for fun?*

Yes, I would take such a student, after explaining some basics to the parents before we began. For example, I would want them to understand that I don't start any beginner with the idea that he or she will become a concert pianist. That is an outcome so rare that it's nothing even to consider at the start; if the talent is there, it will manifest itself despite anything teachers or parents can do about it. In contrast, all students have the potential for a lifetime of joy making music at the piano, so our goal for all beginners is not just playing the piano for fun for a few months or years, but acquiring the equipment necessary to take them as far down the road as their talent, interest, time, and energy will take them.

I would want parents to understand, too, that scales will not be an issue for a long time, and that there should never be any "struggling" to learn to play pieces, large or small. Instead, every beginner must have certain basic learning experiences that are common to all piano students, just as all students in school learn to read and write, whether as adults they become novelists or stenographers; and all students learn to add, subtract, multiply, and divide, whether as adults they become physicists or supermarket clerks.

If the parents seem to understand and agree with my teaching philosophy, I would be happy to work with their child, knowing that as we grow together we will probably come to share the same goals. (May-June 1981)

Beginner quits. *I had a shock recently when one of my best young beginners suddenly insisted right after Christmas on stopping lessons after having completed 12 weeks of apparently happy and successful study. His parents tried to persuade him to continue, but he insisted he was no longer interested and would not practice. The parents corroborated my impression that he had enjoyed his private lessons and had been an enthusiastic spark-plug in the group lesson. Where did I go wrong?*

I doubt if you did. However, when such a situation arises, we do need to look at all the aspects: our teaching, the student's response, and especially the role the parents play at home. The best we can do, having lost at least temporarily on this one, is to try to prevent a similar situation from developing in the future.

From your report, the student has not lost interest in music. Probably he has not lost interest in playing the piano. Instead, he must have reached one of those points at which some children suddenly lose interest in practicing. Here are some possible explanations:

If he was always well prepared, perhaps his parents demanded too much practice at home.

His slump came just after Christmas; is it possible that he was asked to practice regularly during Christmas vacation, even though he was not having lessons?

Perhaps he'd just reached that moment of truth when he realized that suddenly the whole world seemed to be making demands on him: homework, household chores, personal routines, and that terrible awareness that his friends are outside playing ball while he's inside practicing the piano. Meeting and facing these moments of truth are part of growing up. Some children weather them better than others. When the going gets rough, it's often the latest activity, or the one that requires the most self-discipline, that gets scrapped.

In the future, ask the parents to notify you immediately if they see any lack of enthusiasm or resistance to practice. Had you known at the first hint of trouble, you could doubtless have made some change in your attitude or expectations, or in his assignment, that might have averted the crisis.

In a case such as you describe, you might have suggested the student continue lessons for a few weeks without any home practice. This is risky, but sometimes it allows the child to enjoy lessons without the pressure of practice. Naturally, lessons without practice can't go on very long, but once in a while that concession on the part of teacher and parents provides just the breathing space the student needs to change his mind without losing face. *(January 1982)*

45-minute lessons. *How can I explain to parents the advantages of a 45-minute lesson, when the former teacher never gave anything but 30 minutes?*

I'd begin by explaining that you give only 45-minute or 60-minute lessons, if this is the case. When they ask why you don't give 30-minute lessons, you can explain your reasons.

Based on my experience, I would say with conviction that a 45-minute lesson is worth twice as much as a 30-minute lesson. It doesn't look that way mathematically, but I have proved it to my own satisfaction by timing the amount of a lesson in which actual concentrated learning takes place. At first I was surprised at how much time was taken up in greeting the student, discussing briefly something of interest or importance to him (as a way of bridging the gap between what he has been doing that day and the piano lesson), then getting his mind into focus on the music. Again, at the end of the lesson, time is consumed in making the student aware of what has been learned and sending him home enthusiastic about the new assignment.

When I subtracted the time consumed by these important pre- and post-lesson activities, I found that the time left in a 45-minute lesson was almost twice as much as the time left in a 30-minute lesson. In terms of progress, the fee for a 45-minute lesson is actually less than the fee for a 30-minute lesson.

No student is ready for a piano lesson just because it is Tuesday afternoon at 4:30. We have to take time to get him ready to think and to learn. Then, what a pity it is to have to stop the learning, just because the clock says 5:00! *(November 1980)*

Increasing lesson time. *How do you persuade parents to increase their child's lesson time from 30 to 45 minutes when they say the child already has enough music to practice?*

I assume your reason for wanting to increase the lesson time is the same as mine would be. We know that students who leave our studio with clear goals for the week's practice and who feel capable of accomplishing those goals in a reasonable time are the students who are eager to practice.

A longer lesson does not mean a longer assignment. What it does mean is a student who is more ready to work on new music with accuracy and confidence and who understands more clearly how to work to improve review music. Instead of lengthening the assignments, a longer lesson shortens the learning time for new music and thus greatly increases the student's rate of progress.

Before talking with the parents about the proposed change, be sure in your own mind why you are making the recommendation for a longer lesson. Then you can present your case clearly and persuasively. *(October 1986)*

Late for lessons. *What do you do with a student who is always late? I have a wonderful young boy who could be an excellent student if only he'd come in time to get his whole 30 minutes. Sometimes I run over in order to give him his whole time, but of course this ruins the rest of my afternoon schedule. I have talked to his mother, even changed his time to 30 minutes later, but the situation remains the same. I'm at my wit's end. His mother is cooperative in every other way, but this problem remains. Do you have any suggestions?*

It has been my experience that there are two kinds of people who are habitually late (and I believe this applies to their appointments with doctors, dentists, and hairdressers, as well as piano teachers). In the first group are those who have no respect for your schedule but expect you to respect theirs; in the second group are those who take all scheduling very casually, their own as well as yours.

It helps first to discover which kind of person your student's mother is. You might reschedule his lesson, putting him on a different day at a different hour, telling his mother one time but adding him to your own schedule 15 or even 30 minutes later. For example, tell her 4:00, but have him in your own schedule at 4:15 or 4:30.

Now comes the test. If they arrive ahead of the time in your schedule and have to wait, you can soon determine if the mother is type A or type B. Type A will grow restive with the delay and will soon express displeasure with the fact the you are keeping them waiting. At that point, confess your plot and ask her how you can solve it to your mutual convenience. Type B will accept your lateness as casually as she expected you to accept hers, and as long as she doesn't catch on to the difference between your schedule and hers, the student will probably always arrive late according to their schedule, but on time or ahead of time according to yours. With B-type parents I have sometimes gone an entire season with a 15- or 30-minute time difference that went undiscovered and resulted in perfect schedule coordination. *(November 1972)*

Parents reject contemporary music. *I am having a perplexing problem this year. The parents of a young student insist that their child study no contemporary music. In fact, they go so far as to assert that nothing worthwhile has been composed since Beethoven. The father says he will be restless until his 10-year-old son can play Bach Preludes and Fugues. Any suggestions?*

I have found that the best way to solve this type of problem is before it arises – by interviewing a new student and his parents. At this time you can make sure they understand what the student's study program will include, and why. Before tastes have been discussed or prejudices revealed, you can make some telling points about developing a healthy, well-nourished musician through a carefully planned and well-balanced musical diet. If that issue is laid to rest in the initial interview before the student enrolls, it is not apt to develop as a problem later on.

In your case the problem exists; and if I knew the parents well, I would explain the importance of familiarity with all styles and implore them not to let their own prejudices limit their child's musical development. If I did not know them well, I would explain how very little great literature is available for young students from such composers as Bach, Mozart, or Beethoven. Surely a father who is such a Bach enthusiast would be impressed to learn that Bach's own sons were brought up on the music of Bach's contemporaries. You might show him the *Anna Magdalena Bach Notebook* and explain its pedagogical purpose. To strengthen your position, you might also show him the notebooks which Leopold Mozart prepared for Wolfgang and Nannerl, emphasizing that musicians are often trained, as young children, on music written especially for them by contemporary composers. Then show the parents sets of teaching pieces written for today's young students by the master composers of our time. Perhaps this will turn the tide. *(February 1979)*

Aptitude testing. *The parents of two of my students, both juniors in high school, are very concerned about whether or not their children should go to college, what college they should attend, and what they should specialize in. They are my two best piano students, and of course I would like to see them major in piano. The problem is that they excel in everything, and this poses a problem, both for them and for their parents.*

I once heard that there are places where young people can go to be tested for aptitudes, but I am not sure what the tests are called or where one has to go to take them. Both the parents and I will be grateful if you can help.

The most comprehensive aptitude-testing center I know is called the Human Engineering Laboratory. The musical aptitude tests given by the Laboratory are fairly rudimentary, but the range of other known and provable aptitudes they test is very wide and comprehensive. I have known many young and older people (both students and professionals in mid-career transitions) who took the battery of tests and felt they greatly benefitted by the test results and counseling provided. There are Laboratories located in 15 states. Johnson O'Connor Research Foundation, Inc., 11 East 62nd Street, New York) *(March 1974)*

Cost of music. *Parents of new students often ask how much their child's music will cost for a year of study. How can I estimate this before I have worked with the student and can judge his rate of progress?*

At the initial interview, you can quote a probable minimum and maximum figure, based on the average music costs for your students at the same level over the last several years. The estimate can be fairly firm with a young beginner. With students who are transferring to you from another teacher it is more difficult to judge, so be careful to make your maximum figure on the high side. *(April 1979)*

Changing teachers. *I am a parent, not a piano teacher, and would like your advice on how to change teachers gracefully. Our ten-year-old daughter and seven-year-old son have been studying with the same teacher. Our daughter had reached the point where we felt she should change to a teacher who could give her a greater challenge. When I told the present teacher of our decision, she refused to continue teaching our son even though we wished him to continue with her. This has caused discomfort and hurt feelings for all of us, and I wonder how I might have avoided the problem.*

Experiences such as this are worthy of mention because they remind us once again of the necessity for continued contact between the parents of young students and their teachers. This communication needs to work two ways, with both parties initiating frequent discussions, either by telephone or in person.

Such contacts should begin with positive exchanges. For example, the parent might call the teacher to say that the child comes home from a lesson and runs to the piano to practice, or that the student considers the day of his lesson the most exciting in the week, or that the parents are surprised and delighted with the student's progress. The parent might call the teacher to discuss the length of the assignment, how long the students should be practicing, or to ask if there is anything the parent can do to help.

On the other side, the teacher might call the parent to say what a delightful student the child is; how well the student was prepared for the last lesson; or how much the student's technique is improving. Or the teacher might want to ask if the assignment seems too long, too short, or just right; how long the student is practicing every day; or how the student enjoyed a particular new piece.

Should the day come when enthusiasm lags or practice has grown lackluster, it will then be entirely natural for the parent and teacher to discuss the problem before it grows out of proportion. If cooperative effort to solve the problem fails, either party could introduce the possibility of changing teachers without embarrassment or hurt.

Usually the kind of trouble you have just experienced occurs only if we wait until after a problem has arisen before we initiate contact. Of course, this is true of most human relationships, not just those between parents and teachers. *(March 1988)*

Trouble getting sheet music. *This year I have had more trouble getting sheet music than I have ever had before. Those teachers who live in or near large cities can't possibly know how difficult it is for us who live in a small town with a dealer who keeps only a very small stock, especially of sheet music.*

I do appreciate your predicament and from first-hand experience. For many years I lived in a small town that had the same sort of music store you describe, but this experience taught me that the problem you describe can be solved, providing you take the initiative. Begin a comprehensive list of all the music you now teach, listing it by title, composer and publisher. As you discover a new teaching piece that works, add it to your list. When you learn an old favorite is no longer in print, cross it off your list so that you won't order it again by mistake.

From the music magazines to which you subscribe, clip all of the recommended lists of new materials. If a review of a new piece or collection interests you, order a copy. After you have taught it, if you find it successful and think you will want to teach it again, add it to your list to have the pertinent information at hand when you want to order it again.

The same procedure can be followed for music listed in publishers' ads of new music, although these descriptions (prepared by the publisher) are apt to be less helpful than those prepared by a good reviewer.

Any publisher will be happy to mail you a copy of his piano catalogue, in which you can hunt for music you have mislaid or perhaps discover new music you might like to try. All you have to do is send a postcard, asking for a copy of the most recent catalogue. *(February 1979)*

Delays in receiving music orders. *Each year getting the music I need for teaching becomes more difficult and frustrating. This year it approaches being impossible. I am not referring to basic course books, but to the supplementary collections or sheet music I might wish to assign in addition.*

I have ordered directly from the publisher, with delays of weeks, only to receive a notice that the piece in question is no longer in print. I have ordered through dealers, with still longer delays, and again many times find the piece is now out of print. For the record, music I've ordered from seven different publishers that was available last year is now out of print.

This is driving me crazy. What is the solution?

To my real sorrow, I have no solution to this problem and only one suggestion. If you place your music order still further ahead, at least you won't be caught short at the last minute.

Again, let me just cite the system we have found most workable at the New School. Our spring term ends in June. As soon as it is over, and before the teachers leave on summer vacation, they plan the work for each of their students for the fall term. They plan all aspects of each student's work, including the exact repertoire they plan to use with that student in the coming year, especially that important new piece for the first lesson.

Knowing the problem with sheet music, each teacher is asked to hedge his bets by listing a first, second, and third choice piece for each student.

As soon as the entire music list is in, we place the order with our local dealer, giving him about 10-12 weeks to order from the various publishers. During the summer the music begins to come in, along with notices that some of the material is out of print. Whenever a first choice piece is no longer available, we immediately re-order the second choice piece; if we learn that it, too, is out of print, we order the third choice piece, etc. I don't believe with this back-up order system we have ever been caught short without the excitement of a new piece of sheet music for every student at the beginning of the new season. (*November 1972*)

For years my teaching has been hampered because it has not been possible to obtain music for my students in a reasonable length of time. For example, a piece that was ordered in time for Christmas arrived in March. This was a well-known number from one of America 's largest publishers. This is a ridiculous example, but not at all unusual. Recently I conducted an extensive investigation that proved the bottleneck was not between the dealer and the teacher, but was result of the delinquency by publishers in getting their publications to the music dealers. What can be done about this distressing situation?

I understand your problem and can sympathize with it. I am fortunate to deal with a music dealer who orders from his suppliers every day. As a result, I seldom wait longer than two weeks, but I know there are many teachers across the country who share your problem.

Try to plan still further ahead, so that ordering can be done even earlier. Christmas music received in March is distressing, but was it ordered in September or October? The Christmas season is a problem for all people who deal with music, so even earlier ordering would help.

More important, did your investigation of the problem take into account not only your local dealer, and the publishers involved, but also the jobber between them? Does your dealer send off his orders the same day he receives them from you? Many smaller dealers find it more practical to wait and collect orders until they have a sizeable order for a given publisher. If your dealer actually does send his orders as received, it is possible that he orders through a jobber rather than direct from the publisher. If the jobber waits to collect an order, this may become a major bottleneck for your dealer to contend with.

My own research on this subject has led me to the conclusion that, in general, the publisher is less accountable for slow shipping than the dealer or jobber for slow ordering. There are, of course, some spectacular exceptions, but most of the big, reputable publishers have a policy of same-day order filling.

Unknown publisher. *I live in a small town that has a small music store and a cooperative dealer who tries hard but doesn't know a lot of the answers. I'm about to lose my mind trying to locate music if I don't know who publishes it or, in some cases, if I do know the publisher he seems no longer to be in business or at least not at his old address. The hang-ups and delays on music I'm trying to order are just unbelievable, and I turn to you for any possible help you can offer.*

I called our dealer after your letter came, and had a long talk with him about this problem. He suggests asking your dealer to call his jobber to locate the work or asking your dealer to go through major catalogues to find the work; this is time-consuming but not impossible.

When you know the publisher, but are having difficulty locating him, there is a much easier solution. The Music Publishers Association of the U.S.A. prints each year a complete list of publishers, American Agent or Parent Company of Leading Music Publishers. This list is divided into American agents or parent companies (there are 24 of these}, and leading music publishers (there are over 700 of these), identified by a number that refers to its American agent or parent company in the first list. This is an invaluable tool in locating publishers that all music dealers should have. (Music Publishers Association, 609 Fifth Avenue, New York) *(May 1973)*

Piano upkeep. *We are preparing information on pianos and their upkeep to hand out to the parents of all of our students. We want to include answers to questions that we have received from them as well as some information that we think parents should have in order for their children to have decent pianos on which to practice. To help us we would appreciate your answers to the following questions:*

> *How often should pianos be tuned?*
> *Do new pianos require more tuning than old pianos?*
> *Can any tuner voice a piano?*
> *Is a used grand better than a new upright?*
> *Where should a piano be placed in the home?*

How do you clean the inside of a piano?

Is it essential that all students have a piano with a sostenuto pedal?

Rather than answer each of your questions here, may I recommend instead an excellent book published in 1971. It is The Piano Owner's Guide, written by Carl D. Schmeckel, published and nationally distributed by Apex Piano Publishers, Sheboygan, Wisconsin, 53081. So far as I know it is the only book devoted to the subject of choosing and caring for a piano. Mr. Schmeckel is a professional piano tuner-technician and rebuilder with a background of 45 years in music. This book will answer all of your questions far better than I could, and it will even answer questions you didn't know you had. *(March 1973)*

Classroom equipment. *The one thing I have most wanted to do ever since I started high school is to open my own piano studio as soon as I graduate from college. I have just seen one of the videotapes from your school and am very discouraged over the quantity of specialized equipment it apparently takes to teach group piano. I don't see how I can ever afford to furnish such a studio and am wondering if I should give up my dream.*

Don't give up the dream! Most successful piano studios open with one fine, enthusiastic young teacher and one piano, often in a living room. Even to start successful group teaching you don't need two grand pianos, artist benches, specially-built tables, chairs, keyboards, dry-marker boards, rhythm and melody instruments, tape and record players, and certainly not videotape equipment.

Years ago I began teaching with one good upright piano and a revolving piano stool that could be adjusted for height. Some years later, when I began group teaching, I used card tables, folding chairs, and cardboard keyboards. I didn't even have a chalkboard at first.

I'm convinced that all you really need to be a successful piano teacher is one good piano (it can be an upright), one adjustable chair or bench, an attractive room, and the right music for each student. Among the highlights of my early teaching career were the moments when I bought my first grand piano, my first artist bench, my first chalkboard, etc. I remember that they made my teaching easier, but not necessarily more successful. Why not begin with just the essentials and have the excitement of adding equipment as you are able to afford it? *(July/August 1982)*

Electronic pianos. I am thinking of buying an electronic piano to use as a second keyboard instrument in my studio. I teach all styles of music and can see big possibilities here in the popular music field. However, do you think these new instruments are correct for the traditional repertoire? To be perfectly honest, the thought of playing a Bach invention with the harpsichord voice or the "Dance of the Sugar Plum Fairy" sounding like a celeste is enough to send me off with a down payment, but what about Chopin or Debussy?

Congratulations on your admirable willingness to consider an electronic instrument for your studio. I turned your question over to my colleague, Sam Holland, Director of the New School for Music Study and a specialist in the use of synthesizers and electronic keyboards in piano teaching.

"When making a decision about purchasing an electronic keyboard you must first decide how you intend to use this second instrument. Certain types of music lend themselves naturally to performance on a synthesizer. As you have noted, much pop music does. The synthesizer is also ideal for some orchestral transcriptions and even for some original piano music where the piano was used to imitate another instrument. To perform Purcell's *Trumpet Minuet* or Hovhannes' *Mystic Flute*, for example, why not use the actual sound of the trumpet and flute? Baroque keyboard music also transcribes well to the synthesizer. With the realistic harpsichord and organ sounds that are possible, Bach Inventions and Scarlatti sonatas can be delightful.

"The instrument has not yet been invented, though, that can replace or even approach the acoustic piano for the literature of the Romantic and Impressionistic periods. Why? The sound of an acoustic piano is extremely complex — arguably the most difficult of all instruments to recreate electronically. This is because a piano's sound is not simply the result of single hammers striking strings at specific speeds; it is an aggregate of the sympathetic vibrations of many strings plus the resonances of the sounding board and the whole instrument. Adding pedals increases the complexity of this blend.

"Computers can analyze, sample, and recreate piano sounds to some degree. Synthesizers such as Yamaha's Clavinova succeed well at this imitation, but the process remains just that — imitation. In addition, whatever synthesized sounds we hear can never exceed the quality of the amplification and speaker system through which we hear them. Another factor is the player's kinesthetic response to the action of an acoustic piano and to its vibrations. This response does not occur with electronic keyboards — not even those with weighted, touch-sensitive keys.

"A good synthesizer is a serious musical instrument. The options it presents for composing and performing are exciting, indeed. For Baroque literature, pop, jazz, theory, composition, or experimentation, an electronic piano is a wise choice that is right in step with the times." *(April 1986)*

Casio keyboards. A missionary in Africa writes: *I eagerly receive and read* Clavier *whenever my copy arrives. Being somewhat isolated from the Western musical world, I find it* helps keep me inspired to practice. I have the opportunity to teach some children of other missionaries in this area. Due to the unavailability of pianos, they have only a small Casio keyboard on which to practice. Do you think there is value in giving piano lessons in this situation? Shall I conduct lessons on the small keyboard or on my own piano? How long could lessons continue in these circumstances and still be beneficial? What areas would you emphasize or de-emphasize?

If you embark on this project on the premise that what you are teaching is music (not piano and not Casio keyboard), I believe you and your students can have an interesting, challenging, and worthwhile experience.

I would suggest giving the lesson on your piano, but ask the students to bring their keyboards with them to the lesson as well. Of course, you will have to keep in mind the limitations of their keyboards in terms of size, range, quality and quantity of tone, accentuation, pedal, and so on.

If you use a beginning approach that covers many octaves, let students experience your piano's wider range during lessons, then adjust the pieces to conform to their keyboards for home practice. In selecting literature for more advanced students, keep in mind that Baroque, Classical, and Contemporary styles lend themselves best to electronic keyboards, and avoid Romantic literature that is so dependent on tone color, nuance, phrasing, and pedaling.

Your circumstances are unusual, but isn't it better to explore the world of possibilities available to you, and invent ways to expose these missionary children to the joys of music, rather than to settle for nothing at all? How far you and your students can go will depend on the creativity of your own ideas as the days, weeks, and months go by. I'm sure you'll be pleasantly surprised! *(March 1988)*

Use of cassette recorders. *How can I use a cassette recorder to help make my teaching more effective?*

We use ours primarily to help develop our students' critical listening. For example, when a student's performance of a piece or technical etude approaches our standards for that piece or etude, we tape it at the lesson, play it back immediately, then ask the student if he is satisfied with his performance. Students seldom are satisfied. I have heard such comments as:

"I didn't choose a slow enough tempo."
"The piece died at the end."
"I lost the melody when it changed to the left hand."
"I began the ritard two measures earlier than I meant to."
"I flubbed the third phrase — guess I'd better use the fingering you suggested after all!"

After the student's critique, we discuss how to improve the things about the performance that didn't satisfy him. He almost always asks, "Can I play the piece again? I know I can play it better than that!" The second playing is almost always better, primarily because the student has alerted himself to what was missing.

Students who own cassette recorders can use them effectively in their home practice. We often ask them to record specific pieces at least once a week, to listen to the recording and act as their own teacher. Perhaps even more valuable is another type of practice assignment: with pieces being prepared for public performance, it is important to practice the feeling of "just one chance." For this reason, we ask students to record their first performance of the piece each day, listen to it, evaluate it, and work to improve it. This is a great aid in developing secure public performance, as well as the students' ability to listen to their own playing objectively.

We find this use of cassettes truly effective in helping students become their own teachers between lessons. *(November 1981)*

I have just purchased a cassette recorder to help me in my teaching. What are the most effective ways of using it as a teaching tool?

Basically there are two ways in which a tape recorder can be a great aid to the piano teacher. The first is to tape some of your lessons so that you can criticize your own teaching techniques. The second is to use the play-back of students' performances to help your students learn to listen to themselves objectively and criticize themselves constructively.

In using the recorder to criticize your own teaching, I suggest you tape one complete lesson each day, varying the lessons you tape from week to week. The next morning, listen to the tape and make notes on your teaching. You might begin by asking yourself three simple questions:

1. What did I do that should not have been done?
2. What did I not do that should have been done?
3. What did I do that did not need to be done?

Studying the taped lessons from these three points of view will lead to valuable insights into your teaching. Be sure to notice the student's reactions as well as your own teaching techniques. Does the student understand your instructions, or do you have to repeat or clarify them? Is he responding quickly and intelligently to your questions, or are you getting wrong answers due to poorly worded or imprecise questions? Does his playing really improve as a result of your suggestions, or did you only think so during the lesson?

The second way a tape recorder can be used in teaching is to help the student develop self-criticism. Tape one piece (preferably a short one at first) that the student has prepared, then play it back for the student, following the score together. At first you will probably need to lead the discussion, guiding the student to hear himself objectively and making suggestions for improvement. As the student becomes more comfortable with the process, ask him to critique his own playing. Then ask him to play the piece again, making the improvements he suggested. Inevitably, the student begins to listen more carefully to his playing, which is the most important aspect of practice. When the student learns to listen critically he can then determine what needs to be improved and what practice steps to use.

If the student has a cassette recorder at home, record the entire lesson and ask him to listen to it every other day. This will remind him of suggestions made at the lesson and give him a way to measure daily progress.

Even more valuable is the use of home recorders for practice sessions. Students who learn to judge their taped lessons objectively will soon discover that the same technique works wonders in home practice. If you suspect that practice time is not being used wisely, suggest that the student record one entire practice period and use his practice time the following day to listen to and evaluate his previous day's practice. Students are often shocked at the wasteful use of practice time they hear on the tape recordings. (October 1978)

Use of video-tape. *I am becoming more and more interested in buying audio-visual equipment for my studio to help my students' performance. I know you use this equipment in your school and have heard that it is also used in some dance studios. How essential do you consider audio-visual equipment? Please give me some idea of how you use it in your teaching.*

If I were teaching in a private studio instead of in a school, buying audio-visual equipment would be out of the question. It is extremely expensive to purchase and maintain, and learning to use it effectively is nearly a full-time job.

Anyone who has the good fortune to teach where such equipment is available, especially where there is a technician to run it, can profit enormously from the experience of having his teaching taped, then studying it. It's a pretty bad jolt to the ego to see yourself in action on film for the first time, but once you have grown accustomed to how you actually appear (as opposed to how you always envisioned yourself!) you can learn endlessly from the experience.

If you have the opportunity, I recommend filming an entire lesson under conditions as normal as possible, then set aside plenty of time to view and review the taped lesson, studying it from every angle. All too often we hear students' performances as we want to hear them rather than as they actually are. As we become concerned with a student's performance, we also become subjective about it, and frequently imagine we hear improvement (because of what we are doing or feeling) that in reality has not occurred. I have heard very good teachers ask a student to play a passage over again because he didn't really make a crescendo, or because the staccato wasn't really crisp, or the tone not rich enough, then comment on how much better the second performance was when, in reality, there was no difference at all. The teacher was hearing the improvement he desired rather than the performance that was actually taking place. Here the tape can be a harsh and realistic judge.

When audio-visual equipment is not available, it is comforting that much the same help can be derived from a simple audio tape or cassette recorder. We require our pedagogy students to tape lessons and then analyze them. They discover to their horror a plethora of words, lots of wasted time, failure to follow a lesson plan, or worse, strict adherence to a plan that simply was not working for that student on that day. The audio tape alone can be an enormously helpful critic-teacher for anyone who has the courage to listen objectively to his own teaching successes and failures. I recommend this highly on a regular basis, for experienced as well as beginning teachers. *(May-June 1974)*

About Frances Clark

Frances Clark is recognized as the foremost authority on piano teaching in our time. The books and study courses that bear her name and the school she founded and heads demonstrate a measure of her broad influence in the world of piano education. More eloquent testimony are the thousands of young students who have experienced the joy of making music at the piano because of her sweeping improvements in teaching methods and materials.

Clark was born and raised in Sturgis, Michigan. At Kalamazoo College she majored in English, French, and Philosophy, and studied piano and theory privately. Immediately after college she taught English literature in high school and opened her own piano studio; later she pursued graduate study at Juilliard and in France at the Fontainebleau School. Her piano teachers included Guy Maier, Ernest Hutcheson, and Isidore Philipp. On her return from France, she opened piano studios in and around her home town. As her reputation spread, she was flooded with students who came great distances for her special brand of piano instruction.

In 1945 Kalamazoo College appointed her to its piano faculty, and a year later she founded its piano pedagogy department. She conducted the first of many workshops for piano teachers on the Kalamazoo campus in 1948. News of her practical, inspirational approach to piano teaching spread rapidly, and soon her fame was nationwide. Teachers came from all parts of the country and abroad for her Kalamazoo courses, and many other colleges and universities invited her to their campuses.

Gradually the materials she developed were published, and in 1953 the Summy-Birchard Company commissioned what is now an extensive educational series, *The Frances Clark Library for Piano Students.*

In 1955 she became director of piano and piano pedagogy at Westminster Choir College. In 1960 she left Westminster to found The New School for Music Study, a professional training center devoted exclusively to post-graduate training for piano teachers. In 1981, The New School and Westminster began to offer a joint program leading to a Master's Degree in Piano Pedagogy and Performance.

In 1963 Kalamazoo College awarded Clark an honorary doctorate for her achievements in the field of piano education. In 1984 the National Conference on Piano Pedagogy awarded her its first Lifetime Achievement Award. In 1991 SH Productions produced two video cassettes on her life and works.

The following message from Frances Clark appeared in the September, 1992 issue of Clavier:

Dear Readers,

For several years I have thought each spring that the following September issue would be my farewell. This year I made up my mind; after 26 years of "Questions and Answers" for Clavier, this column will be my last. I take this opportunity to try to thank you for the privilege of such a rich experience.

The monthly contact via correspondence has given me the opportunity to become acquainted with hundreds of piano teachers across the country, to know their problems and their joys, their doubts and successes, their ambitions and disappointments. The letters and the questions they contained were, of course, the raison d'etre for "Questions and Answers"; it's those questions that have kept you and me and the monthly column together for so many years. Your questions have challenged me, made me re-think and reconsider what I believe, and forced me to organize my thinking and attempt to express it more clearly. I thank you for these many hundreds of questions; I shall miss receiving them.

Whenever I visit a group of piano teachers, inevitably someone comes up to me and says, "I am so and so, the one who asked the question about..." At that moment my acquaintance takes on a face, a voice. If you will continue to introduce yourselves that way when you see me at conventions, pedagogy conferences, work-shops, or anywhere, this won't be farewell, just "Auf Wiedersehen."

— *Frances Clark*

Frances Clark in action.

CPSIA information can be obtained
at www.ICGtesting.com
Printed in the USA
LVHW022157161118
597372LV00008B/351/P